# Rafe
## A MEMOIR

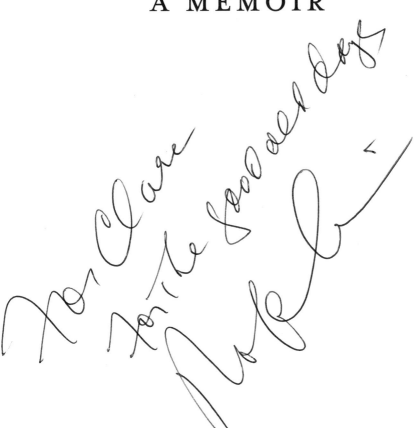

For Clare
for the good old days

[signature]

# Rafe

## A MEMOIR

# Rafe Mair

HARBOUR PUBLISHING

Published by
Harbour Publishing Co. Ltd.
P.O. Box 219
Madeira Park, BC
V0N 2H0
www.harbourpublishing.com

Edited by Betty Keller
Cover and page design by Peter Read
Cover Photo by John Lehmann/*Globe and Mail*
Printed and bound in Canada

Harbour Publishing acknowledges financial support from the Government of
Canada through the Book Publishing Industry Development Program and the
Canada Council for the Arts, and from the Province of British Columbia
through the British Columbia Arts Council and the Book Publisher's Tax Credit
through the Ministry of Provincial Revenue.

**Canada Council for the Arts**

**Conseil des Arts du Canada**

**BRITISH COLUMBIA ARTS COUNCIL**

We acknowledge the support of the Province of British Columbia
through the British Columbia Arts Council

Library and Archives Canada Cataloguing in Publication

Mair, Rafe, 1931-
    Rafe : a memoir / Rafe Mair.

ISBN 1-55017-319-7


    1. Mair, Rafe, 1931- 2. Radio broadcasters--British Columbia-
-Biography. 3. Cabinet ministers--British Columbia--Biography.
4. Politicians--British Columbia--Biography. 5. Journalists--
British Columbia--Biography. 6. Lawyers--British Columbia--
Biography. 7. British Columbia--Biography. I. Title.

FC3830.1.M35A3 2004    971.1'04'092    C2004-903012-4

To Wendy, the love of my life whose patience
throughout the creation of this book was obviously
inexhaustible, and in memory of the unforgettable
Shawn, 1959–76.

# CONTENTS

# INTRODUCTION

THIS BOOK IS MEANT TO BE AUTOBIOGRAPHICAL. Consequently, where what I say collides with the truth, I prevail. I did, however, take particular care with the three chapters about my years in government for I was inspired to write about them by my friend and former deputy minister, Tex C. Enemark, a man as remarkable as his name. (We share the perpetual question from strangers: "Where the hell did you get a name like that?") Tex is and has for a long time been a master of public policy issues in Ottawa and BC. He spent considerable time with my old law classmate Ron Basford when Ron was a federal cabinet minister and, as a result, I don't believe there is anyone in Canada whom Tex doesn't know or who doesn't know Tex. Of course, I do exaggerate a tad, but his contacts in almost every area of public policy are incredible. But Tex has not only been a bureaucrat and a politician's aide, he has done such things as edit a magazine and sink old ships to make neat places for divers to go.

When Tex encouraged me (shamed me really!) into writing about our years together—I as minister, he as deputy minister of Consumer and Corporate Affairs (1976–78)—I asked him for his recollections. Were it not for the fact that I intend to keep all to myself the massive royalties that I know this book will generate, I would admit how much of those three chapters I owe not only to his memory but his composition. Tex is a helluva guy and for three years we had a partnership I'll never forget.

# I
## Some Background

I'M A VANCOUVER BOY, BORN IN Grace Hospital, Vancouver, on New Year's Eve, 1931. My father was a Kiwi by birth, being descended on his father's side from a pioneer family of Scots who had settled in the Bay of Islands on the North Island of New Zealand in the early 1800s. But in 1913 Dad's maternal grandfather, a Doctor Coates, originally from Salisbury, England, a man blessed with that business acumen for which the medical profession is so famous, heard that Vancouver's streets were paved with gold, so he transported the whole family there: my great grandmother (whom I remember in her wrinkled old age), my grandfather Leslie, my grandmother Blanche (called Phyllis or Phyl for some obscure reason), my dad (the first of four consecutive Kenneths), his twin sister Lois, and their younger sister Bertha (who was, mercifully, called Boo all her life). They settled in the West End, which was then the fashionable place to live. Dad attended Lord Roberts, King George and Prince of Wales High School (from which I later graduated though he didn't) and went into the paper box business where he stayed most of his business life. Until the late fifties Dad did well and was well known as a yachtsman at the Royal Vancouver Yacht Club; his old teak, 45-foot, double-ended power boat, the *Gleniffer*, can still be seen around the Vancouver waterfront. (When the huge USS *Iowa* came to Vancouver in 1948, Dad took his little yacht to her stern, saluted by lowering his flag and the *Iowa* saluted back!)

My mother was born in Vancouver to Leonard and Jane (Macdonald) Leigh, and she too grew up in the West End. My Gram had an enormous influence on me. Coming from Cape Breton Island, she was more Scots than the Scots and never for a moment forgot the Massacre of Glencoe in 1692 where members of Clan Campbell murdered their Macdonald hosts in their sleep. To the end of her life she maintained she had never met a Campbell she liked or trusted, and I'm not all that sure she was kidding. She had arrived in Vancouver on the second CPR passenger train and she came here with the same intense dislike of Toronto for which Vancouverites are now so famous. So livid was she when Eatons bought out our home-grown David Spencer's Department Stores that she forbade any of us to shop there! The fact is, every time I went into Eatons, I seemed to have a bad experience which may, I admit, have been because of the Scottish chip she had planted on my shoulder. In any event, when Eatons went belly up I'm sure I heard Gram saying yes! from her grave.

My maternal grandfather, whom I called Gandy, an American by reason of the fact that his English mother gave birth to him as the family was passing through Minneapolis, was also a considerable influence. He and Gram lived on a small farm in Burnaby. Yes, Burnaby. I used to stay with them frequently and learned such invaluable life lessons as it's better to wring the neck of a chicken than cut its head off because it's much less messy. Gandy had a bantam rooster named Jiggs who always chased me and frightened me out of my wits. Then one day Gandy and I went into the nearby woods where he fashioned me a sling shot. We then went back to the chicken enclosure where I found Jiggs parading himself amongst his servile hens. Gandy handed me a cinder from the path, and when Jiggs wasn't looking I fired and got him square in the ass. I can still see that damned bird catapulting into the air then, loose feathers flying, scampering for the safety of the henhouse. Jiggs never bothered me again! It was Gandy, as much as anyone, who gave me a lifetime love of the outdoors. He showed me the moss growing on the north side of trees and what sort of crawly things live in ponds. Gandy also had a "Chinaman"—for that's what they were called back then—named Lee Yuen who lived in a shack on the property. I never did find out what that was all about, but I do know that Lee was unfailingly kind to me, showed me how he smoked his water pipe (what he was smoking I can't say) and the huge oranges he somehow got from China.

(A geographical note: my four grandparents were born in Auckland, New Zealand; Salisbury, England; Cape Breton Island, Nova Scotia; and Minneapolis, Minnesota. Getting them all together took some doing!)

My relationship with my father was, I suppose, pretty typical of the times—stand offish. If I had to confide or confess, it was to my mom, not Dad. Unfortunately, what I remember most were two severe beatings, the last one for stealing two silver dollars from my aunt's bookcase while she was busy driving an ambulance in war-torn Belgium and then lying about it. I was about 12 at the time and was thoroughly ashamed of myself—and still am, for that matter. The bigger shame is that this beating, and that's what it was, is what I remember best about my dad, though he did a lot for me and I know loved me very much. I owe my education to him and a great deal else besides. He was the most honest man I've known—dishonesty for him was unforgivable.

My mother—Frances but always called Frankie—went to Crofton House School, the girls private school, back before it moved to west Kerrisdale. She worked as a stringer for the Vancouver *Province*'s "social page" in the days before such pages fell out of fashion. She knew everyone who lived on the West Side of Vancouver and was your basic snob–but a nice one. She didn't look down on anyone but was simply convinced that God had settled everyone in his place and that we should all simply accept that. Like her mom, she was built of very stern stuff and had character, and she tried very hard to instill backbone into her two sons. (I have a brother Leigh, five years younger. He managed to stay out of the public eye and was a successful businessman, retiring a couple of years ago to live half the year in Russell in the Bay of Islands, New Zealand, and the other half near Vancouver.)

It was my mother who taught me to love reading. Not only did she read to me when I was little—books by A.A. Milne and later those wonderful English boys' books like *The Boys Own Journal* and *Chums*–but she encouraged me to read *The New Yorker*, *Harper's Bazaar* (as it was then known), and my dad's *Time*. She was still reading to me when I was in high school as we tried to master Latin and French together.

Mom had her trials with me, of course. I was inclined from birth to be anti-establishment and anti-authority. I certainly didn't lead a quiet, austere youth, to say the least. But Mom was always there for a listen when I needed it. She lived to 84 and died truly loved by all whom she touched. (She was very close to my first wife, Eve, and her worst moments were the death of my beautiful daughter Shawn in 1976 and the subsequent break-up of my marriage.)

I grew up mainly in Kerrisdale at 6389 McCleery Street, which at that time had the nice rural touch of a working dairy farm—owned by Dutch Baroness Van Steenwyk—at the top of the street. But for a growing boy and his pals it was the woods behind it that was the big attraction: it was a super place to build forts or play doctor.

I went to kindergarten at Jack and Jill at the corner of East Boulevard and 45th Avenue, the fashionable place for West Side Vancouverites to send their kids. A class picture looks like a *Who's Who* of Vancouver 65 years later. Philip Owen, later to become one of Vancouver's most popular mayors, is in that picture and he was with me later at Prince of Wales High School. His family were great friends of ours, Jean (Dowler) Owen having been a pal of Mom's at Crofton House and Walter Owen, later lieutenant-governor, a pal of my dad's. (It was Walter Owen who swore me in as minister of consumer services in December 1975.)

My first four years of elementary school were spent at Maple Grove, a couple of blocks east of Jack and Jill, and my memories are still pretty bright about those days—the softball games, the sports days, the teachers starting with Miss Dunlop in grade one. To this day I still see a lot of the kids who were there with me. At the end of grade four my parents sent me to St. George's, an English-style private school for boys only at 29th and Crown, and there, after coming first in my fifth grade class in the Christmas exams, I was put ahead to grade six in the middle of the school year. I stayed at St. George's until June 1946.

My recollections of St. George's are mixed. The headmaster, John Harker, was a Rugby public school lad (shades of *Tom Brown's School Days!*), and the school's joint national anthem seemed to be "Land of Hope and Glory/God Save the King," plus the most provocative anti-French versions of "The Maple Leaf Forever." Occasionally we sang "O Canada," the version that had us "at Britain's side, whate'er betide."

I came away with a curious split personality in that I was an anglo-phile, which I remain, yet chafed at the feeling that Canada was run by Englishmen. I still get teary when I read Sir Henry Newbolt's "Drakes Drum" or "Vitae Lampada" (Play up! play up! and play the game!) and my hero worship of Winston Churchill has been a lifetime commitment, yet the plummy accents of a superior, snotty-nosed Englishman annoy the hell out of me.

I loved the games at St. George's, especially rugby and cricket—very English games but then this was a very English school. I was the sort that in the English vernacular was "a useful breakaway at rugby" and a "useful all-rounder at cricket." I usually went third or fourth in any pickup games. But I must say that my love was cricket, partly because Dad played for Point Grey, then for Brockton Point, in the local cricket league. My cousin Hugh's dad, my uncle Howard, an Englishman, also played for Brockton Point until he left for Italy where he was killed in 1944. But Don Bradman, the greatest batsman of all time, was my real hero, and I saw him play at Brockton Point right after the war and was horrified to see him "bowled for a duck."

Sometimes when our dads were playing, Hugh and I used to sneak off from the cricket pitch at Upper Brockton Point to play down at the beach. Our favourite game of pirates had us wading out to Deadman's Island, now HMCS Discovery. As I recall, our moms were quite distraught to see their sopping wet, seaweed-covered sons return to the cricket pitch. But parents didn't supervise as much in those days. When Hugh and I were in our very early teens, we and some mates would take the street car to the harbour, catch the ferry over to North Van, take the street car up to the top of Grand Boulevard, then spend the day hiking up and down Lynn Creek. One of our favourite games was to swing out on a rope over the pool that is now out of bounds because of the number of tragedies that have occurred there. And probably our favourite form of transportation was by thumbing rides. (The saved fare could buy you a glazed donut!) We all did it then, girls as well. No one thought anything about it. Those were really very different days.

I came away from St. George's with a terrific grounding in current affairs, and for a boy interested in such things, there was no time quite like World War II. I kept a huge world map on my bedroom wall in which I put pins with little flags on them to denote how the Eighth Army was doing (Uncle Howard was attached to the Eighth, the famous "Desert Rats" of General, later Field Marshall, Montgomery), where the current Russian front was, and how the Americans were doing against the "Japs"—as they were always called then—in the Pacific. My interest in general knowledge was such that I won the school prize for it in grade seven.

St. George's also left me with a powerful love of English literature which in later life I rather abandoned, a bit sadly, for political sciences and biographies, especially those involving British and European histories. Truly sad was the fact that I could never quite relate to the history of eastern Canada. I always said that this was because it was all so far away, but that doesn't really wash because I loved American history, especially that of their War of Independence. As I look back, I think the main reason was that St. George's, which had such an abundance of discipline, most often in the form of corporal punishment, had put me at odds with authority, and I saw the American Revolution as a reflection of my own rebellion against the English authority of my middle schooling. This meant, horror of all horrors, that I rather favoured the American side in the War of 1812. But I think there was more to it than that: I bitterly resented not learning about British Columbia. I remember—I think I was still at Maple Grove, though it might have been later—asking a teacher why we learned all about Iroquois, Hurons and Algonquins but nothing of the Musqueams with whom I used to fish in Tin Can Creek near where we lived. In any event, I became more of a British Columbian than a Canadian, and there I've remained.

Prince of Wales at 25th and Marguerite vied with University School for honours as the smallest high school in Vancouver. I actually lived in the Magee High School district, but Mr. McCorkindale, the perpetual—or so it seemed—superintendent of schools, heard my plea that most of the public school kids I knew went to PW and gave me permission to go there. (His lovely daughter Mary was the childhood sweetheart of my friend Gordon Christopher and they have been married, I'm sure, for 50-plus years by now.) PW, because of its small size, had terrific school spirit and was a hell of a lot of fun. Many of my lifelong friends, men like Philip "Pip" Owen, later mayor of

Vancouver, and John Fraser, later speaker of the House of Commons, were at PW with me. By a strange coincidence, in 1979 when I was environment minister for BC, John Fraser was environment minister for Canada—both of us graduates of that tiny Class of '49 at Prince of Wales.

Vancouver in the pre-war and wartime years when I was growing up there was a very different town than it is today. Most of the houses were heated by Iron Fireman coal-fired furnaces (their logo showed an iron man loading the hamper but in reality at our house that was my job) or sawdust-burners and the heat distributed by cast-iron, horse-collar-style, hot-water radiators. A Chinaman with an old Model T truck delivered our fruit and groceries, and horse-drawn carts delivered bread and milk (and the consequent horse-buns on the road). And in winter—real winter in those days—bread and milk and eggs were delivered on sleighs (and we kids sledded down Macdonald hill onto the "flats"). There were dial-less telephones on the wall and "Central" took the number you wanted and connected you; nice names like Kerrisdale, Bayview and Lakeview preceded telephone numbers; party lines with their built-in lower social ranking were shared with perhaps four other families, each line distinguished by a letter after the numbers. Mail was delivered twice a day on weekdays and once on Saturdays; stamps cost three cents (the same as the daily newspaper) and if you mailed a letter to Victoria in the morning, there was a good chance it would be delivered that afternoon. Businessmen, lawyers and stockbrokers sealed their letters with red sealing wax and a signet. Street car tickets—blue for kids, yellow for adults—were eight for 25 cents for kids, four for a quarter for adults, but everyone hitchhiked to save money. We took the interurban to New Westminster and Steveston.

Those were the days when the *Vancouver Sun* ran swimming classes at Lumberman's Arch in Stanley Park, when a seedy old buffalo roamed the paddock across from the yacht club, when HMCS Discovery was just plain old Deadman's Island, when Teddy Lyons manned the open air street car that showed Vancouver and the park off to tourists. There was no Lions Gate Bridge, and the old ferries to North Vancouver carried vehicles and the West Van ferries were sleek and new. The Granville Street bridge was shared with street cars then and, going through the span, the lanes were barely wide enough for a car to negotiate.

Summers brought the terrifying annual polio scare; and when you caught chickenpox or measles or whooping cough, you stayed in bed and listened to soaps like "Oxydol's Own Ma Perkins" and "Big Sister" brought to you by Rinso White, programs you hadn't heard since the last time you had a childhood disease—and nothing had changed in the plots. In the fall you could hear the steady staccato of shotguns from the Richmond dikes and the foghorn at Point Atkinson lighthouse, still manned in those days, making its regular "eee-yaw" on foggy afternoons.

In those days you could pretty well count on finding a fifty-cent piece in your palm when you shook hands with your kindly uncle, and your birthday cake always had nickels, dimes, and quarters hidden in it. It was like hitting the jackpot if you got the quarter. You spent your money on a Nickel Lunch or a chocolate-covered macaroon or the red pop called Whistle or nickel cokes or jaw breakers that were a penny each. Saturday afternoon at the Kerrisdale Theatre only cost a dime for kids, and after movie serials like *King of the Royal Mounted*, there were yo-yo and bolo-bat contests. We bought Big Little Books and comics starring Superman and Batman and Flash Gordon, and we hollered "Shazam!" in hopes that like Billy Batson, the newsboy, we would turn into Captain Marvel.

In 1939 the King and Queen visited Vancouver and officially opened the new Lions Gate Bridge to the north shore, but my cousin Hugh and I barely got a glimpse of them because the car went by so fast. And then there was the Sunday in early September when, as an eight-year-old up in a chestnut tree, I heard the newsboy coming down the street crying, "Extra! Extra! War Declared! Read all about it!" Another Sunday just 27 months later it was Pearl Harbor. We all saved rolls of silver paper from cigarette packages because this was some-how going to advance the war effort. There were war saving stamps and war bonds, and the billboard of a local jeweller showed carica-tures of Hitler and Mussolini and Tojo and under them the words "Buy Bonds and Stamps to Beat the Tramps, but Send Your Old Watch to Grassie." There were parades—and weekly casualty lists. There was gas rationing, and even worse, liquor rationing and permits which drinkers collected from non-drinkers. With my father I listened to Churchill and to Roosevelt's "Fireside Chats," and heard the wonderful wartime voice of Edward R. Murrow from Piccadilly Circus during the Blitz intoning, "This…is London." One year the big secret around town was the imminent arrival of the then-largest ship in the world, the *Queen Mary*, being used as a troop ship "for the duration," and the entire population of the city lined the shores to watch this military secret unfold. There was the March morning in 1945 when the ammunition-carrying freighter *Greenhill Park* exploded in the harbour. And just when we thought it would never end, VE and VJ days came and the war did end, and the city went nuts with rolls of toilet paper (doubling for ticker tape) thrown from the upper windows of the downtown buildings.

And by then I was all grown up—well, I was fourteen and in high school. What I remember most about my teen years was that the big games in town were played at the Kerrisdale arena or the old Forum with the Kerrisdale Monarchs going up against the Nanaimo Clippers (Nanaimo's star, Red Carr was rumoured to have played a game in the NHL). And one year the Vancouver Canucks with Bill and Bob Carse and Ed McNally in goal actually won the "World" amateur title by beating a team from Boston called the Olympics. At the Capilano Stadium the Tran brothers, Bill Brenner, our own "Casey at the Bat" Frank Mullins, and the best foul-'em-off hitter I ever saw, Jimmy Estrada, played for the hometown Capilanos. And then there were the Vancouver College football games played there against all those US teams like O'Dea and the team from Hawaii featuring the bare-footed kicker.

We listened to Tommy Dorsey and his brother Jimmy on the radio, Ray Noble and the great Buddy Clark, Benny Goodman, Lionel Hampton, Teddy Wilson, Harry James and Gene Krupa. We played our records of Fats Waller's "Honey Hush" backed by "You Meet the Nicest People in Your Dreams," Sonny Dunham and "Memories of You," and Frank Sinatra when he sang for Harry James, then Tommy Dorsey. There was "Jazz at the Philharmonic" with Norman Granz, and greats like Lester Young, Flip Phillips, Illinois Jacquet, Nat "King" Cole (before he went commercial) and those Vancouver favourites, The Mills Brothers. We danced the home waltz, usually Glenn Miller's

"Moonlight Serenade" with our "steadies" at the Saturday Night Club at St. John's Anglican Church in Shaughnessy.

One of the rites of passage into adulthood came when, at age 16, we were allowed to smoke in front of our parents. Before that, we all tried to look 16 so we could get in to see "The Sarong-Stealing Parrot" at the girly shows featured at the Beacon Theatre (later the State), and we learned about girdles and garter belts that held up girls' two-legged nylons so we were ready for the challenges they posed in the back seat of a car at Struggler's Gulch, as the Simon Fraser monument on Marine Drive was called.

And then finally the day came when you looked old enough to drink officially, and the big kick was to smuggle a bottle of hootch into the Cave, the Palomar or the Flame, all supper clubs that piously declared it illegal to drink on their premises—which of course it was—but which provided mixer, even water, at a huge mark-up. Joe Philipone at the Penthouse, which had neat little slots under the tables that exactly fitted a bottle of rye, always seemed to know when the police were about to descend and always advised his patrons so they could take suitable steps to hide anything naughty. There were clubs, too, like the Pacific Athletic Club and the Arctic Club where, before the arrival of cocktail bars, you could get a drink. (Humorist Barry Mather opined that the Pacific Athletic Club was no more noted for its athletes than the Arctic Club was for Eskimos.)

But it was still a "small town." The Marine Building, then as now the most beautiful building in Vancouver, was also the tallest. Dal Richards—yes, the same one—played the Panorama Roof at the Hotel Vancouver, the same hotel that turned Bing Crosby away when he arrived still clad in his fishing garb and the desk clerk (whose fate is unknown) didn't recognize him. Black performers—like the Mills Brothers, Louis Armstrong, Ella Fitzgerald, Nat King Cole, and that little kid with the Will Mastin trio by the name of Sammy Davis Junior who came to play the Cave or the Palomar—were also turned away whether they were properly dressed or not. And the White Lunch was so-called because Orientals were not allowed in.

Those were the days.

# 2

## A Career in Law

I ATTENDED THE UNIVERSITY OF BC and, after a somewhat check-
ered career in Arts, entered law school and graduated, not with dis-
tinction but in the top third, in 1956. This was a class that had far too
many distinguished members than I could name in the space allotted
but included Tom Berger, famous for defending Native causes; federal
Liberal cabinet minister Ron Basford; that dauntless libel lawyer, the
late Peter Butler; and judges too numerous to mention.

When it came time for me to do my law articles, I refused to go
with the establishment firms to which my father was so well connected but articled instead with the late Tom Griffiths whom the "old boys"
hated because he used juries to relieve their fat-cat insurance company
clients of more of their ill-gotten gains than the establishment thought
fitting or appropriate. Tommy became one of the main influences in
my life. Here was a guy after my own heart, a guy who assumed that
the establishment was peddling a load of horse buns until the contrary
had been clearly demonstrated. Like him, I have been a contrarian all
my life. From childhood on, I never liked being told what to do and
challenged authority at every turn. I would argue any politically correct proposition from the opposite side at the drop of a hat, though
more often—as I got older and began doing my debates in the Georgia
Hotel pub—at the drop of a beer.

Thus it was that, when I began my articles with Tommy, I became a performer in the courts of law. Now all performers have one thing in common: when it comes to self-esteem and self-confidence, they're basket cases. They are hugely sensitive, though they learn to put on a brave face, and they take the slightest slur as a deeply wounding insult. Moreover, they have egos that are never fully fed. My favourite example of this concerns e-mail. A performer can read 100 e-mails telling him what a great guy he is but the one that feels like a stake through the heart is the one criticizing him—even just mildly. And he can see his name in a newspaper article and miss every bit of what is said except the uncomplimentary bits.

I started performing one day in 1960 when, as an articled law clerk to Tommy Griffiths, I was sent to Supreme Court chambers (where applications are made to a judge for various legal orders) with the instructions to say when the case of Cusker v. Bouchard was called, "Second reading, Milord." I didn't know where chambers was let alone what went on there, but I was directed to room 235, I think it was, where a judge, not gowned, was on the bench before a roomful of perhaps 75 lawyers. The deal was this: as each case was called by the clerk, the late and delightful George Rycroft, one of the lawyers in attendance, would arise and ask for an order. It might be for letters of administration in an estate, an adoption order, an appointment for a committee to look after a child's interest, or perhaps an application for a jury in a motor vehicle case. The last was what I was on about, while the immensely capable and even more immensely scary Douglas McK. Brown, QC, was there to argue that, because the issues were too complex for the average juror to understand, this trial ought to be by judge alone. "Second reading" meant that argument would be postponed until after all the uncontested matters were heard. When Cusker v. Bouchard was called, I stood up, aware that Mr. Brown had stood up behind me, and chattered out, "Sssecond rrreading, Milord."

Then, in what seemed like no time at all, first reading was over and, because Mr. Brown was the senior barrister in the room, Cusker v. Bouchard was called for argument. I panicked. What the hell to do now? I knew the arguments well because Tom was a constant user of civil juries, but I was just a student! Fortunately, just as the case was called, I saw Tom enter the room, and I asked Mr. Justice Verchere if the matter might wait a moment while I talked to Tom about how to get this thing adjourned if he couldn't handle it right now. "Nonsense, my boy," said Tom to me. "You know the arguments. I'm tied up in the Court of Appeal. I'll see you in the office later."

I apologized to the rather antsy Justice Verchere and made my application, after which the judge called upon Mr. Brown to state his objections. To make a long story short, after a couple of hours of tangling with the best—and, incidentally, beginning to like it as it went on—I won my application with costs. Thus it was that I had a case reported in the *Western Weekly Reports* when I was still a mere articling student—and against the Goliath of the Bar to boot! But, in fact, all of the Browns, including Doug's brothers Ralph and Brent, were good family friends, but you'd never have known that as Doug threw everything but the court bible at me!

From there on I got plenty of court experience. I did all of what were then called police court cases, ones now heard in the provincial court, criminal division. I took all chambers applications as well and had another three reported before I was called to the bar. Indeed, the day I was called to the bar I had to leave my family quickly after the ceremony to argue my first case as an actual barrister in the Court of Appeal. I lost, but the point was fine enough that it too was reported in both the *Western Weekly Reports* and the *Dominion Law Reports*.

As the practice of law went on I spent much of my time in court, but I never overcame being nervous. I am, however, consoled by the thought that the great Senator J. W. DeB. Farris, QC, always threw up just before going into court. And here I must digress with a story about the great Farris. Back in the twenties, so the story goes, he was defending an insurance company in a fire case before a jury. Counsel for the plaintiff entered into evidence dozens of pictures showing the building before and after the fire. Finally, Senator Farris drew himself up, went over to the jury box and said, "Mr. Foreman, I'm afraid I don't have any pictures for you. You see, my client didn't know there was going to be a fire!" It is said that the jury promptly found for the insurance company.

A lot of funny things happen in the practice of law in the courts. (This is also true in broadcasting, these two professions, law and broadcasting, being quite related if you consider that in both they are trying to entertain as well as inform.) Back when I was doing a lot of personal injury law, I represented a client whose back had been injured in an intersection collision, and amongst other ailments, he could no longer—at least not for a very long time—get an erection. (This was long before the days of Viagra.) The case was heard by a judge and jury, and in those days civil juries consisted of eight persons, nearly always men. Since it was always difficult to get an ordinary citizen drawn from the voters list to actually appear for jury duty, the sheriff had a list of what were usually quite elderly men with nothing to do who liked to sit on juries for the eight bucks a day it paid. These men were called "talesmen," and most of my jury that day were of that ilk. My client gave evidence of all his injuries and told how not only could he not get "it" up but that before the accident he had been a once-a-day man. Every day, except for those few "off" days a month, he and his wife had enjoyed sex. Now if this had been some sort of muscled hunk in his twenties, one might have accepted this scenario, but this man was in his mid-forties, small and shy as a church mouse. He looked like the 98-pound weakling the bully always kicked sand into the face of at the beach.

My final question to this timid lothario was, "And do you still have problems getting an erection?"

"No," he conceded. "My doctor gave me some pills and now it works fine."

At this point the foreman of the jury—in his eighties, I would judge—leaned forward and, in a stage whisper heard throughout the courtroom, asked, "What's the name of that pill, sonny?"

Maybe you had to be there.

My family and I moved to Kamloops in July 1969 where I joined the practice of my former classmate Jarl Whist, a Norwegian who must rank right up there as one of the great characters of the world. Immensely bright, with the touch of Midas, Jarl had already made a lot of money. He had also run twice against the then unbeatable Tories for the federal seat in Kamloops and had damned near won in 1963 when, I'm told, one of his planks was his war record as a teenager in Norway. Jarl might have been telling the truth, but to know Jarl is to know that his biggest strength is not modesty. He is a truly larger-than-life man who has enormous enthusiasm for everything he does, not all of which is guaranteed to be in the pursuit of fitness and good health!

Jarl needed a litigator, as they are now called, and I was to be it. I wasn't in Kamloops long before I was asked to take on a legal aid case. Three youths, two girls and a boy, had allegedly bludgeoned a young Italian kid to death on a country road near Little Shuswap Lake. My client was the boy whose name was Hough; the late Maurice Duhaime defended one of the girls, and Terry Shupe, now a judge, defended the other. It was an awful case, and the three of us went into a preliminary hearing that lasted more than two weeks. Because there were so many alleged confessions—all of which wandered all over the lot—there were endless *voir dires*, or trials within the trial, to determine the admissibility of the various statements. It was exhausting work for which we were paid the princely sum of $50 a day, and even in those days that was a pittance.

After the three were quite properly committed for trial, I stood up and advised the judge that I considered that I had served my brief and that I did not intend to take the trial itself. I was quickly joined by Duhaime and Shupe, but because they were much younger than I, the subsequent attention was virtually all mine. There was a huge howl in the local papers and it made the national news. Here was a barrister who had dumped his client in mid-case, and on and on it went. It was crap, of course. I had every right to assume I had been retained for the preliminary hearing only. Besides, I knew I simply could not pull my weight in the firm if I were to devote another two weeks or probably more to the jury trial that would follow. A special meeting of the Kamloops Bar Association was called, and lunch was me. (Ironically, two years later I became president of that same association!) Andy Berna, now a QC and a partner in my old firm of Mair Jensen Blair but at that time with Andrews and Company, sprang to my defence in print, pointing out that those against me never did any legal aid work and that those for me did. In all events, Russ Chamberlain, then as now a very able Vancouver criminal lawyer, came to the rescue and took the case so that the Kamloops bar was saved from my disgrace.

However, some weeks later, Peter Millward, QC, now a Supreme Court judge but then a bencher of the BC Law Society, asked me to come to his office. (The benchers are the governing body of the Law Society.) After the small talk Peter said, "Rafe, it is my unpleasant duty to reprimand you for your behaviour in the Hough case."

"Wait a minute, Pete," I said. "We're missing something here. I don't remember any hearing!"

"Ah," said Peter, "we don't bother with hearings in matters of this sort. The discipline committee thinks it wiser if the local bencher just has a word with the chap."

I well remember my next and last words in this conversation. "Pete, you and the benchers can go fuck yourselves, and that is precisely what I'm about to tell the treasurer!" (In those days that's what the president of the Law Society was called.) I went back to my office just steaming. Jarl asked me what had happened, I filled him in and told him what I was going to do. He and my other partners tried to dissuade me, but I was honestly prepared to face anything the Law Society would throw at me rather than take this sort of patronizing drumhead justice. I duly wrote the treasurer and told him that, without a hearing and a finding of guilt, I was not prepared to accept any sort of action or reprimand from them. Several months passed and I had quite forgotten about the incident when I happened to run into the treasurer, John Bouck, now on the court of appeal, whom I knew pretty well. I asked him if I could assume, in the absence of any reply to my letter, that the matter was closed.

"Yes, Rafe," was the reply, "and the practice of private admonitions from bencher to member has stopped, too." He had the same feelings about this sort of administrative arrogance as I did, so I was not surprised at his welcome approach.

I had arrived in Kamloops just in time for the campaign leading up to the provincial election of August 27, 1969, and it was expected that I would lend a hand to get the local Liberal candidate elected. I had always been politically minded and by the time I started university had become a Liberal tried and true. I had, however, taken little part in campus politics except those of the very best sort—the long, long-winded and somewhat beery debates held in the Hotel Georgia beer parlour. Those were the days of the fall of the Liberals and the rise of John Diefenbaker, and I had fought the good fight in those beer parlour trenches as the Grits were pushed into Opposition between 1957 and 1963. I don't want to overstate my involvement; I was a noisy, argumentative politico, seldom the hard-working "Young Liberal" on the rise, though I did campaign for my friend Bill Trainor as he vainly sought a seat for the Liberals—twice, as I recall—in the sixties, and I campaigned from way back in the bus for John Nicholson, later to become BC's lieutenant-governor, in the back-to-back '62 and '63 elections. But being a young lawyer in those years, my nose was to the grindstone (when it wasn't following a golf ball or into the booze in a poker or crap game), and my active politics had been confined to being a director and then two-term president of Quilchena Golf and Country Club.

From the start, the Quilchena Club had an unwritten rule barring Jews, Asians and Blacks, and when in 1956 the CPR took back the land at 33rd and Pine Crescent, which the club had leased from them, that old unwritten rule was carried over to the new course established in Richmond. After the move the club struggled for existence for several years, and on one occasion the directors made a pitch to a service club in south Vancouver to recruit new members. The only man from that club to come forward and plunk down his $250 membership fee was Jack Diamond, the well-known businessman and patron of the turf, who was, of course, Jewish. The club executive said nothing, just gave him his membership, and though Jack always paid his annual dues after that, he never played a game at the club.

After I became president of the club in 1963, the directors approved a membership in the name of Ken Lee, and a little while later some of the members were astonished to notice Ken on the practice fairway and discover that he was Chinese. I decided I'd had enough of this nonsense, and at the next directors meeting I moved that we no longer discriminate officially or unofficially in any way. I got great resistance from a number of the directors, some because they were simply bigots, some because they were afraid that if it became known that we'd changed this unwritten rule, we would telegraph the fact that we'd had such a rule in the first place. But others worried that, since the new course was near Steveston, which had a substantial Japanese Canadian population, we would signal that they were welcome. "Very well," I said, "we will have a special meeting of the membership and let them decide." This also horrified some directors because they thought it would bring the club bad publicity. My notice of the meeting made it clear what it was to be about, and as a result before it came off I received two phone calls within a few minutes of each other. The first was from a senior lady member who told me that, if we allowed "Japs and that sort of people" into the club, she would resign and take 40 members with her. The next call was also from a lady member and she announced that if the club wouldn't accept her Japanese friends she would resign and take—you guessed it—40 members with her.

We had a full house on the night and there, sitting in the front row, right under my nose, was Bill Campbell, who had spent four horrendous years in a Japanese prisoner-of-war camp. This did not bode well. I made the speech of a lifetime on civil rights, decency and so on. When I finished, I asked for questions. There was silence for what seemed like an eternity. Finally Bill Campbell rose. My heart sank. Then I heard this crusty old Scot say, "Mr. President, when are going to fill in those goddamn ditches on the back nine? I can't afford all the golf balls I'm losing." I could have kissed the old bugger. There was a moment of silence, then everyone started to laugh. The voice vote was unanimous, and thus ended discrimination at the Quilchena Golf and Country Club. It was one of my proudest moments.

While on the subject of discrimination, it strikes me as strange, though I suppose not surprising, that while people complain about affirmative action programs for minorities, they never consider the affirmative action that has favoured them all their lives. For the establishment of our country it has often been a private school, with tutoring if necessary, the right university, the family-financed postgraduate degree, the bonding with future members of the establishment and the doors that Dad can open with just a quick phone call or perhaps a drink at the club. It's the advantage you have when seeking a bank loan or a mortgage for that new house. In fact, it works right on down through the whole White food chain where starting jobs at lower levels can be obtained because of family standing. It is one thing to sit back in the comfort of middle or upper Canadian White society and cluck our tongues at Natives getting into law school because of a quota system, quite another to see how the unspoken quota system has worked very nicely, thank you, for the better-off in our society. For surely we must ask ourselves this question: how can a society be fair when the reality is that it closes doors or makes them hard to open for millions whose only sin is another skin colour or birth outside the ruling classes? The injustice is that of society as a whole and, while it seems unfair that rectifying this must often be borne by the individual, perhaps this only says that much more must be done in other areas. Because above all, society must offer hope, real hope. It's just too easy for us who have never had a door closed in our faces to make the facile argument that all jobs and places in universities shall be granted on merit alone, when it is the White establishment that sets up all the criteria, an establishment that is already snug and warm behind what to others seems an impenetrable curtain. No one ever said life would be fair. It sure as hell hasn't been fair to those born Black in the United States of America or those born Native in Canada. To rectify that, sometimes the tilting of the scales will of necessity be a bit unfair, too.

In Kamloops back in 1969 Jarl Whist & Co. were plumping for Mac Bryson, a rancher who was running for the Liberals against the perennial winner, the just-a-tad-controversial "Flying Phil" Gaglardi, so known because of his penchant as highways minister for getting speeding tickets while "testing the curves" on his highways. The job Jarl assigned me and Ian Meikle, one of my colleagues, was knocking on doors and canvassing for Bryson and the Liberals. The last few nights of the campaign, sensing that the game was up for Bryson— which it was—Meikle and I said to hell with knocking on doors, and we stuffed our propaganda into the mailboxes of North Kamloops, which wouldn't have voted Liberal had it been the only choice in the election, and we repaired instead to the Village Hotel pub. On election night Gaglardi waxed Bryson, and Jarl got into a fist fight with a Socred supporter. When he found out the next day what Ian and I had done, I thought he was going to take both of us on as well.

The following summer what had by then become Whist, Wosniak, Webber, Meikle and Mair parted company with the last mentioned. There simply wasn't room for two egos like Jarl's and mine in one law firm.

I started my own firm at that time, and in 1974 a case crossed my desk that had the double virtue of being most entertaining and bringing me such enormous publicity that it launched my political career. It involved a shapely lass named Linda Adams who had been displaying all her wares in a local night club, Friar Tuck's, run by my friend Liz Biggar, a lady of great character whose chef was her divorced husband Ralph. It seems that Miss Adams, performing her nightly dance, was inclined to take her panties off, thus launching the case of the bottomless dancer. She was represented by the very able Peter Jensen; it was my task to represent Liz Biggar and Friar Tuck's. The prosecutor, Bill Turlock was a navy veteran of World War II, so it was hard to believe that he would take all this very seriously—but he did. The case, which soon became a *cause célèbre* in Kamloops, was presided over by Judge Stuart Van Male (now deceased), a very liberal chap with a wonderful wit, so Peter and I decided that the best way to handle the case was to show how idiotic it was.

The first police officer called to testify, a young and nervous chap, told the court how Ms. Adams had disrobed, exposing her "gentile" parts. In cross-examination Peter presented him with a G-string covered with hair and innocently asked whether the lady might have been wearing a genital hairpiece like this. It brought the house down. My cross-examination went to the question of community standards, a very important point, so I showed him crotch shots from various magazines found on the city's magazine stands, read him the most salacious sections of *The Happy Hooker* by Xaviera Hollander, and then asked him how they compared with what Ms. Adams had done. We called the well-known columnist John Pifer and somehow had him qualified as an expert witness on the matter of community standards. Needless to say, John, being a regular customer at Friar Tuck's, did not rate Kamloops community's standards very high.

The *pièce de résistance* came, however, when we managed to have a Miss X qualified as an expert on dancing, and she gave it as her opinion that ballroom dancing was the only really lewd dancing since it was the only kind where the partners actually touched each other. It was during her cross-examination by the puritanical Bill Turlock that Peter Jensen tugged at my sleeve. "I want to recall the cop!" he said. This being one of those cases where there was nothing to lose no matter what you did, we recalled the young lad who had testified about "gentile" matters.

"Officer," said Peter, "you witnessed the evidence provided by Miss X, Mr. Mair's expert on dancing?"

"Yes."

"Have you ever seen her before?"

He looked thoughtful for a moment, then said, "I don't believe so."

"Isn't it Miss X's picture, in full-frontal nudity, that is on the wall of the RCMP wardroom directly under this courtroom?"

This added an electrifying Perry Mason sort of edge to the case as Judge Van Male and the whole court then had to adjourn to the wardroom where, lo and behold, there was the picture in all its full-frontal glory!

When all the evidence was in, Peter and I urged the judge to postpone his decision until a case from Alberta that was on all fours with ours was dealt with by the Supreme Court of Canada, and he agreed. Several weeks then passed, and finally the judge could contain himself no longer. He gave a brilliant and witty judgment, asking among other things just how much public money had been spent on this nonsense, before he found Ms. Adams guilty and fined her one dollar. When the media asked how Peter and I felt about this decision, we announced that we would appeal. Never mind the one-dollar fine—there was a principle at stake here. We duly filed our notice of appeal, but before the case could be heard, the Supreme Court of Canada came down in the Alberta case in our favour. In those days appeals from the provincial court went by way of a new trial before the county court. But when the case was called, the new prosecutor, Pat Dohm, now associate chief justice of the BC Supreme Court, called no evidence, our appeal was allowed and the dollar returned. Peter and I got Linda to agree that the dollar was part of our fees, and I lost the toss for the province's cheque in that amount.

The amusing sequel to this story involved a prominent Kamloops law firm that had a clause in its partnership arrangements allowing for a partner to be tossed out if he was guilty of immoral behaviour. Well, it turned out that the senior partner, whom we will call Mr. R, did indeed have a bit of a go with a lovely female articled student, resulting in another *cause célèbre* with divorce proceedings and the like. Mr. R's partners duly locked him out of his office, wound up the old partnership and formed a new one. Mr. R sued, and when Mr. R's old partner, now the senior in the firm, was examined, he was asked about this morality clause.

"Very serious matter," said Mr. H. "Very serious." Mr. H was, in fact, a very straight and religious man who, I hasten to add, had no direct knowledge of what was to be put into evidence.

"Is it the firm's policy to have a Christmas party, Mr. H?"

"Yes indeed, though I only put in a token appearance myself."

"At the Christmas party last year, is it not true that the young lawyers auctioned off a night in bed with one Linda Adams of recent fame?"

The examination for discovery dissolved, I'm told, and Mr. R received a handsome settlement.

Shortly after the Friar Tuck's case, which had made me—though a fairly recent arrival in town—famous, I was at my favourite watering hole, the Stockmen's Hotel, having a mild libation, when I was informed by Roger Hook of the famous Hook ranching family, the Kamloops equivalent of television's Cartwright family, that it was the wish of the regular tipplers that I run for council of the newly amalgamated City of Kamloops. I was opposed, but my will was broken as the evening wore on. There were to be twelve aldermen, as they were then called, six representing separate regions but elected at large, another six at large, plus a mayor. I was duly nominated for Brocklehurst and was elected by a landslide of 57 votes. One of my brethren on council was my good friend Nelson Riis, later a long-time NDP member of parliament.

This council's first term started on July 1, 1973, and was to run until December 31, 1974. During that time I distinguished myself on only one issue, but I must admit it brought a lot of publicity. The city was in the throes of preparing an official plan called "KamPlan," and the quarterback to lead us was an engineer from "X" Engineering Ltd. I soon discovered that this company did all of the city's work, but they were also the engineers for the two largest proposed developments in the area, both of which were breathlessly awaiting council's decision on KamPlan. As you might expect, I raised the question of some pretty serious conflict of interest. I got nowhere. The mayor and the city manager wouldn't countenance any slur on the fine firm of X Engineering. In due course, our quarterback placed his recommendations for KamPlan before us, and by the strangest of coincidences both of the developments of his company's clients had made it! I hollered until I was blue in the face, to no avail. Shortly after that, without any plan having yet been approved, a huge sewer and water contract was let to go to one of these developments, and guess who got the contract? You got it: X Engineering!

When the end of term drew nigh, I announced that I was not seeking re-election. I had not been a good alderman. My attendance was spotty. In fact, it was non-existent for the secret afternoon sessions because I found out, early on, that they were only held to pass the motions that would later be trotted out at the public meetings accompanied by a phony debate before the already done deal was voted on. In my subsequent campaign for the legislature my rather indifferent attendance record was cited by my Liberal opponent, but it had little if any impact as the voters seemed more interested in the fact that I had stood up to the city establishment.

Before I leave the subject of Kamloops civic politics, let me tell you about the mayor we elected in 1976 to replace the one I had served under. By that time I was in the legislature, but back in Kamloops my friend Bud Smith, later attorney general under Bill Vander Zalm, was going stir crazy in his law office. (He had become a member of my old firm when I left.) He, being a political animal to end all political animals and with no provincial or federal elections to get involved in, had become interested in the local scene. Over a drink with him and several of my other supporters, we decided to start a civic party called the Kamloops Voters Association (KVA) and, casting about for a mayoralty candidate, we decided on Mike Latta, a very popular businessman, though a neophyte in politics. His opposition was a former mayor of both Brocklehurst (before the amalgamation) and Kamloops named Al Thompson, who looked like and was thus known as Mr. Dressup. Thompson was sure to win but Mike ran a game campaign.

On the day of the election I came home to Kamloops for the vote, and in the taxi on the way into town from the airport I asked the driver how the election was going.

"The media all say Thompson," he said, "but I have a feeling Latta might win."

When I got to town, I went over to Al LaChance's barbershop. Same question, same answer word for word. Latta's headquarters was a room in the Stockmen's Hotel, and just as the polls closed he arrived, and I asked him how he thought he would do. Mike was sure he would lose big time. "Mike," I said, "I have it on the authority of a taxi driver and my barber that you're a shoo-in. They know about these things."

And so it proved.

Jarl Whist's path and my own crossed again in early 1975 when, under Jarl's impetus, a number of us formed the "Majority Movement," which was designed to unite all those opposed to the NDP government of Dave Barrett. The notion was grabbed by Vancouver politicos but, while it moved like a brush fire across bc, it didn't take hold. However, it did focus the mind of the bc voter and, in my opinion, had a hell of a lot to do with the ability of Bill Bennett and Grace McCarthy to bring most of the "right" back under the Social Credit banner. Grace was highly regarded by all of us in the Majority Movement and considered a saint by some. Rightly she was seen as the person most responsible for the revival of the Social Credit Party after it lost the election in 1972. After 1974 she travelled the province so many times she must have lost count. She was a whirlwind when she descended into your riding, barking orders—always with that huge smile—and giving advice you hated to hear but you knew was right.

Bill Bennett had decided that Kamloops would be the first riding to select a candidate, mainly because he wanted to show the province that Phil Gaglardi was finished. Though Phil was a great character from W.A.C. Bennett's days, he had come to represent all that the public assumed was wrong with the Social Credit Party. The selection of a candidate was set for March 17, 1975, and the race was on. A young man named Pat Desmond from a pioneer family was the early favourite. His declaration of intent was followed by that of Dave Kozoris from Barriere who would bring a lot of support from the North Thompson communities. At the last moment Helmut Allert joined in; he was never a serious candidate, but the old guard was hoping that he would take support away from me. And there was I with an unstoppable machine that had been built up by my friend Dick Lillico, a former broadcaster from Moose Jaw, who had been an insider public relations man with W.A.C. Bennett and more recently with Bill Bennett.

The local party brass arranged a series of meetings, one of which would be my chance to show my stuff. I was awful. My speech, if that it could be called, was written in longhand and contained every platitude known to politics. I remember being at about page four of a twenty-page script, sweating profusely, and deciding to bail, which I did. I learned what the sound of one hand clapping was all about. I was mortified. As it happened, I was driving to Vancouver that night with Claude Richmond, later to become speaker of the house, so I could talk this all out with a friend.

"Was it as bad as I think, Claude?"

"It was fucking awful," he said. And he suggested that I speak to political crowds as I would to a jury—off the cuff but supported by a few notes in my hand. He also suggested brevity, commenting none too kindly that the only good thing about my speech was that it was short.

As I look back, I ask myself why I had decided to run for this job. I was scarcely a real Social Crediter and had, in fact, consistently voted Liberal. Indeed, the first vote I ever cast for Social Credit was for myself! What I was, I think, was a reasonably bright lawyer with a big chip on his shoulder when it came to authority. I was, to put a word to it, an opportunist. I was trying to get nominated to get rid of the hated NDP, and it seemed to me that the revived Socreds with Bill Bennett at the head and ably assisted by Grace McCarthy were the best bet.

That nomination contest had a huge following in the constituency and there was such a crowd at the nominating meeting in the Kamloops Senior Secondary High School that microphones had to be placed outside for the overflow. The speech I gave that night was, in remarkable contrast to those of my four opponents, very brief. My representative counting ballots was a chap named Ted Smith, and we arranged that, if I won, he would give me the high sign. Grace McCarthy chaired the meeting that was, to say the least, raucous. Dave Kozoris came with a caravan of supporters, most of whom (though not Dave) had clearly been into the refreshments. As the crowd came to order, Grace looked over at me and said, "Rafe, all I see are Kozoris and Desmond fans. Where are yours?"

"Mine," I said, "are the quiet ones waiting to vote."

After the voting, I looked at Ted and saw nothing. "What the hell?" I thought. I'd been sure I was going to win. When Grace was handed the results, she launched into one of her famous, unscripted, almost endless rallying speeches. I was, of course, beside myself. How could I have lost? And on the first ballot, too! Finally Grace opened the paper and said, "You have selected. . .Rafe Mair!"

When Ted came up, I was too happy to be angry with him, but I asked, "What the hell happened to that high sign?"

"Hell, Rafe," he said, "you were just a bit too overconfident, so I figured I'd let you sweat it out awhile!"

I had been on the wagon for the campaign, but when we all repaired to the Stockmen's Hotel, I made up for a bit of lost time.

# 3

## A Novice in Provincial Politics

D
AVE BARRETT, TO THE SURPRISE of all, especially the members of
his own party, called an election that fall, and on December 11,
1975, I was elected to the legislature, along with enough of us to form
a government. A few days later I was informed by Peter Hyndman,
a Social Credit insider and later a cabinet minister, that Bill Bennett
wanted to meet with me at the Harbour Towers Hotel in Victoria at
1:30 that afternoon. I arrived to see Jack Davis, a former federal Liberal
minister in the lobby; we didn't know each other but we both knew
why we were there. Jack went in to see Bill Bennett first, and then there
was I, 44 years old, a lawyer who had been used to tough spots in front
of judges, quaking in my boots as I went in to see this severe-looking
man, six months my junior.

When I had first met Bennett in Kamloops back in 1974, he had encouraged me to seek the nomination, but he had also made it clear that
he didn't interfere in such matters. After I was nominated, I had met
with him in Victoria and he introduced me to the House, but when we
went for a drink afterwards, he—rather brusquely, I thought—made
it clear that no one was being promised anything, much less a cabinet
seat. To be truthful, I was more than a bit scared of him—and I was by
no means alone in this feeling, as I was to find out in later discussions
with colleagues.

So there I was, knees shaking, as I went into Bill's room where I was told in about 30 seconds flat that I was to be his minister of consumer services, the smallest of all the ministries, that I was to tell no one, not even my wife, and that if the news leaked out, I might find myself out of a job! But for all of my discomfort at that moment, I still felt very attracted to this man and felt he was a leader I could follow. But I was sure as hell scared of the guy!

The night before the swearing in, my friend Dick Lillico, the former broadcaster from Moose Jaw, went with his wife Joanna to dinner at a local hotel, along with Grace and Ray McCarthy, Garde and Helen Gardom and other prominent members of the about-to-be-sworn-in cabinet. As they all walked into the dining room, a lady ran toward them hollering, "Excuse me, excuse me!" The assembled dignitaries all smiled beatifically, assuming that the dear soul wanted one, or perhaps all, of their autographs. But the lady homed in on the only unknown in the party. "Excuse me," she cried, "aren't you Dick Lillico, that wonderful broadcaster from Moose Jaw?" It was an early lesson in humility that was to be repeated many times in all our young political lives.

December 22, 1975, was one of the strangest days I have ever lived. At about 11:00 a.m. my wife and I arrived at Government House amid camera flashes and a general look of "Who the hell is this guy?" from the working media who I would so quickly get to know. We went into the giant reception room where we shook hands and talked with future colleagues, most of whom I knew only barely, if at all. Then the deputy provincial secretary, Laurie Wallace, who was the quintessential civil servant, guided us all into the main room where my family's old friend Walter Owen, now the lieutenant-governor, was standing behind a large oak table. One by one, starting with William Richards Bennett, we were duly sworn in. I was the very last. I remember standing in front of "Uncle Walter," as I had always known him, with a bible in my right hand and my knees shaking so much that I was sure everyone would notice. (My later wife pointed out that they did.)

After the swearing-in, there was a brief social gathering with the customary champagne; then the premier and his new cabinet repaired to the Empress Hotel for our first cabinet meeting. After lunch, under the guidance of Laurie Wallace, we all went to the cabinet room in the west wing above the premier's office, and as we assembled around the table, Wallace said, "Mr. Premier, your father always had the provincial secretary on his immediate left and the attorney general on his immediate right." Bennett's response? "Mr. Gardom, my attorney general, will sit on my immediate left, and Grace McCarthy, my provincial secretary, will sit on my right." Bill Bennett was pissing on trees and establishing his position from day one, and the lesson was not lost on any of us.

Having settled us into our assigned seats, Bennett immediately announced that at four that afternoon a group of ministers and their deputies would be leaving for Ottawa in one of the small government jets. There they would meet with their federal counterparts and make it clear that BC was behind the war on inflation and that the rent, price and wage controls brought in by the NDP government were here to stay. The travellers were to be labour minister Allan Williams and his deputy Jim Matkin, finance minister Evan Wolfe and his deputy Gerry Bryson, and me with my deputy Bill Neilson.

It was a horrible trip as we had to refuel in Calgary, Winnipeg and Thunder Bay and didn't arrive in Ottawa until 5:00 a.m. We were taken to the Château Laurier where we just had time for a shower and shave before being escorted to countless meetings with God-only-knows how many people such that I have no real memory of any of it. At about 5:00 p.m. we went back to the plane, which stunk of the Limburger cheese that Bill Neilson had brought, and off we went to Victoria with three stops for refuelling. It now being December 23, I had rather hoped that the plane could drop me off in Kamloops, but no such luck. The premier wished to be debriefed. We would all go on to Victoria. Just what he made of the reports delivered by his sleep-deprived ministers I'll never know. But finally at 4:00 p.m. I was back on the plane heading for home, the only other passenger being the premier. The pilot told us that it was about the same distance from Victoria to Kamloops as it was from Victoria to Kelowna. Which would we prefer? Needless to say, we dropped the premier off in Kelowna first.

In the first months of 1976 the wage, price and rent control issues, which we had gone all the way to Ottawa to discuss, became acute for our new government. Among the more stupid things the NDP had done was, after freezing prices, create a mythical "food basket" that was valued every month to see how things were going. For me this "basket" became a sort of Chinese water torture as every month the media descended on me demanding to know why the darn thing cost more this month than last. Rent control, however, was not without its amusing aspects. When I met with the officials in charge, I expressed interest in how they had arrived at, as I remember it, something like a 7.9 percent allowable increase in rents for the year. There were shuffling feet and nervous coughs. I said, "Don't tell me you all just threw numbers in a hat, divided them by the number of people, and Presto! that was it?" And that is exactly what had happened! But it soon became increasingly clear that no new apartments would be built until the rent freeze was lifted. As a result, in mid-1976 we decided to grasp both nettles and announced the end to wage, rent and price controls. To our considerable surprise, apart from tenant and consumer groups, it was a one-day story.

Bill Bennett was as shrewd as they come. I well recall finance minister Evan Wolfe's first budget after we were elected. Evan had a mess to clean up, and as he outlined his budget to us in cabinet, he got around to the usual "sin taxes" that were always the first port of call for a hard-up finance minister. He would raise taxes on cigarettes, Scotch whisky, rye, gin, vodka, beer. . . .At that point Bennett got that steely look for which he was famous. "Evan," he said, "leave the working man's beer alone. Do you want every patron in every pub around the province cursing us, if only silently, as he sips his beer?" The tax on beer stayed the same. (If the Gordon Campbell government had the kind of cabinet we had, he would have avoided so many of the silly things he has done—like hitting seniors' bus passes and audio books for the blind.)

When we took power, one of the things that annoyed a number of my colleagues was the term "Mincome" given to social assistance for the elderly. There was nothing wrong with the program itself—it helped the elderly in need—but the name was too identified with the NDP, and in those early days we were pretty eager to eliminate as many good memories of our hated enemies as we could. So we spent an entire cabinet meeting coming up with a new name. We all agreed it had to be an acronym, so there we were, the 18 men and women who ran the province, huddled around a blackboard looking for a name much as one might do a cryptic crossword puzzle. Eventually someone—I think Pat McGeer—came up with Guaranteed Annual Income for the Needy: GAIN. We were as proud as Jack Horner with the plum on his thumb. To celebrate, we gave the seniors a bit of a raise. The next day we got a lesson in what happens when you try to be cute in politics. The big black headline on the Victoria *Times* read: MINCOME WIPED OUT. It took considerable effort to explain that one away to the elderly, I can tell you.

In 1975 the NDP had brought in a rule change that limited to 130 hours the amount of time that could be spent altogether on debate over the budget estimates. Prior to that time the debates had been limitless as each minister presented his estimates, in those days to the whole House sitting as a committee, and defended such of his items as the Opposition wished to question. It often became a terrific battle between the Opposition and the ministers who, for one reason or another, they wished to attack. Only rarely does such debate disclose anything unusual of a financial nature. In effect, it is just a never-ending question period where Opposition can batter ministers and hope it all gets into the media.

When this rule change was brought in, the Socred Opposition cleverly ran out the whole 130 hours before it was the finance minister's turn, so that when he stood up, the speaker passed each of his estimates without permitting debate. Naturally Bill Bennett, as Opposition leader, took this well-scripted play to the people, shouting, "Not a dime without debate!" It had a devastating effect for here was the NDP, already proven by the Socred Opposition to be wastrels in government, now denying the Opposition the right to debate the finance minister's estimates. This may have been the straw that broke the camel's back, especially since the NDP then foolishly made a martyr out of the well-off Bennett by depriving him of his legislative stipend while he was on the road. The whole thing was stupidly handled by the Barrett government. Early on, it was obvious what the Socreds were up to, and the NDP could easily have scotched it by simply saying, "We waive the 130-hour rule. Debate away to your heart's content." This would have successfully spiked the Socreds' guns and taken away a huge and devastating election issue. But the story doesn't end there. On March 17, 1976, when our first session as the government began, we looked at the 130-hour rule and decided, "Hell, this makes sense!" Needless to say, the NDP gleefully pounced on this and ran estimates interminably. What goes around comes around.

The legislature was a scary place for me, very scary. This was particularly so since the NDP Opposition had racked up years of experience in the place. I was scared stiff of Dave Barrett, Gary Lauk and Graham Lea, but I soon got the hang of it because it was bombast and rudeness, not carefully articulated arguments, that carried the day. Once I had learned that, contrary to all I had learned in school, the legislature was only good for the figurative spilling of blood, I understood the game and had a hell of a good time.

However, relations between the Socreds and the NDP were little short of vicious during the years I sat in the House. They reflected the intense dislike between Dave Barrett and Bill Bennett that had started in 1973 when Bennett had won a by-election to replace his father. There are countless stories about this ill will. In the 1976 sitting Lorne Nicolson, a usually quiet and thoughtful NDP MLA from Nelson, was speaking when our House leader, Allan Williams, stood up and drew the Speaker's attention to the clock, the appropriate signal to request the usual adjournment for dinner. We duly adjourned and reconvened, whereupon Williams, a well-respected man with impeccably good manners and stately bearing, rose again to advise the Speaker that Mr. Nicolson had the floor. Something went badly wrong at this point because Nicolson thought Williams was usurping his right to speak and all hell broke loose. He stood on a point of order while bedlam reigned. The Liberal leader and that party's only MLA, Gordon Gibson—whom I suspect had been well served at dinner—arose and, snapping his famous red suspenders, gave a classic speech on the rights of parliamentarians going back to Simon de Montfort. This aroused Bill King to a furious intervention, and the crescendo mounted as with gusto he tore up his rule book. Nicolson then flung his at the Speaker who, rising to attempt to restore order, just managed to duck in time.

But the incident I remember best occurred in the 1979 session. There had been an electoral boundary change made in time for the 1979 election as the result of a report done by provincial court judge Larry Eckhardt, who no doubt had been appointed to the bench by

Bennett Senior as a reward for his support. By an amazing stroke of luck, the change Eckhardt recommended added a sliver of staunch Socred territory to Grace McCarthy's swing riding. This addition the NDP labelled "Gracie's finger." If the Socreds had won the 1979 election by a wide margin, this issue would never have had legs, but the margin was only five seats, and the NDP felt they had been cheated out of victory. It then transpired that Grace had spent some time talking to Eckhardt while he had been deliberating on the changes. There was nothing wrong in this—all MLAs had been encouraged to do it—but the NDP painted a word picture of a clandestine meeting and Grace carefully guiding the judge's finger along the line of her choice. This was something that she stoutly denied, as did the judge.

In all events, one evening session after everyone had returned to the House, having had the usual moist dinner, the battle began. One NDP member—I believe it was the eminently likeable Bill King—accused Eckhardt of manipulating Grace's riding boundaries to her advantage and decried the political nature of Eckhardt's appointment. The shouting rose to unbelievable heights, at which point I shouted across the house, "What about Judge Norris?" Mr. Justice Tom Norris, by then long gone, had done an electoral revision for the NDP, and although Norris was a Tory (his wife and son were staunch NDPers), he hated the Bennett family with a passion, so the Socreds had always sworn that this had been obvious in his redefinition of the boundaries. My hollering of his name brought the gentlemanly Stuart Leggatt to his feet. Now Stu, who later became a most liked and respected judge of BC Supreme Court, had only recently arrived from a stint in Ottawa and he couldn't believe the hatred that existed in the BC Legislature. When he tried to point out that what I had said was outrageous since Norris wasn't alive to defend himself, a near donnybrook ensued, such that Speaker Harvey Schroeder, much respected by both sides, abruptly adjourned the House. The debate then spilled out into the corridors where I immediately ran into—almost literally—the former NDP Attorney General, Alex Macdonald. I disliked Macdonald from another movie. He had clearly libelled me but had done so within the privileges of the legislative chamber, which to me added cowardice to the defamation. So on this occasion I went toe-to-toe with him while the television cameras happily buzzed away. Then the very tough—both physically and mentally—Frank Howard stepped in and I decided that this was a good time for an orderly withdrawal. (Howard had been a federal MP, and it had been disclosed that he had as a youth done time for robbery. He had lived that down and went on to a fine legislative career.) Unfortunately, my withdrawal was not timely enough because the damage had already been done. For several days thereafter the television news showed me shouting, "You slanderous bastard!" at Macdonald, and the incident spawned a marvellous cartoon by *Vancouver Sun* cartoonist Len Norris.

Neither of these incidents could be considered among our finer legislative moments, but they did underscore a truism: all laws are really arranged behind cabinet doors. The legislature itself is meaningless except as it allows the figurative spilling of blood that might otherwise literally flow in the streets.

# 4

## The Minister of Consumer and Corporate Affairs

WHEN I BECAME THE MINISTER of consumer services in December 1975, the first pressing issue to cross my desk was—are you ready for this?—canning lids. It seemed that in those days every woman in BC canned all her family's own food, and there was a shortage of canning lids that I was somehow responsible for! As with all crises, this too passed, but for a couple of months I was the bad guy refusing to come up with the requisite number of lids for the season.

In time I went on to bigger problems, among them the "tax discounters" who, often in times of consumer stress, paid a few cents on the dollar for a poor chap's tax rebate. There was nothing per se wrong in discounting credit, but the horror stories I was hearing begged for action. Thus, when in February 1976 there was a meeting of Canada's consumer ministers in Toronto, and the Ontario minister who was chairing the conference, Sid Handleman, kindly asked me to breakfast on the first day, I took the opportunity to ask him to put this tax rebate issue on the agenda. He was puzzled; he'd never heard of this scam, but he agreed we should discuss it. When it reached the table, it turned out that no other minister across the country had heard of it either.

Back in Victoria my deputy Bill Neilson and I decided to seek amendments to the Consumer Protection Act that would protect taxpayers, which we did. At the next meeting of consumer ministers I was surprised to see the issue of tax rebate buyers heading the agenda.

It seems, you see, that in the interim this evil practice had hit Toronto, so it was now a formal problem.

Another serious problem for consumers in those days was the charter flight business. It had become all the rage for entrepreneurs to rent airplanes and sell package tours to Reno, Las Vegas, Honolulu and such places, but often they didn't have enough money to bring the passengers (often elderly people on fixed incomes) home again. After each such scam occurred, the owner would go out of business then show up the next day at a new address with another charter business. Obviously something had to be done. Neilson and I looked around the country and discovered that Quebec had dealt with this problem by setting up an assurance fund for use when a default left passengers stranded. We put together a pilot bill that proposed a small surcharge on every ticket sold, and we sent it to the travel agents association for comment. The agents who attended my office in Victoria were not pleased, to say the least. But the idea had caught the imagination of Premier Bill Bennett who, coming from Kelowna, a retirement haven, knew something of the distress the lack of protection was causing. His blessing strengthened our resolve, and the Travel Agents Registration Act was duly passed. Gustav Kroll (Okay, I admit it! He was a former partner of mine!) became its first commissioner and a very big problem was thereby resolved. In the years that followed some agents bitched about the fee and said there was no need for it as there was no longer a problem. I had to point out that the reason there was no problem was because the Act and the fund were in place, which meant that travel agents who had once been rather casual about putting passengers on fly-by-night carriers now took matters much more seriously.

In the 1980s, when Jim Hewitt was minister of consumer and corporate affairs, he complained bitterly after a large group was stranded and the fund had to be used. Interviewing him on radio at the time, I said, "Jim, if you had any political sense, you would be out at the airport getting your picture taken along with those happy consumers. That's sure as hell what Grace McCarthy would have done!" In all events, it was a good piece of legislation that sharpened up the industry and took good care of consumers.

In October 1976 Premier Bill Bennett decided to gut the attorney general's ministry of the part that administered industry, and he combined that part with consumer services to create the new ministry of consumer and corporate affairs. In November I became its first minister, and Tex C. Enemark became deputy minister of consumer and corporate affairs after I, as minister, hired him. Correction: in November 1976, I thought I had hired Tex, and he very definitely thought he had been hired, until I got back to Victoria to face an angry Premier Bill Bennett who reminded me that all hirings at that level had to be discussed by cabinet and approved by him. In short, I had to "unhire" Tex. I was going through a pretty bad patch as my 17-year-old daughter Shawn had been killed in a car accident only the month before. Grace McCarthy interceded with Bennett for me, and he, understanding my anguish over the Enemark situation, kindly said I could hire him instead as an assistant at the deputy's salary, with the entire situation to be reviewed in a few weeks. Bennett was not being difficult; he knew Tex, and some of his writings on constitutional matters had him worried. In the end, however, Bennett relented, and thus began a remarkable association, one that neither Tex nor I will ever forget.

Tex Enemark is one of the pre-eminent experts of his time on Canadian public policy. I haven't space here to list all his accomplishments but of recent memory was his landmark review of BC liquor policy. When I hired him, he was freelancing as a consultant in Ottawa, having previously been federal minister Ron Basford's executive assistant.

Tex had come to my attention in rather a strange way. My first deputy had been Bill Neilson, a first-class legal mind who would later be dean of the University of Victoria's law school. He had left academia in 1974 to become deputy to Phyllis Young when the tiny Department of Consumer Services had been set up by the NDP government. He did this because "consumerism" was all the rage, and he saw many areas needing reform—not least of which was the retail automobile industry. He and his minister brought in the cutting edge Trade Practices Act, an excellent piece of legislation not least because the car dealers hated it so much. He went on to have a remarkable tenure in that job, and I inherited him when I took over that ministry on December 22, 1975.

When Premier Bennett's plans to combine Consumer Affairs with Corporate Affairs were developing, Bill Neilson came to tell me that he didn't want to be my deputy when the new ministry came into being. This was not because we didn't get along—in fact, we got along famously and made a good team. But while Bill enjoyed being the reformer, he wasn't much interested in being the administrator of a huge ministry that included such things as liquor, securities (including the Vancouver Stock Exchange), companies, credit unions, co-operatives, insurance and so on. And that was when he recommended that I talk to Tex Enemark.

Tex and I had our first meeting in a bar in Ottawa. It was clear from the start that he and I were—at least in this field—a match made in heaven. Both of us wanted to make reforms and he had the added attribute of knowing how to go about it. He hated bureaucratic bullshit; so did I. I hated the federal government; he didn't hate them but he knew where the bodies were buried and was quite happy to help me pass provincial legislation that often skated very close to federal jurisdiction. He was both a "big L" and a "small l" liberal so we were philosophically on the same, or at least a similar, page. We made quite a team, which only ended when I took over the ministry of the environment in November 1978. So in 1998 after my book, *Canada: Is Anyone Listening?* was published, I was pleased to receive a letter from him. But Tex was writing to chide—not congratulate—me. Here, in part, is that letter.

> I was given your book for Christmas, and I am now in the middle of reading it. But I am now feeling really badly. Was working with me in Consumer and Corporate Affairs such a traumatic experience that you have completely forgotten two years of your life? In the narrative, you go from a newly minted Minister of Consumer Services to Minister of Environment with nary a mention of the ministry in which you actually accomplished something of very long-term lasting value.
>
> Let me remind you, for when you retire to your dotage and write the long version. You sponsored 22 bills in the legislature in two sessions, a record never equaled by anyone else before or since. Your administrative changes are equally substantial.
>
> You rewrote the fundamentals of the province's liquor

*licensing laws. Despite the Knight Street Pub scandal [which came after my time –R.M.] after which the then government made some bad decisions, most of those changes have stood the test of time.*

It was interesting that Tex should mention the changes we made to liquor laws first on our list of accomplishments together. With the creation of the new ministry of consumer and corporate affairs had come the responsibility for everything related to liquor licensing, regulation and distribution. And no later than the next day demands had come from just about every liquor interest in the province for a hearing of their particular grievances. Liquor interests are particularly persistent and self-serving. They'll go to great ends to create issues where there are none, to enlarge issues that, left alone, would shrink and disappear, and perpetually put forward the idea that governments are the cause of their problems rather than it being government regulations that, by creating constrictions in supply (and licensing), are almost without exception the reason they can sell their products and services for more than they would be worth in an unregulated market.

Bill Bennett, in appointing me to the ministry, specifically warned me of the pressures that would be coming from the liquor industry, reflecting on his father's perception that liquor scandals were one of the things that had defeated the coalition government in 1952 and brought the elder Bennett to the premiership. W.A.C. Bennett, in fact, took rather a shine to me and often phoned me to warn me about "those liquor people." His son, though determined to avoid any appearance of impropriety, had recognized that it was time to make substantial changes in the province's long moribund liquor laws and directed me to bring in a new liquor policy as soon as possible.

So for two years beginning in October 1976, my main job was minister in charge of booze in BC. My previous experience in this area had been confined to consuming, which is why I'd had considerable experience with one particular facet of the liquor business: the traditional beer parlour. As a UBC student and—I must confess—before I was of legal age to imbibe, the Georgia's beer parlour had been my frequent haunt. The Georgia, however, looked a bit like a pub with its wainscotting, high ceilings and genial atmosphere, whereas in the

average BC beer parlour the smoke hung low, the decor was…well…
absent and the noise was unbelievable. Usually the stench of smoke
was gently yet thoroughly mingled with the odour wafting from the
men's nearby urinal.

Beer parlours had come out of BC's short experiment with prohibition at the end of World War I. It had been adopted because of
strong objections by the Women's Christian Temperance Union and
other anti-liquor groups to the growth of "saloons"—places where
one could go to drink any sort of liquor without eating and that offered no social benefit to the community. So a prohibition law was
enacted in 1916, it was approved by a referendum a year later, the
saloons were shut down and liquor became difficult to obtain. At
least, that was the theory. Before long, human ingenuity, weakness
and greed made liquor available to most who wanted it. Between
the booming trade in homemade beer and wine, a fair number of
illegal stills, the bootlegging of smuggled liquor and prescriptions
from friendly doctors, drinks could be had. Just before BC ended this
unsuccessful experiment in 1921, the government held a referendum
that narrowly approved the sale of "packaged liquor" through government liquor stores. It wasn't long after that when it became clear that
something had to be done to make "liquor by the glass" available as
well. Politically, however, the government of the day could not dream
of returning to the saloon model. They didn't want places serving liquor by the glass on every street corner, either. How then to structure
something that would work, bring benefits to the community to offset
the harm—or moral evil—of liquor sales, limit the numbers of outlets
and return an adequate amount in taxes to provincial coffers to pay
for it all? It should be made clear that as well as harm there were actual
costs involved: policing, inspection and more jails for drunks at the
local level. The resulting legislation was a marriage of convenience
between the government—that is, the finance ministry—the hotel
industry and the breweries. Having decided that beer, because of its
lower alcohol content, was a less dangerous beverage, the government
would issue licences to sell beer in "public houses" that also offered
hotel services. Thus, beer parlours were born, the sale of beer sky-
rocketed and government tax revenues rose significantly. While the
province made bucks out of the sale of booze, the community made
money out of taxing the hotels.

I digress here to observe that governments don't make money from liquor. In 1978 I was challenged by the former Attorney General, Alex Macdonald, to explain why we were allowing Scotch whisky to go up in price, thus increasing the "profits" to the government. I asked Tex to canvass the deputies in the "social" ministries, such as health, human resources and attorney general, to see how much booze actually cost the Treasury. This was back in 1978, remember, but I learned that the government took in about $400 million from liquor sales and licensing and spent about a billion in pretty direct costs from alcohol abuse. Some profit!

In the aftermath of the post-prohibition liquor legislation, hotels sprang up all over BC. Undoubtedly they were a boon, particularly to non-metropolitan BC, because a full-service hotel offered a restaurant, good accommodation and meeting rooms in communities that otherwise would not have had them. And most hotels offered better surroundings in which to drink than did the run-of-the-mill bootlegger, although some bootleggers operated whorehouses, which added a whole other dimension to the business! Of course, some hotels offered these enhanced services as well. In fact, in Vancouver the apparently high-class Devonshire and Ritz hotels did little but warn ladies of the night when the Vancouver Police's morality squad was coming to the bar. They really needn't have bothered since nothing was easier to spot than a cop in civvies. They were a nuisance to the girls but did little to discourage them from plying their trade in the bars.

I had a golfing pal we'll call Al who was a big-time bootlegger. In those days, liquor offences could cause the forfeiture of any vehicles involved, so Al used a number of old rattletraps valued at less than nothing to reduce his exposure. He used to come by the liquor store on Broadway near MacDonald where I worked part-time when I was a university student, and when he arrived, it was like a visit from an oriental potentate. The vendor would invite him into his office, doors closed, then Al's boys would take their rickety hacks up to the back ramp and they would be loaded up. No waiting in lines at Christmas or any other time, for that matter. Surely the police knew where Al was and recognized his cars. I often wondered...but I never asked! Bootleggers stayed around until fairly recent times when broadened liquor store hours put them out of business.

The unintended consequence of that post-prohibition legislation was that in some areas there were too many "hotels." Even today, there are more licensed drinking seats in the Downtown Eastside of Vancouver—where most people cannot afford to drink—than in the west side of the city. On a surprise tour of the Downtown Eastside in 1978 with the late Bruce Eriksen, the alderman who had done so much for this area, I found unbelievable drunkenness before noon. In one beer parlour I watched as the bartender woke up a sleeping patron to get him to drink his two beers so that another two could be delivered. I learned that most hotels in the area survived almost entirely on their beer sales with little effort made to operate the hotel side of the business. As hoteliers were asking for more and bigger outlets, this visit had a really profound influence on me.

Beer parlours were strange institutions. Bland and ugly, noisy and often filthy, they were divided into two sections—one for men, the other for "ladies and escorts only." This segregation was ridiculous but nonetheless enforced, though at least the provision for ladies was better than on the Prairies, where women were confined to a separate room in which men were strictly verboten. Still, in BC a considerable amount of ingenuity and stealth was required for men and women to link up. Some owners, knowing that boys and girls together was very good for business, cleverly facilitated "trolling" by locating their men's toilets in such a way that a fellow had to detour through the ladies and escorts section to get to a place made all the more necessary by the amount of beer he was consuming.

Beer parlours smelled of stale beer, cigarette smoke and, in many of them, the sweat of hard work. There were no dart boards, pool tables or the like to distract the clientele from guzzling beer; in fact, there were neat signs quoting a section of the Liquor Act that said that it was forbidden to dance, sing or play musical instruments. It might as well have said, "Just sit there and drink, damn you!" Food, if that it can be called, was confined to potato chips, salted peanuts and pepperoni sticks, all guaranteed to increase thirst. Beer was delivered two glasses at a time except near closing time when most waiters, wanting as many one-for-yourselfs as possible, would simply fill the table to overflowing. Cost reductions were made by short serving—easily accomplished because the glasses were thick at the bottom and gave the impression that there was lots of beer there. One could, and sometimes did, demonstrate this by blowing smoke into the glass, which, when held upside down, revealed the size of the fake bottom. A slightly short fill could easily deprive the customer of as much as one-third of what he thought he was getting. Many customers refrained from complaining because they were minors. Besides, however short served you were, it was still a lot cheaper to get drunk with draft than with hard liquor. In the late 1950s, as a sneaky way of increasing prices, the hotel industry adopted a larger glass and doubled the price. But they hadn't doubled the volume, and with an even more exaggerated taper to the glass there was a greater opportunity for the bartender to cheat. And as the "beer slinger" could as easily deliver a ten-ounce glass to the table as a six-ounce glass, the owner saved on labour as well.

The cocktail lounges that were permitted in the so-called private clubs and at the race tracks had a slightly different but effective substitute for the short serve. A skilled bartender could get 75 or more mixed drinks out of a bottle of gin by putting very little, if any, gin into the glass, then sticking his index finger into the gin bottle and wiping the gin around the inside of the glass. The effect was such that the patron thought he was getting one hell of a drink when, in fact, he got very little, if any, liquor.

The scams pulled by the hotels would fill a book, but one anecdote bears repeating. It concerns a liquor inspector from northern BC who, when on a holiday with his wife, passed through Kamloops. It was a hot day and, since beer parlours were often the first places in town to install air conditioning, they stopped off for a beer and, in the wife's case, the use of the facilities. When she came back, she told her husband that there was a condom dispenser in the ladies' room, and as she had never seen the unique coloured product offered, she had deposited a coin, but no condom emerged. She tried twice more. No condoms. She wondered if she should tell the bartender. Her husband, smelling a rat, phoned the local liquor inspector, invited him for a beer and related the story. The local inspector asked the bartender to open the condom dispenser. It was, as expected, empty. "How long has it been in here?" asked the inspector.

"About six months."

"How long since you put any condoms in the machine?" asked the inspector.

"We've never put condoms in that machine," replied the bartender.

"How many complaints have you had from the ladies?" asked the inspector.

"None," said the bartender. It was the perfect scam. Few female customers thus cheated were likely to pound the bar demanding their money back because the %#@&* condom machine didn't work!

Since the sale value of a hotel depended little on its assets but rather on the number of kegs of beer it could sell, and since sales depended on the number of seats, there was constant pressure on government liquor officials to approve increases in the size of the hotels' licensed areas. This meant that liquor inspectors had immense powers to enforce rules that frequently were not written down anywhere and that usually could not be effectively appealed. The system also led to bigger and bigger beer parlours, many of them with over 300 seats and a few with 400. One pub near Victoria was so big its waiters delivered on roller skates! It was the closest thing in the world to having a licence to print money.

Of course, while the owners were forever pressing for more seats without also expanding the food and accommodation facilities, they would also then complain that they had to have "entertainment" so they could fill the seats. This entertainment was most often strippers and such like performers, which added to the squalid atmosphere of the place. This trend peaked in the 1970s with a pair of girls who were able to do quite amazing things with ping-pong balls. Crowds of men came from miles around just to witness what they believed (or their girlfriends had told them) was impossible.

By 1976, indeed long before that, the beer parlour had become an anachronism as well as a social blight. What to do? The answer from the hotel owners was simple: let us serve hard liquor, too. The problem with that was political. My caucus, never terribly moral themselves when out on the town, foresaw terrible consequences, the worst of which, evidently, was that men would put rye into their beer, thus making a potent mix called a boilermaker, then lurch home to beat the crap out of the wife and kiddies. I told the hotels that I had higher priorities but, representing as I did a constituency with several small towns, I knew how tough things were getting for the small, rural hotel.

My own view was that beer parlours were bad enough as they were. We would not be advancing public policy to further entrench the traditional beer parlour by permitting hard liquor sales. That would just further enrich the hotel lobby. But I was on a collision course with the politically powerful hotel interests, and tough decisions—which had been avoided like the plague by my predecessors—had to be made. And when my deputy minister, Tex Enemark, and I made those decisions, I was fortunate to have the unfailing support of Premier Bill Bennett.

The end came unexpectedly. In 1978 I was faced with a crisis out of which we managed to grasp opportunity to solve at least three problems simultaneously. This crisis came in the form of a labour dispute—the second in two years—that for the first time in the province's history closed all three major breweries at once. For beer parlours to be shut down in summer was catastrophic, but by that time brewery wages had reached the point of obscenity, the result of the breweries being picked off individually by the unions over the years. Since no brewery could afford to be shut down in the summer, a series of very generous but unsustainable wage settlements had been made. Finally, having had enough, the three breweries agreed to bargain jointly: if one brewery were struck, the other two would lock out. With the exception of a trickle of foreign beer and production from a small brewery in Prince George, which together accounted for about eight percent of BC beer sales, there would be no beer. And summer was coming. The union, of course, knew this and thought that the hotels, without beer, would mount an irresistible lobby to have the government force the breweries to end the strike/lockout. They expected a two-week dispute then back to work at much better wages for all. They were in for a surprise.

Tex was in Vancouver acting as general manager of the Liquor Distribution Branch (LDB) that spring when one day he was invited to a meeting of the three regional general managers (vice-presidents, actually) of the major breweries at the office of their lawyer, Eric Harris. They explained their strategy and pointed out the pressures the government would be under to step in. There would be about 50,000 people in BC whose jobs would be affected, but the breweries had made up their minds: they were going to take a stand. Tex, of course, promised nothing. The government had interests as well, he told them, and he and I would be taking care of them.

My deputy was, of course, worried about how the dispute would affect liquor sales revenues—people could, after all, always drink something else—as well as the reaction of the hotel lobby and the hotel unions. He asked the LDB staff to make inquiries about the possibility of obtaining large volumes of beer from the US and then hied it back to Victoria to brief me. Tex and I had long mused that BC had no constitutional authority to keep out American beer and that keeping it out was probably contrary to international trade rules. It now seemed to us that there was only one course of action: open up the border and aggressively seek out whatever US brands could be bought wherever supplies could be found—not an easy job for it was summer there, too. This would mean expensive distribution costs for the LDB, since the BC breweries had been doing much of their own distribution by direct deliveries both to beer parlours and to liquor stores. Tex suggested surcharging US beer by a dollar a case to recoup these extra costs. We reviewed the politics of the situation. At best the union would call us "scabs," so I decided to talk to the premier about it. He agreed with our analysis, I gave Tex the go-ahead, and before the day was out, we had a plan in place. A few days later, the BC beer industry shut down. We estimated we had about two weeks' supply in the pipeline, so we limited sales to two cases per customer to try to cut down hoarding.

The buyers for the LDB performed magnificently. They discovered beers nobody had ever heard of before, and it came from places that had never heard of BC before. Ultimately, we imported 22 new brands of US beer from as far away as Kansas City, Missouri, and we settled in for a long dispute. By and large our plan worked. The pubs had their beer, albeit bottled and American, and consumers were able to slake their thirst. There was one interesting side game in all this: the union sicced the feds on us, and they threatened to stop US beer coming into the country because it was not bilingually labelled. When I observed that French speakers probably knew what a bottle of beer looked like and told the feds to get stuffed, the problem vanished into the ether.

Meanwhile, Tex and I had been discussing how to overcome political objections to serving liquor in beer parlours; if we could solve that problem, the hotels could survive all strikes indefinitely. Why not, we asked ourselves, allow selected "first-class" hotels to serve liquor during the present labour dispute providing they cut down the size of their beer parlours? These smaller beer parlours could then be left just serving beer, but in the new space the hotels would create facilities much like the neighbourhood pubs that the NDP government had introduced in its final days. Each would have a maximum of 125 customers, and the hotels would have some fixed time—say a year—to draw up plans and have the construction done. Tex and I took our ideas to Vic Woodland, our Liquor Control and Licensing Branch "czar," and together we came to the logical answer: why not tell any hotel that agreed to close its beer parlour and put in the equivalent of a "neighbourhood pub," reduced to 125 seats, that they could sell both hard liquor and beer? The appropriate licence was quickly passed. We told the hotel owners that while we expected nice decor and atmosphere, we would judge such matters on the locality involved: we would not expect the same decor in, say, Kleena Kleene as in downtown Vancouver.

Some hotel operators really liked our solution. Some said we were blackmailing them, to which we replied, "Take it or leave it. It's your decision." The suburban and rural hotels, hit the hardest by the strike and not big enough to have dining licences and cocktail bar licences, quickly saw that this was a pretty good deal. It satisfied my caucus colleagues and within the next year the new "hotel pubs" gradually became a reality around the province. In the meantime, their ability to serve mixed drinks reduced the pressure on the hotels to put pressure on the breweries, and everybody was happy—except, of course, the breweries and their unions. And their dispute dragged on with little evidence that there would be a settlement in the foreseeable future.

There was an interesting "unintended consequence" to all this, but it was handled with his usual tact and flair by Tex. On August 15, with no warning at all, the breweries settled. Tex gave immediate orders to cut off our orders from the US, but there were about two million cases of beer already in transit and nothing could be done to stop them. We were just going to have to flush them through the system. And two million cases would not have been too much to flush except the weather changed. It started to rain, and when it rains, beer sales plummet. As well, it was clear that a lot of British Columbians had taken the opportunity to buy more US beer than they really needed; many, in fact, anticipating a long drought, had accumulated a basement full. So suddenly nothing was moving in our liquor stores. It took a few weeks for the breweries to get production going again, then they announced they were back in business and were ready to ship product to the liquor stores. Sorry, they were told, we have lots. We will call you when we run low. Faced with more pressure to "do something," we discounted our US beer, which ordinarily sold at a premium to Canadian beer, by a dollar a case. Though it was still raining, the bargain was too much for many to resist.

More weeks passed. Then one day the brass from the breweries arrived in Tex's office with representatives from the unions, whose members were now facing layoffs because the only sales the breweries had was that of the kegs they sold to the hotels, and kegs are much less labour-intensive to produce than bottled and canned beer. Tex explained the situation to the group. "The stores are full. We are doing what we can to flush out the system, but this has been a significant investment and the government is not going to dump it down the sink." When one of the union representatives protested that "Canadians want to drink Canadian beer," he was coldly told that this had not seemed to be a concern of the unions when they started the labour dispute. They should realize, they were told, that the government's policy of flushing all surplus beer out of the system before ordering domestic beer was firm. In fact, though many British Columbians wanted their old beers back, quite a few had come to rather like their Budweisers and other American beers. Enough customers really did want Canadian beer, however, so we started stocking it again in limited amounts sooner than I had wanted. Then to accelerate the clear-out of the US beer—we were short of shelf space—we discounted it by a further dollar. More basements filled, and many licensees took the opportunity to offer "specials," but by the middle of October the LDB was back to business as usual.

The whole episode has had three lasting positive effects on the BC liquor industry—and on liquor policy. First, what the brewery unions thought would be a two-week dispute went on for over two months and then, because the government refused to roll over and start ordering beer as soon as it was available, the effects of the dispute lasted another two months after that. It was a painful lesson to the union leadership, and the result was that there has been almost complete labour peace in the brewery industry for the last 26 years. Second, the era of the big beer parlour ended. Even the few that remain are better than they were—better decor, improved ambiance, more hospitable. But third and most importantly, it reduced the reliance of the hotel industry on beer. Hotels discovered that they could sell lower volumes at higher prices in nicer surroundings, and while this didn't make a great difference financially to the large urban hotels, places like the Clearwater Hotel in my riding were perhaps saved by the hotel pub. And somehow we heard no reports of the old man pouring rye in his beer then going home to beat up on his family. In fact, all this civilizing led to lower consumption, so it was an advance in the public policy of liquor regulation. I suppose there was another consequence as well: consumers now had a bigger variety of beer to buy. One thing was for sure: the day of the traditional beer parlour was over.

There is a postscript to this story. Because the three major breweries controlled virtually all beer production and sales in BC, I came to dislike them intensely. Gone were our favourite beers and gone were the lovely small interior breweries in places like Princeton (which had two) and the Kootenays. Moreover, the "Big Three" had combined to form Pacific Delivery Ltd., which shipped all their products to liquor stores and licensed premises. This was fair enough, except they refused to permit Ben Ginter, the colourful construction titan from Prince George, to deliver his "Uncle Ben's" beer through their system. The phoenix-like rise of the local brewery during the past couple of decades has given me great pleasure, and I simply won't drink Molson's or Labatt's as long as there is a BC micro-brewery product available.

Tex Enemark's 1998 letter to me tells the rest of the beer parlour and neighbourhood pub story. He wrote:

> *You began a well-financed advertising program support-ing a more responsible attitude towards liquor that, among other things, was designed to keep beer and wine advertis-ing off of the airwaves. On the liquor distribution side, you privatized the importation of imported products, opened the world's largest liquor store, and began to modernize the prov-ince's liquor distribution branch. And you listed 40-ounce*

> *bottles of liquor. (Well, maybe this latter is not so important.)*
> *Establishing the Marine Pub policy for the solace of fisher-*
> *men was a small, single afternoon's endeavour.*

And then Tex went on to talk about the success we'd had with our cottage wine industry legislation, and I recalled how, within days of my appointment as minister of consumer and corporate affairs, the various liquor interests—"friends of the government" all—had descended on my office demanding my time and attention. But it was the BC wineries that presented the greatest challenge and resulted in our most successful policy initiative: the development of a cottage winery policy, which, in turn, resulted in what is of pride to all British Columbians: the many very successful, world-class estate wineries of today.

Until the Barrett government of 1972–75 came along, BC wineries pretty well had things their own way in the province's liquor stores. While they generally produced only cheap plonk, the Liquor Distribution Branch listed very few imported wines, meaning that there wasn't much of a culture of enjoying a fine wine with a fine meal here. It was still a rye and water/beer parlour kind of society. But even W.A.C. toward the end of his premiership had recognized the shortcomings of the BC wineries. Though the senior Bennett was a non-drinker, he had been an original investor in "Cap" Capozzi's Calona winery. Cap's son, Herb, who inherited the winery, was a bon vivant, a former BC Lions football general manager, and during W.A.C.'s final years in government one of his Socred backbenchers. The story goes, according to Bennett Senior, that one day Capozzi said, "Mr. Premier, you shouldn't be too hard on wine. You know, it is mentioned with approval in the Bible."

"Now," Bennett continued his storytelling dryly, "I never thought of Mr. Capozzi as being much of a student of the Bible, so I asked him, 'Where in the Bible is wine mentioned with approval?'" Capozzi's reply was that it was the section where Jesus performed the miracle that turned water into wine. "Well, Herb," said Bennett Senior, "it would take a miracle to turn that stuff you sell into wine as well."

But it wasn't until the election of the NDP that change actually began. The new Attorney General, Alex Macdonald, was a genteel socialist—a parlour pink, my father would have called him—with some refined tastes. At his insistence as minister responsible for liquor distribution, the choice of imported wines increased. Big time. By the time he left office, there were about 500 imported wines available and, much to the consternation of the long-cosseted BC wineries and despite a discriminatory pricing policy, some of them were cheaper as well as better than local wines. The owners of the British Columbia wineries screamed like stuck pigs. They were going to be squeezed out of business; what they needed, they said, was a lower markup in taxes so they could compete against the imports.

Although the premier represented part of the grape-growing Okanagan, and the minister of agriculture represented the rest, neither said anything to me. However, Liquor Distribution Board data was showing falling sales of BC wines. We had to react positively and quickly, so in late March 1977 I went to the cabinet with a 25-page document addressing issues of liquor licensing, licensing appeals, revision of the neighbourhood pub policy brought in by the NDP and a proposal for a program to encourage a more moderate approach to alcohol consumption. Among other things, I recommended giving BC wineries more than they asked for, partly because if they failed—as seemed likely in the face of growing consumer demand for better product—it would have adverse political ramifications. But mostly Tex and I were confident that with the right kind of encouragement good wine could be produced in BC.

The cabinet discussion was lengthy, with a couple of ministers with more educated palates than their colleagues arguing that the BC wine industry was not worth the effort of saving. However, I had the all-important support of Bill Bennett, without which nothing was possible in our government. (The converse was also true: if he didn't support you, forget it.) Thus I was able afterwards to call in the industry and tell them that we would be lowering the markup on BC wines from 66 percent to 46 percent, while lowering the markup on imports from 110 percent to a mere 100 percent. We would also be putting a floor price under the cheaper imports currently listed and would not be listing any more cheap imports. We also told them that the LDB would not carry large-sized bottles of any imported product so they would have exclusive access to the jug wine market. (This latter is now called the Château Cardboard market, this being the industry term for the four-litre bag-in-a-box). They were encouraged to open tasting rooms and sell wines on premises at no markup, offered display racks in liquor stores for their promotional literature and given advantageous placement in stores. But we warned them that this extraordinary relief would probably be temporary. My deputy Tex was convinced that the foreign wineries would take BC before the international trade body, then called the GATT(General Agreement on Tariffs and Trade), alleging discriminatory treatment, so the favourable markup structure we were offering could last no more than 10 years. Thus, he advised the industry that "they had better get busy producing a decent, internationally competitive product."

The existing wineries objected. It was out of the question, they said, to make better wine in BC because our soil and climate made it impossible to grow better grapes. We asked them to give it a try but received no positive response. Within a month Calona increased its prices. We refused to process the increase for several months, in effect leaving prices as they were before the reduction in markup. But effectively, they were now transferring money the government had been taking in to their own pockets—much to my embarrassment! What had been intended, at least in part, to be a consumer benefit of lower prices went instead to Standard Brands, by then the owner of Calona. The other wineries followed in due course. They'd had little credibility with me before; now they had none!

Tex and I turned our minds to the bigger, longer-term picture. There had to be something that could be done to improve the quality of BC wines. We did not for a moment believe what the wineries had told us about BC not having suitable climate and soils. We both knew people who grew good varieties of grapes and made superior wines as a hobby. Vic Woodland, the general manager of Liquor Control and Licensing, had been fighting this battle for years. Sig Peterson, the deputy minister of agriculture, also agreed. Could it be that the big guys just didn't want to make better wine but that smaller guys could?

At the heart of the problem were, in fact, the grape growers who marketed their product through a co-operative and, because they were a monopoly, could demand very high prices for distinctly inferior grapes. The other reality was that the BC wineries were not allowed to import wine for other than blending, so they had to buy these inferior BC grapes and pay what the growers demanded if they wanted to stay in business. Most of the wineries had very few acres of their own vines so, in effect, in talking to the wineries we were talking to the wrong people. The existing growers had everybody trapped. The wineries were obliged to buy their grapes, but had no bargaining power on price and little on quality—such things as sugar and acid content. But if the government allowed a free flow of imported grapes or bulk US wine to come into BC just to be bottled, the growers would be driven into bankruptcy, and we couldn't allow that to happen.

Meanwhile, the Okanagan Valley had been developing another problem: the fruit grown there, long a staple in the province's economy, could no longer be farmed advantageously because of competition from the subsidized state of Washington. Many tree fruit farmers, unable to subdivide their land because of the "land freeze" and unable to make a decent living from producing orchard fruit, were in a hell of a jam.

We decided that we had to explore the options, and Woodland in his Volkswagen camper set off for California to research the situation there. Upon his return we started toying with the idea of changing our winery licensing requirements by putting a maximum size on the small winery. For reasons long lost—though it was probably to prevent "basement operations"—there had always been a minimum size on wineries and this had successfully kept the small operators out. In addition, obtaining a winery licence required proof of substantial capital investment and a commitment to volume production. Now, over some weeks of talks, an alternative approach emerged. Could we make a policy work that was based on small-volume wineries with low capital costs and premium-priced product?

We put together the financial pro forma of how a small winery would look. We knew we had to keep it small to avoid the trap of increased volumes chasing cheaper prices, and we did not want any more large commercial wineries producing more plonk. We decided that the small winery—the term "cottage winery" emerged at this stage—had to be wedded to ownership of the land and the production of wines had to be based on grapes that the owner grew. Otherwise, it would not work. There had to be pride of quality in the final product. But in the pro forma, given the lack of the economies of scale with a small winery, the price of appropriate land in the Okanagan Valley, the expected retail price of the wine (including the 46 percent markup) and the long lead times needed to plant new vines and see them to maturity, the numbers just did not work. There was also the recognition that the phrase "good quality BC wine" would be seen as an oxymoron and greeted with laughter. BC wines had become so identified with poor quality that anybody trying to break out of the mold would have a difficult time. My colleague, veteran MLA and potent cabinet colleague Pat McGeer was especially derisory of our plans to make good wine.

So now we had a general agreement on an appropriate upper-size limit on a cottage winery but not much else when we met in my office one day in the late summer of 1977—Tex Enemark, Vic Woodland, Keith Warnes, general manager of the LDB, and myself—to discuss a solution. None was forthcoming until Enemark put forward the radical suggestion of just not charging a markup. That is, there would be no revenue it in for the government. Woodland and Warnes were both aghast. "Why carry a product if we don't get any money out of it?" said Warnes. "The whole purpose of the government selling liquor is to make money," added Woodland. The thought of giving up the money machine was anathema to both of them.

But Enemark persisted. "Look," he said, "the volumes are going to be very small. The impact on your bottom line, Keith, will be next to none. But, say we tell the cottage wineries, 'No markup on what you sell yourselves directly to restaurants or to consumers at the farm gate, and a nominal markup—say 15 percent—on whatever goes through the LDB.' You, Keith, will at least cover your costs. Besides, what are we trying to accomplish here? We are trying to encourage innovation. Better we spend the money this way than on some Department of Agriculture demonstration program."

We recrunched the numbers, and it looked like it would work financially. I thought this was the best approach and took it to cabinet. Within weeks of our announcement of the new policy, the Claramont winery was established and was successful in making better wines from better grapes. Several others started up in the following year. Then came a generous program of assistance from the federal and provincial governments to help cover the costs of tearing up the old, poor-for-winemaking Labrusca grapes, which allowed for the replanting of the new varietals and hybrids that were needed for making better wines.

The cottage wineries matured, morphed into "estate wineries," and the BC wine industry took off in international competitions, consumer preferences and financial returns. The loss in revenue from markups has been more than made up by a booming tourism industry based on the cognoscenti doing wine tours. The last time I checked, there were over 80 estate wineries in BC! Had we not radically changed policies and pushed the industry toward better grapes, there would be no indigenous wine industry in BC today at all. And the big BC wineries? They mostly survived because the province loosened the regulations concerning the importation of bulk US and Chilean wines to be bottled here. Under pressure from the Free Trade Agreement, the markups on these so-called "BC wines" increased to the point where there is—except for the special position of the estate winery situation—the same markup on both domestic and imported wines.

Premier Bill Bennett was supportive throughout. His only concern—remembering what had happened to neighbourhood pub licences—was that we might be creating a licence that could be flipped for a fast and substantial capital profit before a grapevine was planted. I explained to him that because of the long lead time between planting and good wine being made, this was not a problem. And it never was. It was a perfect case of a win-win solution for everyone to a depressing and intractable problem. I look upon the estate winery industry today as one of my proudest achievements as a policy maker.

Tex Enemark also reminded me that together we had "brought the troglodytes in the Canadian banking industry to understand that they had to comply with the consumer protection laws of the province. That alone," he wrote, "should have got you the Order of Canada!"

I had grown up believing that Canada's chartered banks were paragons of all that is right with Canada. Unlike the US and most other countries, they didn't fail in bad economic times, taking their depositors' money with them. And if they seemed reluctant to loan you money unless you could put up collateral equal to about twice the money loaned, well, that was all part of the way things should be done. I then practised law for about 15 years and learned that, in fact, our bankers were mostly greedy, malicious, unfair, grasping and overly eager to seize all those assets the poor borrower had pledged, thinking his bank would treat him fairly and honestly. By the time I became minister of consumer services, I was already very wary indeed of trusting the banks. Then I found out just how really nasty they could be. The fact was they simply refused to comply with BC consumer protection laws and no amount of friendly persuasion could convince them to change their ways. Ultimately, it was the publicizing of their behaviour in an outraged front-page story in the *Vancouver Sun* that brought them to heel.

The root of their high-handedness lies in British common law that gave creditors remedies that in modern circumstances had become unfair. Under common law a lender could hold a lien on the title of the goods, say a car, for a loan. If the borrower defaulted, the lender could seize the car and sell it and, if he didn't realize all that was owed, could sue the lender for the balance—plus costs, of course. The situation might look like this: borrower gets a loan of $10,000. After making $5,000 in payments, he loses his job and defaults. His car is seized and the lender sells it for $3,000 then sues the borrower for the $2,000 difference. In the end, the borrower has paid $7,000 and has no car to show for it. And bailiff, legal and court costs might have added another $1,000 to his debt. Several provinces had already passed what became known as "seize or sue" legislation, meaning the lender had to choose between suing for the full debt or seizing the asset. If he chose to seize the car and didn't realize enough to satisfy the debt, it was just too bad; he couldn't sue for the difference. But after BC adopted a similar law in 1974, the chartered banks continued as though nothing had happened. They seized and they sued.

By the time I became minister, the department was already trying to deal with this via the Trade Practices Act, primarily through what were called "substitute actions." In essence, when a borrower was sued, and the borrower complained to my ministry, the director of trade practices would act as a "substitute" defendant. At one time the ministry had 17 cases going against the Canadian Imperial Bank of Commerce alone and, though it was a huge drain on our meagre legal services budget, we felt that if we could get a favourable judgment we could bring all the banks to heel. The trouble was, as soon as the bank's lawyers discovered that we were defending, they would just drop the action. Other banks—the Bank of Montreal, for instance—were complying with the strict wording of the law but were circumventing it; they would, for example, get the borrower's wife to provide a personal guarantee for the loan, even though she might have no income. Nice guys. In one case they loaned money for a pickup truck to a husband, and money for a camper to the wife, and got cross-guarantees from each.

Thinking it might be just poor communications, I took it up with the Canadian Bankers Association representative in BC—a kindly gentleman named Victor Dobbs, a retired executive from the Bank of BC. He listened to me patiently then explained to me—as though I were an idiot—that banks were federally chartered and regulated and that our consumer protection legislation did not apply to them. I explained with equal patience that we had in Canada a federal system, and, yes, as long as they were just taking deposits and lending money, they were indeed operating under valid federal law because money and banking were federal powers. But once they took security on a loan and registered it, they were required to comply with BC laws. Hell, I said, just because you're federally chartered doesn't mean you can drive on the left-hand side of the road. We wrote letters to senior executives of the offending banks—primarily the CIBC and the Bank of Nova Scotia—asking for a meeting to discuss the issue. They dodged, bobbed and weaved. The local vice-president of the Bank of Nova Scotia wrote me a very nice letter but it ended with "I prefer not to meet with you to discuss this issue." The CIBC didn't reply at all.

During my first year as minister I was so busy learning the job that the banks problem didn't get any special attention. With the creation of the new ministry of consumer and corporate affairs in late 1976, I became responsible for 3,000 public servants instead of 94, a number of new, substantial and urgent problems were thrust upon me and my determination to sort out the problem with the banks anytime soon slipped a bit. However, I did find time to take the matter to the federal finance minister, Donald MacDonald, in early 1977, and he said he would look into it. Meanwhile, my new deputy minister, Tex Enemark, who knew his way around Ottawa infinitely better than I, took it up with federal consumer affairs officials and with the superintendent of banking. He might as well have been talking to the Peace Tower clock. (At least you know where the clock stands.) The fact was, within the federal government the chartered banks were untouchable. Whatever they had wanted in each decennial Bank Act revision since the mid-1800s, they had pretty well got. They did not even deal with federal ministers, other than the minister of finance, such was their institutional superiority and arrogance.

By mid-year, having made no recognizable progress, Tex used his past connections with the powerful Vancouver law firm of Davis & Co., who were the CIBC's lawyers in BC, to get a meeting with the senior officials of the bank to discuss the issue. It was his feeling that the Davis & Co. lawyer sitting in on this meeting would be able to explain the simple principles of the law to them. During the meeting Tex raised the possibility of our ministry simply refusing to accept for registration any of the bank's documents that did not comply with BC law, but even that made no impression. The bank wouldn't budge. As summer turned to fall, my frustration level began to rise perceptibly. I was good and pissed off, and I wasn't about to let the bloody banks win.

The matter came to a head in December in spectacular fashion. I attended the annual press gallery Christmas party, and after a few seasonal toddies I began expounding on what a bunch of sons of bitches the chartered banks were, describing in graphic detail the unethical and illegal things they were doing. It's unwritten law that anything said in the press gallery is off the record, but a couple days later an enterprising reporter from the *Vancouver Sun*, Hall Lieren Young, asked me if I wanted to go on the record with my case. Tex Enemark and I talked it over. Why not? Nothing else seems to be working, so we sat down with the reporter for a couple of hours and took him through our evidence—names, banks, bank forms, cases, legal opinions, exchanges of correspondence—in fact, everything we had. We thought the story was too complicated to make a feature story and expected six column-inches on page 18 of the business section. Wrong! On December 23 the *Sun* published the story on the front page in its entirety with huge headlines much like the "War Declared" headlines you see in movies. Across the whole top half of the page were the words "Banks Cheating BC Consumers Every Day." Inside, there were almost two full pages that quoted extensively from the briefing book and from my interview explaining the law and why I thought the banks were covered by British Columbia law notwithstanding their protestations to the contrary. To give the whole thing a human touch the story quoted liberally from interviews with victims of the banks' scams.

I was delighted, though I did wonder what Premier Bennett would say. Premiers don't like being caught by surprise, and since the CIBC was the bank the province did most of its banking with, I knew he'd be getting an earful from them. Moreover, though the bank problem had been a thorn in my side for nearly two years, I'd never discussed it with either the cabinet or my colleagues in the caucus—a small oversight that might be a large one now! I called Bennett and explained the background and the situation. To my relief, he was immediately supportive and totally unconcerned. It is a truism, I suppose, that a politician can hardly get himself in trouble by criticizing a bank, but Bill Bennett was a businessman whom the banks had no doubt felt would support whatever happened in the marketplace. Not for the first or the last time was Bill Bennett's political courage and sense of fairness a surprise to the business community.

The next day, the late Len Norris, the *Sun*'s wonderful editorial cartoonist, outdid himself. His cartoon showed a pair of intimidated consumers holding a copy of the previous day's *Sun* with its headline castigating the banks. Seated on a raised desk was an angry figure reminiscent of Ebenezer Scrooge; over his head was a sign with the words "Chartered Banks." Scrooge is looking down at the two trembling souls and saying, "Of course, I have a comment. HUMBUG!" It was the perfect summary of the banks' nasty attitude.

The other media jumped on the story, but not a peep came from the banks. The single exception was the Bank of Nova Scotia. The BC vice-president who had refused to meet with us had recently retired and been replaced by a chap named Cavanaugh. He had been in Toronto when the story broke and was appalled that the bank was doing something illegal that he knew nothing about. He was equally embarrassed that the story pointed to his bank as the second worst "cheat" in BC. He tried to phone me Christmas Eve day and, when I was not available, reached my deputy, insisting we had to meet to get this thing sorted out. He wanted to meet "tomorrow." When Tex pointed out that would be Christmas Day, Cavanaugh said, "Well, the next day then."

"Okay," Tex conceded, "but that's Boxing Day."

"That's fine with me," was the response. So a meeting was set for my office in the legislature for Boxing Day morning, making necessary special arrangements to open the building. Cavanaugh arrived promptly at 10:00, accompanied by Arthur Pattillo, a very senior Toronto lawyer whom I had known when he was the chair of the Ontario Securities Commission. Pattillo burst through the door and came at me announcing, "Before you say anything, Mr. Mair, let me say you are right and we are wrong!"

Why then, Tex and I both wondered, was there a need for a meeting?

Well, it seems they wanted to make things absolutely clear and sort out what steps needed to be taken. Over coffee we explained in a friendly way how the whole thing had evolved and how frustrated we had become with the lack of response from the banks. We then discussed the timing and process necessary for replacing the misleading bank forms. The Bank of Nova Scotia was going to be issuing instructions to their branches concerning the obliterating of some clauses immediately, which seemed fine to us. They were also going to issue instructions to loan officers and their lawyers not only to refrain from proceeding under the old forms to sue if they had already seized but also to review all outstanding collection actions. It was more than I could ask for. But then Tex put forward the idea that, as long as the Bank of Nova Scotia was rewriting their forms, why not do them in plain language? He said the ministry's lawyers had been working on "plain language" for government forms and would be happy to help. Cavanaugh accepted the challenge and the resulting forms were excellent examples of clearly written legal language, with phrases of particular importance to borrowers printed in red ink. They continue to be used today. Unfortunately, most of the other financial institutions did not follow suit. In fact, so indifferent were the banks to provincial lending laws in those days that bankers in BC's section of the Peace River district often borrowed forms from Alberta banks, with the result that BC borrowers had to fulfill the requirements of the Alberta Dower Act in order to get their money!

We were happy that the Bank of Nova Scotia was now on board, but what about the other banks? Mr. Pattillo assured us that he would talk to them all, that they would go along and that he would advise. We kept in constant touch as Pattillo wanted no more bad publicity, and in early February I received a call from him asking what the weather was like. "A beautiful spring day here in Victoria," was my reply.

"Good," said Pattillo. "The weather is terrible here so I'll be out on Friday to present the sword of surrender."

"How about 12:30 at the Union Club with Tex and me?" I asked.

"Done," he replied.

We duly met and the sword of full and absolute surrender by all of Canada's chartered banks was put into the hands of our government. There was, however, one piece of unfinished business, and Tex, who no more liked being pushed around than I, got the last word on that score. "When will you have your new documents ready?" he asked.

"Mr. Enemark," said Pattillo, "we'd like six months."

"Make that three months, Mr. Pattillo," said Tex.

"Right," said Pattillo.

The battle with the banks was over. And it felt very, very good indeed.

Tex Enemark finished his letter to me with a long list of all the work we had accomplished together: the Travel Agents Registration Act; the strongest motor dealer licensing statute in North America; much stronger supervision of the VSE; the amalgamation and transfer of all the ministry's business supervisory functions to Vancouver where the market was; funding the computerization of the Companies Registration office; moving the province's Central Registry (of security interests) from the Motor Vehicles Branch to Consumer and Corporate Affairs (CCA) where it belonged; sponsoring a new Societies Act through the legislature; introducing a program of microfilming documents; amending the Consumer Protection Act to deal with health clubs and dance studio scams; and, before anybody ever heard about "deregulation," we began reducing the costs of compliance with the 37 statutes for which my ministry was responsible. In the corporate affairs program, for instance, 44 forms were reduced to four. A "plain language" review of all statutes had begun. Standard times for the processing of permits, licences and so on had been established in some programs, leading to less business frustration. Tex concluded:

> *It is quite a record, Rafe, incomplete as it is since I write from memory. It is a record you should be proud of because a great many people will benefit for a very long time because these were things you believed in and saw through to implementation. There were no Commonwealth Trust-type of scandals when you were minister (remember Abacus Cities?) and every time a tough decision came up, you made the right decision. You didn't flinch or waver, and you never procrastinated. You always had your eye on the ball. Your departure from the public life of the province was a sad loss, in retrospect. I am sorry that, when you asked my advice on how to manage your departure, I did not counsel greater patience. But, having given up on the government myself with some bitterness, my own situation coloured my advice. I think that, if you were able to have stood the pain of your teeth biting your tongue, you could have been premier. It would have been a better province and a better country had you been able to stand the discomfort.*

Tex's reminder of Abacus Cities took me back to one of the more vexing problems to cross my desk. Abacus was a Calgary company that had been responsible for a considerable amount of condominium development in both Alberta and BC. It was run by two brothers named Rogers, said to be brilliant financiers, who had developed a very complicated "security," for want of a better word. But when they applied to float a sort of bond on the Vancouver Stock Exchange, the superintendent of brokers was leery of their scheme because frankly he couldn't understand it. It was not normally my job as minister to get into these sorts of problems, and with this one I had an added problem: one of the lesser principals in Abacus, Pal Levitt, lived in the same condo complex as I did and as a consequence we had become friends. Hal Hallett, who was Abacus's lawyer and Pal's friend, had thereby also been added to our circle of friends. A few days after the superintendent of brokers brought his problem to me, I flew to Ottawa on constitutional business and was surprised to find Hallett sitting next to me in the first-class section. Hal was, and probably still is, a courtly gentleman of the old school and he patiently tried to explain the Abacus scheme to me. I said "Hal, if you can't make me, a lawyer, understand what the hell you're talking about, I don't think it's a safe investment to offer to the public."

But the Rogers brothers were nothing if not persistent, and they demanded and eventually got a meeting with me. Tex, the superintendent of brokers and I duly assembled in my office, and Dr. Bill Rogers went to work explaining this new money-raising security to all of us, then left us with the usual supply of printed evidence. After he left, the three of us started to mull the matter over, but we were all asking, "What the hell was that all about? Did you understand any of that?" At last I made the decision, backed by my colleagues, that if the three of us—one trained securities man and two lawyers—couldn't make head or tail of what Abacus was up to, how could we expect the public to make a fair evaluation? The application to the superintendent was rejected. Not long thereafter the Bank of Montreal in Calgary pulled Abacus's credit, and the company went bust. Fortunately, the government of British Columbia and, more specifically, the minister of consumer and corporate affairs, were in no way involved. Sometimes it pays to be dumb.

Although I fear that Tex was being too kind to me in his letter, I must say that for two years we made a hell of a team and got many things done that had long needed doing. What made us work so well as a team, I think, is that Tex, unlike other senior bureaucrats, had the guts to speak out on—and more importantly, prepare position papers to support—the reforms we both wanted to make. My role was to have the guts to fight them through cabinet and caucus. The years I spent with Tex, from a work perspective, were the happiest of my life, with the added bonus that I gained a great friend and colleague. To know Tex and to have had the privilege of working with him intimately on matters of considerable social importance made all my political efforts worthwhile.

In early 1978 the first BC Winter Games were held in my constituency, Kamloops. I really had nothing to do with the town getting the games, but that didn't seem to matter; people seemed to think I did, so who was I to argue? The opening ceremony was held at the Kamloops Memorial Arena, and just as Governor General Edward Schreyer, MP Len Marchand and I were ready to be introduced, the lady in charge, a noted and dedicated local Liberal, informed us that Len and I would go out onto the ice together. To the chagrin, I'm sure, of the governor general, I announced, "No way!" These games were a province of BC effort to which the feds had contributed not a single dime. I was following the GG and Len was following me and that was that. The conversation got a little nasty, with Mr. Schreyer looking more and more embarrassed, so the lady at last relented.

We had, of course, the same reason for our opposing points of view. At that time the federal Liberals, at the end of their mandate, were unpopular, and so was Len. I, on the other hand, was, if I may say so, in pretty good shape with the electorate. Why should I share my fleeting popularity with someone everyone was mad at? It turned out as I expected it would: I went out on the ice to a very nice round of applause and Len, following me, was booed. I had learned a bit about politics by that time.

I had not, however, learned anything about curling. I was to throw the first rock. (Forgive me if the jargon is wrong here; I've never played the game and I think that watching paint dry beats watching a game of curling.) There were the usual speeches about how wonderful this all was, and then I was given this very heavy hunk of rock with a handle. Down I went and gave the thing a mighty heave. Too mighty. Way too mighty. The spectators watched in horror as this missile I had let loose rocketed down the ice and smashed into the boards, breaking two of them. It was not my best athletic achievement.

It had been determined that my cabinet colleague and friend Jim Hewitt and I were to open the court games with a game of squash. We did fine until at what turned out to be the midway point I forgot momentarily that Jim was left-handed and got smashed in the face, head-on, by his racquet. Blood from my nose flew everywhere, and after the local first aid man came down with wet cold towels, it was suggested that we call it a night. "Like hell we will," I said. I was leading 7-2, as I recall, and the game would be finished. It did with a victory for yours truly. I am a tad competitive!

It was also in 1978 that Grace McCarthy planned a Captain Cook bicentenary celebration and, typical of Grace's endeavours, this was to be a really big event. Now it happened that early that spring, in the run-up to the celebration, Hugh Ryan from Park and Tilford Distilleries made an appointment to see me, and as was my habit, I made sure that my assistant, Tony Stark, was with me in the office when Hugh arrived. This was a precaution I had learned from W.A.C. Bennett. When I became the minister in charge of liquor control and distribution, he had phoned and warned me, "Don't you get fooled by those liquor people and never ever meet with them without someone else present." And I never did.

I had known Hugh a bit and he was a decent sort of chap, so after the greetings, he said, "Minister, I've just come by to make sure my ducks are all in a row and that our new Captain Cook brand of rye will be on the shelves."

"Have you," I asked, "gone through all the procedures at the Liquor Distribution Branch?"

"No, Minister. I was told by Mrs. McCarthy that this wouldn't be necessary, that her colleague Rafe Mair would sweep all the red tape aside."

I reminded Hugh that there was a reason for all that red tape. There is only room for so much product on the shelves of the liquor stores, and if we were to put his Captain Cook rye on the shelf, what was I to say to the person whose rye I took off the shelf to accommodate his? He left, obviously disappointed.

Within moments Grace's executive assistant, Ed Sweeney of the famous Vancouver cooperage family, was in my office. "Mrs. McCarthy sent me, Minister, because she's sure you must have misunderstood about the Captain Cook rye."

"No, Ed, there is no misunderstanding. If Mr. Ryan can qualify under the rules, I'm sure all will be well."

Sweeney left and in a few moments my phone rang. It was Grace on the line. Though, of course, I couldn't see her, I could imagine that famous smile of hers as she said, "There must be a mistake here, Rafe. You know how much the premier wants this Captain Cook celebration to be such a success."

"There is no mistake, Grace. Ryan has to go through the hoops and that's that."

About ten minutes later the red phone on my desk rang. I didn't like it when it rang, but I picked it up and said, "Yes, Premier, what can I do for you?"

"What's this about the Captain Cook rye?" I explained what had happened and he growled, "Of course you're right, dammit!" and put the phone down.

In the end Ryan got his rye listed in time for the event by going through the right steps. It seems there was a listed rye that had been selling poorly and the general manager, the utterly incorruptible Bob Wallace, was able to delist it and all was well.

It was around the same time that Herb Capozzi, the former Socred mla and heir to the Calona Winery, phoned my secretary to find out when it would be convenient for me to have dinner with him. I told her to check with Tex Enemark because he had to be with me when I dined with Capozzi. A few moments later my secretary came back on the line to advise that Mr. Capozzi insisted on seeing me alone. I told her this wasn't going to happen. It was not long thereafter that I got a call from Grace asking why I wouldn't have dinner with Herb. After all, he was one of us, a former Socred MLA and a friend of the Bennett family. I told her that I simply would never allow myself to be put in a compromising situation where things might be heard that weren't spoken, and that was that.

And it happened again. That damned red phone rang and I heard the premier's somewhat angry voice asking me what this Capozzi business was all about. I told him. He said (and these words were getting familiar to me), "Of course you're right." And he hung up. I found out later that while Cap Capozzi might have been a chum of Bill Bennett's old man, Herb was no particular friend of Bill's.

I have to say that I always admired Grace McCarthy immensely and knew I could count on her as a good friend, but the reason I have stories to tell about her is because she was such a strong and able minister. Thirty years after she was tourism minister she is still spoken of with awe in tourism circles for what she did. And remarkably to many on the left, she was an outstanding human resources minister, if only because, as a business woman, she made sure the money went to the right people. But more than that, despite her personal wealth, she has a deep and abiding concern for those less fortunate. In my opinion Grace McCarthy has been one of the outstanding public figures of her time. Had it not been for her, the Socreds would not have recovered from their defeat in 1972 and among other consequences of that, I would never have had the exciting political career I had.

I served for five years with what I argue was as good a premier and cabinet as has ever served British Columbia. (Fie on any who say that is damning with very faint praise indeed!) It is not my intention to do a show-and-tell or in any way trash any of my colleagues. I hope I would do so were it warranted but it simply isn't.

The cabinet of which I was a member had a number of outstanding members. Allan Williams, first labour minister then attorney general, was one. Bob McClelland, an excellent minister wherever he served, was another. There was Garde Gardom, Hugh Curtis, Tom Waterland and others. And there was Grace. But we had one man who was invaluable: Alex Fraser from Quesnel, where he had been a successful businessman and long-time mayor. Alex was a competent minister of highways—the Alex Fraser Bridge bears his name—but his greater value to our caucus was as a man who knew about politics where it counted: the main street of rural BC. Many's the time I heard Bill Bennett say, especially if we had been busy congratulating ourselves, "Alex, what are they saying in beautiful downtown Quezznel about this?"

"Wal, Mr. Premier," Alex would reply, "they think it's a bunch of bullshit!"

Invariably his comments would rock us back, and we would rethink the matter, knowing that Alex's judgment of the politics of the matter was a hell of a lot better than our own.

I remember another occasion when the wind was taken out of our sails. Usually when in cabinet meetings we had sandwiches brought in, but one day we broke for lunch and Bennett, who stayed at the Harbour Towers, a few blocks west of the legislative buildings, walked home. When we resumed our meeting, he told us that he had just had a reminder that you can never afford to get too cocky in this business. He described how on his walk to the hotel and back he had been stopped by four people, all of them wanting to tell him what a wonderful job he was doing. "Then," said Bill, "just as I was crossing the street to come into the cabinet room, a truck driver pulled alongside, rolled down his window and hollered, "Bennett, you're a big bag of shit!"

Bennett had a firm understanding of the traditions of parliament, and it came to the fore when Jack Davis, a brilliant man and a scientist who had served as a cabinet minister in the early Trudeau governments, was under police investigation for a silly, yet serious, matter. It was alleged that he had ordered first-class air fares through his ministry and privately converted them to economy and pocketed the difference. I was sitting in the House one afternoon when the premier came in, caught the Speaker's eye, and announced that the Honourable Jack Davis was no longer a member of the Executive Council (that is, the cabinet) and was now sitting as a Social Credit MLA. Evidently Attorney General Garde Gardom, having been informed that Davis was under police investigation, had so advised the premier—which is precisely what he should have done—and the premier had asked Davis to resign pending the outcome of the matter. Davis had refused to resign so Bennett, quite properly, had done it for him. In the event, Davis was found guilty and, as I recall, was fined $1,000 and put on some sort of terms. He never got back into a Bennett cabinet in spite of being a very good and thoughtful MLA—which could be why, in 1986, he stood apart from all his former colleagues by supporting Bill Vander Zalm's quest for the party leadership. His reward when Vander Zalm won was a cabinet post.

Bill Vander Zalm was one of the more interesting of my colleagues. Populist to the core, he based his 1975 campaign on getting "welfare bums" back to work by "putting a shovel" in their hands. When the Socreds won that election, Bennett was in a quandary: he knew he had to put the enormously popular Vander Zalm, whose area of political influence was wide and important, into cabinet—but where? Bennett might have made him minister of municipal affairs since Vander Zalm had been mayor of Surrey, but that would have caused great angst in the Union of BC Municipalities who saw him as a very loose cannon at best. And so he was made minister of human resources. Amid great fanfare he immediately set up a task force to find jobs for those "welfare bums," but predictably he was utterly unsuccessful.

In the five years I sat in cabinet with Vander Zalm, I can honestly say that I never heard a single good idea from him upon which the government acted. For all that, Bill was popular, if only because he was a thoroughly decent man who was pleasant to be around. But because he tended to destroy a consensus rather than build one, he found himself virtually without support from cabinet colleagues when he ran for the party leadership in July 1986. He won the leadership only because average party members tend to look more for "winability" qualities in a candidate than leadership qualities. But I cannot leave "the Zalm" without saying two more things: he was always very good to me, especially when I lost my daughter in October 1976, and he was the best fundraiser of all of us as he auctioned off autographed shovels at constituency meetings.

One of my more remarkable colleagues was Dr. Patrick McGeer, without any question the most cerebral of us all. Like Winston Churchill, for every hundred ideas Pat came up with, 99 weren't great, but the one remaining was spectacular. He was given the unenviable task in 1976 of bringing order to the chaotic Insurance Corporation of BC (ICBC), which had been set up as the government's motor vehicle insurance monopoly two years earlier. In that time it had run about $186 million (about $300 million in today's dollars) into the goo. I sat on the cabinet's insurance committee with Pat, and we soon saw that no matter how much we wanted to let the private companies back in, it wasn't going to work. The principal reason for this was that the companies, having been sent packing back over the Rockies, wouldn't come back. They would sell through agents but they wouldn't reinvest any money in BC.

We made the decision, therefore, in February 1976, to assess all policy holders enough to renew this deficit. For most British Columbians this was a hefty kick in the wallet. One day after that decision had been made and publicized, Pat and I went to the Union Club for lunch. As we walked out, former premier W.A.C. Bennett walked in. "Mr. Bennett," asked Pat, "there is going to be a huge demonstration on the legislature's lawns tomorrow. What should I do? Should I speak to them? Should I send my deputy to speak to them? Or should I just ignore them?"

"Turn on the sprinklers," was Bennett's response.

"But," replied Pat, "it's February."

"Turn 'em on anyway," responded the former premier. "Turn 'em on, that's what I would do."

And I believe he would have.

The Miscellaneous Statutes Amendment Act is a traditional bill brought in just before the House rises at the end of the session and it is intended to tinker with wording of acts so as to make their intent clearer. Sometimes the government will, however, slip something contentious in with the hope that the Opposition won't notice. Thus opposition members look this statute over pretty carefully. This is what Charles Barber, then NDP MLA from Victoria, did in 1980 when, lo and behold, he discovered that we had eliminated Seaboard Insurance! It was quite by accident, of course, but it was hugely embarrassing to the government. By the time Charles had made his find, MLAs were all over the place starting their vacations, and they all had to be called back. That emergency session started at 6:00 p.m. and went on until two in the morning. That's the way the House worked in those days—no quarter given. We got the bill changed and put Seaboard back in business, but we paid!

Just before proceedings in the House begin, the speaker always asks members if there is anyone in the gallery they would like to introduce. One afternoon the late Patricia Jordan was handed a note telling her that one of Vernon's finest citizens was in the Speaker's Gallery. Pat rose and, reading straight from the note, asked the House to welcome one of her most distinguished constituents, Mrs. Cunny Lingus. The place erupted in laughter, and because Pat didn't know what she had done, she sat down bewildered at the reaction.

But not all the incidents in the House were in good fun. I well recall the night the NDP set up Tom Waterland. Tom was and is a hell of a good guy, and he was a good forestry minister, but he wasn't a sophisticated sort of a chap. He was in the midst of his estimates, and his questioner was Norm Levi. It happened that for many months the NDP had been on George Kerster's case for no better reason than he'd beaten Dave Barrett in the 1975 election, and because George preferred warmer climes than that of Victoria, he was always needled as the "Member for Hawaii." On this day someone slipped Tom a note saying it would be good fun to needle Norm Levi by calling him the "Member for Whitechapel." Tom had never heard of Whitechapel, which is the Jewish area of London, and he thought he was doing something amusing. On cue Barrett and the more vocal on the NDP front bench shouted that Tom should resign and that the matter was one for a Motion of Privilege. It was all nonsense, of course, and hugely embarrassing to Tom. It was a low trick, but then the legislature was known for such things at the time.

Not many of us could understand why Bill Bennett called the May 10, 1979, election. There didn't seem to be an issue, certainly not one that helped us much. There was, however, a good one for the NDP, which was raising hell all over the province about uranium mining. There were potential uranium mines in several constituencies, including mine and the premier's, so this issue tended to take the public eye off the real issue, which, as we saw it, was good government as opposed to the bad old NDP. Therefore, to take some starch out of the NDP's campaign, in April 1979, as environment minister, I appointed Dr. David Bates of UBC as a one-man commission to look into uranium mining. (After the election when the Bates Commission was no longer necessary for us politically, we found that the good doctor had taken quite a liking to the assignment and we had a hell of a time getting him to shut down!)

Once the election was called, of course, I had to get nominated again. The Kamloops Socreds had a terrific constituency organization, and I took particular care to see that the directors were all on my team. I called my excellent constituency secretary, Sandra Moskwa, and asked if anyone was going to oppose me. She didn't think so, but I decided to play it safe. "Sandra," I said, "hire the smallest meeting room in the Stockmen's Hotel, and I want that room full to the brim with my people half an hour before meeting time. I'll pick up the bar tab." She did, I did, and I won unopposed.

Every time I get on my high horse and spout about political morality, I bring myself back to earth by reminding myself that not long before that election I used $50,000 in lottery money to get the British Columbia Wildlife Federation out of sure bankruptcy. As environment minister, I had the Fish and Wildlife Branch under my wing and was keenly aware of how many fishing and hunting licences were issued each year, and I knew that these licences went to people who voted. The day before the election I also made a deal on behalf of the government with Seattle Light and Power whereby we compensated them for not raising the Ross Dam on the Skagit River, thus preventing the flooding of that beautiful stream on our side of the border. That made a good front-page story.

That 1979 election had an eerie feel to it. I was supposed to have my seat fully under control, so I was sent to campaign all over the province. Then with five days to go, I returned to Kamloops and from the looks on people's faces, including my campaign workers, I realized that my seat wasn't as safe as I had thought. Sandra had me going flat out in the short time left before the election. I was everywhere and in the event I actually won handily. However, on election night I rather upset some of my supporters because, instead of watching for the early returns, I watched the Canadiens beat Boston in overtime in the Stanley Cup semi-finals.

Though our percentage of the vote rose, that election reduced us to a five-seat majority. I stayed on as environment minister though I was moved to the health portfolio that fall. Then in the summer of 1980 Premier Bennett asked all of us to let him know if we planned to run in the next election. He was concerned that a couple of heart attacks in our caucus might threaten our slim majority. I told the premier that this was my last term, and he advised me to let my directors know so that they would have some replacement candidates in mind. I didn't care to run again for several reasons. I was then nearly 50, and I didn't want to spend the rest of my days counting the pensionable time I would have to put in as I could see older MLAs doing. (In fact, when I quit I received no pension at all because I hadn't put in the requisite six years.) I also had no ambition for any other portfolio. As a lawyer I had no craving to be attorney general, a job that was in line down the road. In fact, the only political ambition I had was to be premier, and Bill Bennett, four months younger than me, had a pretty good lock on the job. Moreover, I was a Bill Bennett man through and through, so I wasn't going to be challenging him for it any time soon.

# 5

## A Career in Radio

I HAD NO HANKERING AS A KID to be a broadcaster. Until World War II ended, I wanted to be a sailor in the navy. When I was in my last year of high school, I took some aptitude tests and was told I should be an accountant with law a distant second. University demonstrated that I couldn't understand a balance sheet so it was law. But never broadcasting. I have never really understood how sound travels beyond earshot whether by wire or not. I can't get my brain around wave lengths, however long or short, let alone the absurd, yet true, proposition that, while sound travels about 1,060 feet per second in the wild, so to speak, when you broadcast it over electric wire, it goes at the speed of light. I was a precocious kid and during the war I followed international events keenly. I remember sitting next to our Phillips radio to hear Winston Churchill address our Parliament on December 30, 1941, the day before my tenth birthday. This was his famous "Some chicken...some neck" speech. What I especially remembered about it was the CBC announcer telling us (and how about this for trivia, even from the CBC?) that because sound over the wires travels faster than ordinary sound, we at home would hear the great man at just an ever-so-slightly, itty-bitty bit of a second before our parliamentarians heard it.

Now while I had no desire to be a broadcaster, I did love to listen to radio. I was mesmerized by the voice of Mel Allen announcing a baseball game and listened with seething hatred to that base-homer Foster Hewitt broadcasting the despised Leafs' games. (And why isn't it "Leaves," may I ask?) Afternoons were taken up with boys' programs—girls were out of luck in those days with the exception of "Little Orphan Annie." There was "Jack Armstrong, the All-American Boy," "Terry and the Pirates," "Superman," "Batman" and, of course, "The Green Hornet." The mystery stories, where theatre of the mind really came to the fore—shows like "The Shadow," "I Love a Mystery," and "The Inner Sanctum"—were really, and I mean really, scary. The family Sunday afternoons and evenings were filled with "Amos 'n Andy" (try to get away with that parody of Blacks today!), "Edgar Bergen and Charlie McCarthy" (imagine a ventriloquist on radio), "Henry Aldrich" and the shows of Fred Allen and Jack Benny.

Music played a big part in my teenage years. Locally a fellow named Al Reusch had a show on CKMO, now CFUN, called "Name It, Play It," which was, as the name implies, a request program but with a twist, and it became a way for kids to use pseudonyms like "The Joker" and "Batman" to exchange greetings. I well remember one day in 1945 when the big hit was Freddy Martin with Jack Fina doing "Bumble Boogie." There were so many requests for it that it was the only song for which there was time left on the program and then it was only half-way through. The big men with music in those days were Jack Cullen on his "Owl Prowl," Jack Kyle, Bob Smith, Vic Waters and the perennial Bob Hutton as CKNW's morning man. Monty McFarlane and Red Robinson came a bit, though not much, later.

But television came to town and to our house as early as 1950, and radio slipped back a bit. But you couldn't play the TV in the car or on the beach, and the new wave of sixties music brought from Blighty by the Beatles, plus that "white Black man" Elvis Presley, kept radio a-humming. In the late fifties and sixties "talk radio" became the rage with pioneers like Pat Burns, Gary Bannerman, Barrie Clark, Ed Murphy, retired federal cabinet minister Judy LaMarsh, Jack Wasserman and the inimitable Jack Webster, the giant amongst them all. It began as a North America-wide fad, but somehow it never petered out on the West Coast as it did elsewhere. Through the seventies and eighties Webster, Burns and Bannerman, along with lesser lights, kept the flame of talk radio very much alive indeed.

My radio career had actually started in 1974 although I didn't realize it at the time. I was practising law in Kamloops and was by then also an alderman—a noisy one. One of my clients, CFJC-AM, owned by golfing buddies Dave Clark and Jack Pollard, did a one-hour talk-back show called—oh, how originally—"Talk Back" with Ben Meisner. He was, and is, bright, articulate, ill-mannered, sometimes gentle, often abrasive, knowledgeable, opinionated and for all that a truly "gentle Ben" and a good friend—in other words, the perfect talk-show host. It happened that Ben took a hunting holiday in the fall of 1974 and overstayed his holiday, leaving Dave and Jack without a host. Would I try it? they asked.

Why not? But as this was strictly a call-in show with no guests, I asked what would happen if no one called, but Jack and Dave promised to have people ready to call if necessary. We need not have worried. On the first show, we got onto whatever fuss of the week was fashionable, and I got so into it, I missed the 10:00 a.m. break. No big deal, you might say. But CFJC was a CBC affiliate, and hundreds of people set their timepieces by the CBC ten o'clock national time signal! In any event, I did Meisner's show for five days and had a ball.

Over my political years, I became a frequent guest on radio shows in Kamloops, first as an alderman then as the local member of the legislative assembly; in Victoria and Vancouver I was invited to appear as a cabinet minister, appearing pretty regularly with Joe Easingwood, Gary Bannerman, Pat Burns and, of course, the raging Scot himself, Jack Webster. I enjoyed the sparring very much, especially with Webster. We seemed to spark off each other and we liked one another.

My first meeting with Webster had been back in the mid-sixties after a car belonging to a client of mine had been seized by the government for a liquor offence. My client had loaned his car to his son on a Saturday night, and the boy got pulled over by the police. His passenger was found to have a mickey of vodka in his pocket. As the law read, if the passenger in a car was convicted of being a juvenile in possession of liquor, the owner of the vehicle in question would lose his car! (The legislation at that time would have made Henry VIII blush!) I tried everything imaginable but after the passenger was duly convicted, the sheriff seized the dad's car and, under the Liquor Act of the day, he forfeited the car to Her Majesty. There was a procedure whereby the father could have his car returned, but he had to apologize for the offence he hadn't committed, and we were hard pressed to figure out just what that offence was. Eventually the following spring the attorney general generously gave my client his car back along with a letter saying, "Let that be a lesson to you." To add further injury to the insult, the car was returned with a cracked block because the government hadn't put any antifreeze in it over the winter. When my client asked for compensation, the government's reply was, "When the block cracked, it was our car and we could do or not do whatever we wished with it."

The law, as it was written, was even more outrageous than this. If someone climbed onto your boat at a marina, broke into your booze locker, then sat out on the stern drinking your liquor, in addition to more serious charges the trespasser could be charged with consuming liquor in a public place and then, even though he was trespassing, upon his conviction Her Majesty could seize your boat and sell it! I kid you not! I told this whole story to Jack and he ran with it for a bit, which was no doubt why my client got back what was left of his car.

In the end my induction into radio was all Jack Webster's fault. It happened that in December 1980, when I was BC's health minister, I was a guest on his BCTV show, and afterwards he took me to lunch at the old Timber Club in the Hotel Vancouver. He asked me if I was happy in politics. I told him in confidence that I had already advised the premier that I would not seek re-election in the next election, which as it happened was still two and a half years away. He asked me if I had ever considered a career in radio. "No," I said. To make a long story short, I next found myself talking to Mel Cooper, the owner of CFAX in Victoria. He then introduced me to billionaire Jimmy Pattison who owned what was then CJOR 600 and is now CKBD 600, known as 600AM. Before I knew it I had signed a one-year contract to take over the morning show at CJOR from the legendary Pat Burns—who learned of his demotion when the story was reported on the 10:00 a.m. news. This bit of "media class," incidentally, taught me very early in the game how management behaved. With them only one thing counted: your ratings.

After I came, Pat Burns did the evenings. He was a consummate actor and a fount of knowledge. And he did things differently, if not always soberly. He preferred not to have guests but do open line and wait until he had the right caller to bounce off. I remember listening one night as he played with the kill button while he interviewed a kindly old grandmother who was describing her little granddaughter's first day of school. "The little darling came out of school after her first day and said, 'Grandma, ******!' Then I said, 'That's nice, dear, and was little Jimmy in class with you?' And she said, 'Yes Grandma, he's my best friend and *****!'" What could that sweet little six-year-old in a pinafore be saying? Nothing naughty, of course, but Pat was always the showman, and he knew how to get and hold an audience. He was also a great sports fan, especially loving baseball and horse racing. You dare not make a mistake on a sports subject or Pat would call on the open line and correct you. Though he was past his best years when I knew him, he was a great broadcaster and a real gentleman. When he heard while listening to his own CJOR 10:00 a.m. news that I, a bloody politician, was replacing him, he must have been devastated, but he had real class. Moments before I was to go on air, he called me. "Go get 'em," he growled. "Break a leg." Hell of a guy.

After a rocky start on day one in February 1981, when all the lights went out but the signal was still being transmitted (talk about being tested early!), I found I loved my new job. The early reviews were pretty good, and my first ratings were good, too, second only to Gary Bannerman at CKNW but not all that far back. The station management was so happy they tore up my one-year contract and gave me a three-year deal with a hefty raise along with a cost of living clause I was later glad I had. (Unfortunately, that marked the high-water mark of my days at CJOR 600.)

By 1981 the "Information Age" was just getting into full swing. The computer, though not yet the PC, was with us. We were beginning to watch overseas events live by satellite. Ted Turner and CNN were stirring, getting ready to revolutionize TV, throwing all that had gone before into a cocked hat. I could not foresee the Internet, of course, but it was clear to me that the public wanted more information and more knowledge, so when I was hired by CJOR , I vowed I'd be different. No more "dollar-a-holler" radio. I would do sound interviews with interesting guests who would provoke people to think. Of course, nothing happens easily or quickly. My producers, conscious of what had always worked, still brought in numerologists, psychics and astrologers, and I, fearful of every new step, didn't initially fight them too hard. One of these guests was a numerologist named Cord McIntyre, a man of the Kabbalarian persuasion who would analyze names and birthdays and that sort of stuff. I also, from time to time, had astrologers and psychics on the show. Callers would, of course, jam the lines but I had to ask myself if that meant that those not calling liked what they were hearing. For a few years I also used a couple of psychics who went by the names Crystal and Kristophir, and it used to scare the pants off me. Here were people asking other people over the phone whether they should make a business deal or get married or see the doctor. And I asked myself if I was being responsible in putting such people on air. On the one hand, I was entitled to expect my audience to use their heads, but what about people who might suffer because they were desperate to hear good news from someone—anyone? It was hard to know, but as my show became more and more involved in serious matters, I ceased using these people and received very little complaint from my audience. As a result of moving on to more serious topics, early in my career I was pleased to see a review of talk radio in which I was said to have the most interesting guests. Hitherto that had not been seen as much of a criterion.

After that I began to do an editorial off the top of each program. This was scarcely new. Jack Webster and Pat Burns, two of my heroes, had been doing editorials on an irregular basis for years. What I did that was different was to use my program as a "bully pulpit" for my own ideas, and they often went far beyond local issues to provincial, federal and world controversies.

There were two bits of radio arising from my CJOR days I shall never forget. My guest one day was Lord Diplock, a member of the House of Lords and a Law Lord, meaning he sat on the judicial bench that was the highest court in the UK. I had no real producer at the time so made the best of it by asking a very broad range of questions about the House of Lords, the Judicial Committee of the Privy Council, decisions he had made and so on. As the interview proceeded, I could see that his lordship was puzzled—clearly I was missing something! Today I would simply have swallowed my embarrassment and asked during a station break what it was I was missing. But those were the days when I thought a microphone conferred infallibility, so I did nothing. About half an hour later—after he'd gone—the light went on. THAT Lord Diplock! The man who had authored the legislation permitting the British authorities to throw suspected Irish terrorists into jail incommunicado and without any rights whatsoever! The man that Bobbie Sands and company were starving themselves to death over! And because of my arrogance I'd missed the entire story!

The second event was more complimentary to me. My guest was Paul Watson, the Sea Shepherd Society's whale protector—then and now one of my heroes. Except that on this occasion, far from being in my studio, Paul was at sea off the Kamchatka Peninsula in Soviet Russia and was being buzzed by the Soviet Air Force and chased by a couple of Russian warships. Paul and his crew, you see, had just landed on Soviet soil and destroyed a mink farm that used illegally killed whales as food. It was one of those crackling conversations on a ship-to-shore when each intervention was punctuated by "Over." One could hear the planes as Paul calmly described what had happened and what was still going on. It was truly riveting radio.

There were a lot of famous names around CJOR in those days. Monty MacFarlane was doing the afternoon show, and he was truly one of the funniest men in radio or anywhere else. And he was "tough" funny for, unlike other funny broadcasters, Monty never needed a straight man to bounce his humour off. He did it all alone with nothing but a microphone to bounce off. By the time I arrived, he was ending his career and, as so often happens in this business, was not going out with any understanding and compassion from the industry to which he had contributed so much. Art Finley, a San Franciscan radio veteran, did the news talk show before me, and he helped me a great deal with some of my many technical shortcomings. After a time he was replaced by Kim Calloway, whose lady, then wife, was Maggie Chew—my producer. Some hard feelings developed when I thought I detected some voices on air with Kim that more properly should have been guests on my show. Who knows? But happily we all turned out to be friends when the smoke cleared.

All this great talent wasn't enough to nail CJOR's competition, CKNW. Not by a very long shot. Jimmy Pattison, and indeed everyone involved, underestimated the power of CKNW. In those days, under the magnificent leadership of Warren Barker, they had the best private station news department in the country and in George Garrett arguably the best news reporter. Everyone listened to Frosty Forst for the morning drive, and even more listened to the eight o'clock news read by the man everyone loved, Hal Davis. The news was followed by sports with the unorthodox "Big Al" Davidson. To hear people talk, you would have thought that Al was the most hated sports guy on the planet, but those who hated him obviously listened to him anyway. This was bad news for me because radio listeners are not easily moved off their place on the dial. Going into my 8:35 a.m. start, I was up against a station that had a whole bunch of listeners already wired. But it got worse. During my editorial, my opposite number at 'NW was Earl "The Pearl" Bradford, who did a sort of gossip column of the air and, unfortunately for me, did it brilliantly. As if all that wasn't bad enough, Earl was followed by Bill Hughes doing a bit of radio that was inexplicably and hugely popular. He would go down to the bus depot and interview a busload of people.

"From?" he would ask.

"Hillbilly Flats, Kentucky."

"Wonderful place. My wife and I were there just last month. . ."

And this gripping stuff had people glued to their radios!

But it got even worse. The monster Clifford Robert Olson killed at least eleven Greater Vancouver youngsters between November, 1980 and August, 1981. Before he was captured, every parent and grandparent was frightened that their child or grandchild might be next. As the suspense built, it was CKNW's George Garrett who always seemed to have the news even before it happened. Over the years he had built up a trust with the police that had them often using him as a conduit to leak news. He would get information off the record and thus be in a superb position to frame the questions when the news was released. In the Olson case, George always seemed to know just when a police statement would be made, and he would quickly break into regular broadcasting to give an update. By this time people weren't just listening to CKNW's morning show with Gary Bannerman—an experienced and good (if rather dull) broadcaster—because of Gary but to keep up-to-date on this terrible sequence of crimes. And I couldn't come close to Gary in the ratings thereafter.

I would readily admit that it was my inexperience that caused some of CJOR's lack of ratings, though I was building a loyal audience that would help me later in my career. But what counted for more, I think, was that CJOR 600 just didn't have the firepower to deal with CKNW. Every day Gary inherited a huge audience from Frosty while I was getting next to zilch. He also had first dibs when important people came to town because his ratings attracted them. Moreover, if they went on Jack Webster's BCTV show first, because BCTV and CKNW were both owned by WIC (Western International Communications), Gary would get them next. It became great sport to try to scoop these two giants but, alas, we seldom did.

In the fall of 1983, after going through three managers in the two years I had been there, Jimmy Pattison hired an Ottawa man named Harvey Gold who was going to set things right at CJOR. And that's when I made a mistake that I was never to make again: I thought that Harvey and I had become friends. The fact is, the only friend a broadcaster ever has in this business is a recent and very good ratings book. Nothing—and I mean nothing—else matters. Some broadcasters never learn that lesson in a lifetime. I learned it very early and never forgot it.

Harvey became part of Patti's (my second wife) and my social life. In fact, he spent Christmas Eve 1983 at a party at our house that included only our closest friends. There's little to be gained by saying more on the subject other than to say that Harvey led me to believe that he was going to renew my contract and didn't. He hired former BC premier Dave Barrett to take my place. I sued Jimmy and, when he heard my side of the story, promptly settled with me in full. I have always liked Jimmy and thought a lot of him for being so honourable when he was such a powerful man. Later events were to prove my judgment correct.

I was effectively fired by CJOR as of July 1, 1984. I was devastated. Like all performers I was a cross between a cocky know-it-all and a frightened little boy with the self-confidence of a rabbit. I was also devastated to learn that not only was I stony-assed broke, I was $250,000 in the goo. I resolved not to go bankrupt even though I had a major bank loan and several lesser ones, owed the income tax department about $75,000 and the mortgages on my house exceeded the value of the place.

# 6

## *What About Those Goddam Yanks?*

IN 1984 I HAD TWO VERY IMPORTANT and influential things happen
to me: I lost my job at CJOR radio in Vancouver and I was recipient
of a grant from the US State Department to see whatever I wanted to
see of the American system, all at the expense of the us government.
This grant was arranged by a man who had become quite a good pal,
Jack Cannon. A Boston Irishman and friend of Ted Kennedy, he was
attached to the office of the US Consul General in Vancouver. Being
without a job and with the ass out of my pants I should have been job
hunting, but thankfully I took the trip.

I am an Americanophile, one point that sets me apart from the
left, which I support on many other grounds. I have long been fascinated by politics in general but especially transfixed by the American
Revolution and the drawing up of the US Constitution in Philadelphia,
then the capital, in 1787. It always seemed to me that the men who
made this great document constituted one of the most remarkable
gatherings in history. They had little to go on except some zealous encouragement by men like Tom Paine and his *Common Sense*, the beautifully crafted *Declaration of Independence*, mostly by Thomas Jefferson,
and the writings of a few people like John Locke. All their culture had
taught them up to that time was that there was a king and that the king
could do no wrong. To move from that culture to democracy was quite
a step. There's a long-out-of-print book, called *Miracle at Philadelphia* by

Catherine Drinker Bowen that tells the story beautifully. A search of your favourite online used bookstore ought to get you a copy, and you ought to get it if you want to understand why the United States is the way it is.

I also was fascinated by the Civil War, which not only settled the question of slavery but also the question of which had the primary power—the federal government or the states? And was this union a mere confederation of states that could opt out if they felt so inclined or was the whole truly greater than the sum of its parts? The Civil War determined what is still a fairly open question in Canada. I wanted to find out how the American government worked, in fact. I was interested in knowing how the administration—that is to say the president and the legislatures, which is to say Congress—worked out what the budget would be. I wanted to know something about how a state government worked and I wanted to see a bit of American history.

So I flew down to Washington and, at the neatly numbered 1776 Massachusetts Avenue, I met my hostess, whose name unhappily I have lost. I then spent four days in the company of a young intern in the office of a California congressman, and I had a ball. I stood in the Senate Chamber and watched the proceedings. In the House of Representatives I sat in the chair that John Quincy Adams sat in after he had left the presidency and was elected to the House. I met members of the budget office of the president and a bureaucrat who was in charge of liaising with the administration. I also saw how the committee whose mandate it is to bring the House and the Senate together on all legislation worked. It was a mind-numbing but exciting time.

On the weekend I was taken by a Civil War expert to Virginia where, in addition to seeing many battle sites, George Washington's Mount Vernon, Thomas Jefferson's Monticello and the home of James Munroe, I watched Ted Kennedy address the graduating law class at the University of Virginia, which campus had been designed by Jefferson. I then had a couple of days on my own to bask in the atmosphere created by the White House, the Capitol and the Supreme Court Building where I sat in the chief justice's chair (I'm big on that sort of stuff), and visited the Library of Congress and the Washington, Lincoln and Jefferson memorials. I also had time to nip over to Baltimore to see the Orioles beat the Mariners.

I then went to Philadelphia because I was anxious to get the feel of this most important revolutionary city. I went into the state Senate Chamber where the Constitution was formed and sat in George Washington's chair. I saw where John Adams was sworn in after Washington retired; this was a great moment for it was the first time in modern history that a democratically elected person succeeded another democratically elected leader. The story has it that after Adams was sworn in, he stood aside for Washington to leave saying, "After you, Mr. President," whereupon Washington said, "No, after you, Mr. President. I am Citizen Washington now." I saw the Liberty Bell and visited Valley Forge where George Washington and his troops survived—there is no other word to describe it—the winter of 1777–78 while the British officers cavorted with the ladies in the warmth of Philadelphia. I saw Benjamin Franklin's grave. And another baseball game, the Phillies versus the Dodgers, and my beloved Dodgers won. Next came two days in Columbus, Ohio, and several sessions with politicians, including the governor. It was a truly wonderful experience and I was astonished how free with their time all who helped me were.

I came away with a few prejudices that are with me today. The Americans got their constitution under fire of both the Revolution and the Civil War and in doing so came up with a federal arrangement that is as close to perfect as you could expect humans could come, which is to say, of course, a hell of a long way from being perfect. But the checks and balances, the states versus the federal government, the three-ringed struggle among Congress, the presidency and the Supreme Court have created a unique democracy in the sense that there is a strong interconnection amongst the various branches of government and there is a very strong connection between the elected and the electors. Unlike Canada, where ordinary MPs or MLAs are mere appendages to a system run from the top down, in America the most obscure rookie congressman might well receive an invitation to the White House to discuss proposed legislation with the president because the president dearly wants his vote. After all, it was a single senator, Edmund Ross, from the newly minted state of Kansas who, in the impeachment trial of Andrew Johnson in 1868, went against the party whip, voted for acquittal and thus saved Johnson's presidency.

The importance of this incident had been lost on me until this visit. Ross didn't vote against conviction because he liked Andrew Johnson. He didn't. He cast his vote as he did because he thought that to convict a president of "high crimes and misdemeanors" was a very big step indeed and ought only to be done in "very extraordinary circumstances" which in his view these weren't. It was this precedent, I believe, that made Nixon resign and that saved Clinton's bacon.

I have been told critically that I have spent more time studying the American government than our own. And it is true. That's because the American system, in preserving the power and dignity of the elected politician, has a system of moving parts, all of which demand the attention of the observer. The Canadian system, with all power—and I mean *all* power—exercised by the prime minister in consultation with (if he consults at all) unelected political hacks, is only interesting in that it is an appalling denial of democracy. Our constitution, being unamendable in practice, has given us a perhaps fatal dose of constitutional constipation.

I have the strong feeling that if every Canadian could have taken my 1984 excursion they would readily see that, flawed though the American system can sometimes be, it is representative and democratic. It is a system in which the politicians must respond to the people, not the party whip. Its shortcomings—for example, the importance to the electoral process of scads of money—are not the fault of the system but the refusal of those elected by the big bucks to do something about it. All in all, the Americans have a system from which we could learn a great deal.

I often ask myself why I go on as I do about constitutional and government reform. We in Canada will do nothing to change things and will, unless I miss my guess, disintegrate as a country before the midway mark of this century. Since this will only affect my children, and their children, and their children's children, combined with the fact that the world may be blown to bits in the meantime, perhaps I shouldn't worry. But I do. I'm a worrywart. In many other places I have written and spoken about how we now have an absolute dictatorship tempered only by the constitutional requirement that there be elections for the sheep who follow the shepherd every five years. The leader exercises every bit of power exercisable at the federal level and does it personally. And to the extent he can be restrained by the Senate and the Supreme Court of Canada, it must be noted that it is he who appoints the restrainers.

Here's my point: while I and many others don't believe there is enough gumption in the Canadian people to make the massive changes necessary for the country to be a democracy in fact as well as form, why cannot we at least make it possible for the Canadian people to select their leaders? The best way to do this, of course, is to have a republican system in which the head of government is directly elected but this isn't going to happen. And even republics, as below the line, have difficulty getting people involved in the naming of party chiefs. But if we are bound and determined to continue with this hopelessly outdated, indeed medieval, system of ironclad disciplined parties in this country, can we not at least make this small step: get the public involved in who leads our political parties. At present this job is left entirely up to those who are members of a political party, and even then the influence of the ordinary member is poisoned by the system. Huge membership drives bring in members who will never be heard from again after the leader or favoured candidate is named. New Canadians, whose only words of English are *Liberal* (or whichever party let them into the country, but this means mostly Liberal) and the name of the candidate they are supposed to support, suddenly sign up as members in droves. Whether they are paid in future promises or whatever, the process is haphazard, unfair at best and fraudulent at worst. And it isn't just ethnic minorities who are co-opted into the game; it could be drunks, the mentally disabled, not-yet landed immigrants, or just anyone who will do anything for a lark as long as there's a drink in it. In any case, leadership conventions are fixed. It is not just the delegates selected as above who vote. A large percentage of the voters at conventions at the federal level are MPs, party hacks, senators, local executives and so on. In short, the average voter has no input in the selection process which, among all other sins, is designed to ensure that someone acceptable to the central Canadian establishment is made The Leader.

So why not a primary system as there is in much of the United States? All one need do is register as a Liberal, Conservative or whatever, whereupon in the party primary, which sends delegates to the convention, all who declare themselves to be of that party are entitled to vote. Won't that mean that Conservatives or NDPers could play games and all join the Liberals so as to make mischief? Not if it is against the law to register for more than one party. In fact, in many states south of the border it is not required that a voter be a registered Democrat or Republican in order to vote in a primary. Besides, most people are honest and would simply register for the party they favour. Many probably would not register at all, just as many Canadians don't vote. The end result would be that those Canadians who want a voice in who becomes a candidate or who leads a party would have one. Is even that modest proposal too much for this anally retentive, supine electorate that proves year after year that it will put up with anything?

# 7

## *Saved from the Law*

THAT SUMMER OF 1984, BROKE AND JOBLESS, I thought my prayers had been answered when a large chunk of pie-in-the-sky arrived. A mining promoter for whom I had done a bit of legal work in Kamloops had decided that, in spite of the fact that Craigmont Mines near Merritt had been closed down, there was still plenty of ore left which, if he combined it with ore from another mine in which he was interested, would be marketable. I was slated to be president (at $100,000 a year) of the company he was putting together. This started a four-month period of chasing rainbows that led nowhere and it all fizzled out in the end, but what it did was keep me busy and in a place where I could look for other work.

I really didn't want to go back to law, but one after another my prospects fizzled out. I was asked to do some public relations work for St. Paul's Hospital—very kindly offered, I might add—but the need for my services evaporated before I could start. I was offered the then safe Conservative seat of Capilano in the forthcoming federal election—in fact, I was "rushed" hard—but I turned it down, partly because I wasn't sure I was a Conservative but more because I knew I would win and I had no desire to go to Ottawa. Other consulting work, thanks to my wonderful friend Richard Hughes who was then involved in Sunshine Cabs in North Vancouver, put a little food on the table. I gave some speeches and did a little more consulting, but it soon became obvious that I would have to go back into law.

With that in mind, I made an appointment to see my old friend and colleague Brian Smith, who was now attorney general. When I had last practised law, the NDP government had stopped giving out Queen's Counsels, and by the time they were restored, I was in government and not eligible. Had I stayed in law, I would certainly have been so honoured. A QC now would help me get a position in a law office; it would cost nothing and would give me a bit more cachet on my resume. So I asked Brian to give me one. He was very sympathetic but quickly and firmly made it clear that he could never get it past cabinet. I had, of course, over the three previous years been critical of the government, that being my job as a talk-show host, and had given offence. There it was, a bauble I was entitled to but one that was beyond the reach of my friend to give me. (In later years Brian Smith, with whom I had remained on excellent terms, appeared many times on my show. He had received a QC while in law practice and then became entitled to one as attorney general. Whenever we met I would laughingly ask him for one of his QCs.)

Then one day in October a former classmate of mine, Mark Soule, called to ask me to join him for dinner. I hadn't known Mark all that well in law school, but here he was offering me a good job in his law firm of Campney, Murphy. I still really didn't want to go back to law, but I gratefully accepted and met the partnership committee that dealt with these things. The deal was all but done when something happened that turned my life completely around. My two dear friends, Dick and Joanna Lillico, came to visit us from London. Dick, having done public relations for both Bennetts, had been rewarded with a posting to BC House in London, and he and Joanna, who was English, had settled into Chislehurst, a London suburb. While they were back in Vancouver, Grace and Ray McCarthy held a cocktail party in their honour and invited my wife and me. At that party was John Plul, the public relations wizard for CKNW, whom I knew very casually. During the conversation he asked me if I wanted to return to radio. Upon hearing my enthusiastic "Yes!" he invited me to go out to CKNW the next day, a Monday, and meet Ted Smith, the manager, and his colleagues. I did and was surprised to hear Ted offering me a talk show from midnight until 2:00 a.m. for $90,000 per year, about half what I'd been making at CJOR. I would provide my own producer, namely, my then-wife Patti. As Ted tells the story, I asked to use his en suite loo, then came out and accepted promptly. Actually, I think I went home and talked it over with Patti first, but no matter. I was delighted, accepted Ted's offer and called Mark Soule and thanked him very much for his kindness, a kindness I've never forgotten.

I owe a great debt to Ted. To be honest, he wasn't just doing charity among indigent broadcasters. He could see the seething anger that existed between Gary Bannerman and Barrie Clark and wanted some backup. But that aside, I would not have had my great 19-year career with CKNW had it not been for the confidence Ted and his new program director, Doug Rutherford, showed me.

I started with 'NW around November 1, 1984, and within a few days was in trouble with McDonald's for making a crack about their product. I was interviewing James Barber, the Money's Mushroom Man and well-known gourmet, when a caller mentioned McDonald's. How that name would come up in a piece on decent cooking I'll never know, but there it was. A big fat pitch to belt at, and I swung from the heels. "I remember eating a McDonald's burger about eight years ago," I said, "and now whenever I burp, I can still taste the damned thing." Stupid. Unnecessary. The good news was, surely, that no one from McDonald's would be listening at 1:30 a.m.

Well, they were, and all hell broke loose. McDonald's demanded that at the very least I should be fired and threatened to disengage themselves from a long-standing and mutually advantageous business relationship with CKNW. Ted Smith called me the next morning to advise me of the deep shit we were all in but making it forcefully and abundantly clear that the station stood behind its broadcasters. I refused to apologize because the reaction of McDonald's had been excessive; the fact that they had written the station's owner, Frank Griffiths Senior, demanding I be fired had been, in my view, overkill to say the least. That was also how my lawyer saw it.

Yet there I was, dead broke and teetering on bankruptcy, the new boy at CKNW and eminently expendable, standing up to McDonald's with my manager firmly and unalterably behind me, even though I was wrong as hell! About two weeks into this mess, Ted called me and asked if I would talk to Ron Marcoux, the big push at McDonald's, not to apologize but just to see if there was some way out of the goo. "Fuck him, Ted," I said. And Ted just said, "It's your call, Rafe. No pressure from this end."

I thought about this for awhile. "Rafe," I said to myself, "just who the hell do you think you are? Here's a station that out of the goodness of their hearts opened up a new show for you, just to have a bit of a farm league going, and you're telling one of their largest customers to get fucked. But worse, are you putting your benefactor in a hell of a spot over what was your stupid big mouth? The big boss has supported you all the way, and you won't swallow your pride and make a gesture!"

I phoned. "Mr Marcoux," I said, "I'm not apologizing to you!"

"Mair," he replied, "I'm sure as hell not apologizing to you!"

Now where can you go from there? There was a long awkward silence, and then we both started to laugh. At the end of the day we arranged to have lunch—no, not at McDonald's—and found we really liked one another. I discovered the story of McDonald's was so fascinating that I invited Ron on the show to tell it, which he did.

There the story ended happily, but it really wasn't about Rafe Mair or Ron Marcoux, of course. It was about Ted Smith, who stood behind me when it would have been child's play to toss me out on my ass under circumstances in which I wouldn't have had a word said on my behalf. Don't get me wrong. Ted and I had lots of pretty good disagreements over the years; I am a prickly, hard-to-get-along-with bugger with an excess of pride and, I suppose, ego, and it was Ted's job to deal with me. Lucky guy.

My late show, "Nightline BC," was a gas. Before I went on air for the first time, I was told that Ted Smith hated two things: politics and baseball. So who was my first guest? Senator Ray Perrault discussing the possibilities of getting a major league baseball franchise for Vancouver. Afterwards, I learned that Ted didn't really care all that much for Ray Perrault either! Though I didn't get a single good night's sleep for a year, I loved doing the show. It's amazing who will come on the radio in the middle of the night. Former Vancouver city councillor, George Puil, was a frequent visitor, requiring only that I have a couple of bottles of beer ready for him. And one of my key guests was Rick Hansen who came into my studio to announce his Man in Motion trip around the world in his wheelchair. What he was about to do didn't seem to be that big a deal to Gary Bannerman and Barrie Clark. And no one else wanted him. But when Rick returned, world-famous for his awesome and inspired trip, Gary wanted him for his morning show. By that time I was doing the afternoon show and Rick said plainly that I had been the only one interested in him at the beginning and mine was going to be the first show that interviewed him. A class act all the way.

My audience was the "night people" out there, and they are different. I got calls from cops and hookers, cowboys and millworkers, taxi drivers and lonely souls who had nowhere to go. But the largest group by far were wives who had done a full day with kids, husbands, pets and perhaps a job of their own and just wanted some company in the wee hours of the morning. When I talked to any of them, I had the mental image of a frazzled woman who had ended the formal part of her day, and now the old man was passed out in bed next to her and she finally had a moment to herself.

One night we decided to play "sexual trivia": I encouraged callers to tell funny things of a sexual nature that had happened to them. Now talk-show hosts have a "kill" button which, because there is a six-second delay from broadcast to listener, gives them the opportunity to delete stuff they deem too naughty. I was and remain hopeless with this button (and all other buttons for that matter). When the moment of truth comes, I panic and can't remember whether I'm supposed to hit the button and wait six seconds, wait six seconds and then hit the button, or just what the hell to do.

On the night in question I told my listeners that, though it was late at night and we could get away with things they couldn't get away with in daytime radio, I hoped that they would exercise discretion. The show went swimmingly with a lot of funny stories. I especially remember the one where the guy told of how, after his girlfriend's parents had gone to the theatre, they went up to the master bedroom and after making love, had blown up condoms as balloons. As they were—starkers, of course—batting these condoms around the room, a car came up the driveway. It was the parents, who had discovered that they had the wrong night for the play!

Then just before 2:00 a.m. one of my callers said the words "blow job." Now this was back in 1984, long before President Clinton made it forevermore unnecessary that a boy explain to a girl what a blow job is. Oh-oh, I thought, I'd better hit that button! With wavering finger and after an uncertain time lag, I firmly punched the "kill" button. The next afternoon I received a call from Doug Rutherford, CKNW's program director. "Rafe," he said, "I don't usually stay up late enough to hear you, but I was fascinated by your sex show and stayed up for the whole thing. Great program, but what was it you bleeped out?"

"Why do you ask, Doug?"

"Because what came out was bleep, bleep, bleep, bleep BLOW JOB! If that's what you allowed, what the hell was it you killed?"

Radio does indeed have its lighter moments.

I learned a lot from this show, the main thing being that the radio is a very personal thing. TV is like a movie theatre in your living room, but the radio is generally an intimate part of the family. And then there are other times when it's not part of the family but the way a family member can escape. Night people especially will talk to you as if the conversation were private. In fact, it was here I first noticed—as many other broadcasters have—that somehow you can tell the mood of the audience by the feel of the studio when you go on air. Many people think I've taken complete leave of my senses when I say that, but it's true. I don't know how it works but it does—not all the time or even a majority of the time but often enough to make it eerie.

Until I came to CKNW, their "talk" had ended by mid-afternoon. The afternoon drive was hosted by the late Rick Honey, an enormously talented man who died a few years ago at far too young an age. Among other things, Rick was a world-class magician and a very sought-after master of ceremonies. After Rick's show came Dave "Big Daddy" McCormack, now a colleague of mine at 600AM, who did a fine music show, and after him we got into Jack Kyle and Jack Cullen. After I had been on "Nightline BC" for a year, Doug Rutherford asked me if I would like to do a news-talk show from 6:00 to 9:00 p.m. I was promised an increase in pay which, as commonly happened to me, didn't materialize, but I jumped at the offer. This meant "Big Daddy" McCormack had to go and, as usually happens in circumstances like this, many members of his audience resented my arrival upon the scene. If Dave resented it, he didn't show it for he's a class act and knows that this is part of the business.

But it was at this point that my private life nearly ruined me. I was, as mentioned, more than broke. Though both my lawyer and accountant said bankruptcy would be the sensible way to go, I was doing all manner of things to stave it off. I gave speeches (at much more moderate rates than now, I might add), acted as a consultant on government and media matters, became associated with a large public relations firm putting on seminars on how to deal with the media and became involved with a couple of Vancouver Stock Exchange companies. One of them, Terra Nova Energy, ought to have made us all very rich but didn't. The company, taken over in a proxy battle by a couple of guys I know, had gained worldwide rights to distribute a formula for the natural sweetener, Stevia. This sweetener has become well known now and will, I predict, be the non-sugar sweetener of the future. The story is really a long one but to make it short, let me just say that someone ran off with the money, several hundred thousand dollars that we had placed in London in order to buy the rights in many Arab countries. As a director of the company I was worried at what seemed to me to be pretty loose arrangements, considering we really didn't know who we were dealing with there, so I made a quick trip to London and talked to our financial adviser, the manager of a large Canadian trust company. This man assured me that the money was in a lawyer's trust account and would not move until all the necessary documents were signed. It turned out that this was bullshit, and in a matter of a few days the money disappeared. It happened that this was the time for the company's annual report, and the accountants, a huge multinational firm, decided that they would not announce this shortfall because it happened after the year-end. I threatened to take the matter to the superintendent of brokers. In the meantime, several of the directors, seeing that it was cover-your-ass time, resigned. They had done nothing wrong but knew that it was a good time to check out. Turned out they were right. The superintendent suspended the remaining directors' right to trade stock in the company, and that order brought me a hell of a lot of bad publicity. While I had not done anything remotely dishonest and had, in fact, been the whistle-blower, I looked like the bad guy. In any event, the company I had such faith in went down the tube, and someone else will now make the millions that are bound to flow from the rising popularity of Stevia.

My evening show on CKNW took me right up to Expo '86 and into the station's new studios at the Plaza of Nations. To this day, when my wife Wendy reminisces about the wonders of Expo, I do my version of Bah! Humbug! because to me Expo '86 meant battling huge crowds when I was going into and out of work. In fact, when Patti and I went to Australia in 1988, we saw more of the Expo in Brisbane by far than we saw of our own.

In May 1986, Premier Bill Bennett announced that he intended to resign and that there would be a leadership convention in July. Subsequently, the Socreds announced that it would be the last week in July at Whistler, an inspired choice for it gave the delegates the opportunity to mix socially as well as on the convention floor. Through the ingenuity of John Ashbridge, we patched together a radio station and I covered the event for CKNW. John's patchwork, however, had an interesting and unintended consequence. Evidently the entire broadcast, including our off-air time, was piped into all the hotel rooms. We were finally informed of this on the last day and were told that the off-air stuff was much more interesting than that intended for broadcast! I can believe it!

There were some fascinating moments at that convention. Going into it there were four clear favourites, in no special order: Grace McCarthy, who was the grande dame of the party; the colourful Bill Vander Zalm; the attorney general, the publicly dour but privately very funny Brian Smith; and the best political mind in the province, Bud Smith. As the media saw it, Grace and Bill would probably make some deal and, if possible, so would Brian and Bud. Indeed the two Smiths, though unrelated, were referred to as the "Smith Brothers" after the cough drops of the same name. It turned out that the media had it badly wrong—not for the first or last time. The first ballot had Vander Zalm in the lead but with nowhere near a majority, followed by Brian Smith, Grace McCarthy and Bud Smith. They would go to a second ballot.

As anchor I was getting reports from the floor. Suddenly I got a frantic signal to switch to George Garrett who told me and my audience that Bud Smith was about to move over to Bill Vander Zalm's camp. "Ridiculous," I said confidently on air. "That wouldn't happen in a thousand years." Whereupon a rumble started in the crowd and there, sure as hell, was Bud Smith in Vander Zalm's corner shaking hands. I could not believe it! Bud, in his kinder moments, had said that Vander Zalm was an idiot. What had happened? Pretty soon Bud sent a message that he wanted to see me by the CBC mobile broadcast studio. He and I are close friends; he had managed my two winning election campaigns in Kamloops. "Rafe," he said, "I had no choice. All my supporters said they would stick with me in the next ballot, but their second choice, almost to a person, was Vander Zalm. And, unfortunately, my people tell me that I have very limited potential for growth on the next ballot." I asked Bud if there had been a deal made. "No," he said, but I didn't know whether I could believe him. As it turned out, there was no deal and Bud was not in Vander Zalm's first cabinet.

Before the balloting I was on Bill Good's show on CBC-TV to which I was contracted to do commentary. (Later Bill and I were colleagues for 15 years at CKNW). He asked me what I thought would happen if Vander Zalm were selected. "Bill," I said, "in two years he will have destroyed the Social Credit Party." And so it proved.

With the exception of Jack Davis, the maverick who had been bounced from the Bill Bennett government for cheating on expenses, none of Vander Zalm's former cabinet colleagues supported him. It wasn't that they didn't like him. They mostly did, but they had worked with him and knew he was a my-way-or-the-highway kind of person, who not only couldn't build a consensus but instinctively tried to break them up when they appeared.

After Grace was knocked off on the second ballot, we all waited in a terrible bit of mass boredom until Vander Zalm murdered Brian Smith on the last ballot. And why did Vander Zalm, so mistrusted by his colleagues and much of the party, win? There is no doubt that Bill had the looks and the charisma. He was very good one-on-one and in small groups. He was excellent in trivializing complicated issues. But the main reason was more practical and timely: on the eve of the final vote, both the *Vancouver Sun* and BCTV published polls showing that of the four major candidates, only Vander Zalm could win the next election and that he would win it if selected. That information ran through Whistler like a brushfire and, in my opinion, had an enormous impact. In any event, the public and the media were in for four and one half of the most politically raucous years in BC history.

In the fall of 1986, when I went to London to investigate the Stevia matter, I got a call from Patti to tell me that Barrie Clark was leaving CKNW to write a book and the host position was open. In fact, one of the main reasons Barrie quit was that he and Gary Bannerman hated each other's guts to the point that CKNW had been forced to erect a wall in the old Holiday Inn Harbourside studios in order to keep them from killing each other. I had been promised by Doug Rutherford that if Barrie's job came open, it would be mine. I immediately phoned Doug to say, "I assume I will be moving to the afternoon show." Doug mumbled some inconsequential platitudes, and I was shocked to find that the job wasn't necessarily mine after all. When I got back, Doug advised that there were over 70 applications for the position and that the station would be evaluating them all. To say that I was very pissed off is putting it very mildly indeed.

A few weeks later I got a call from Doug just before I went on air asking me to come out to the main studio in New Westminster the next morning at nine to discuss the afternoon show. I told him to get fucked. I said that I wasn't going to be like some mail-order bride being looked over on the wharf by potential mates and that, if CKNW didn't know what I could do by now, to hell with them. Needless to say this shocked Patti who, being the one-person producer of a show that often had as many as a dozen guests, couldn't wait to get a show that was easier to produce and carried at least one assistant. That evening at virtually every break in my show Doug phoned again begging me to come to the meeting. My answer was consistently the international phrase for "go away." I was truly angry because I had earned my spurs and with them the right to move up the ladder. In any event, Doug called me again at nine as I signed off to plead with me one more time. I could see that he was on the spot because he had assured management that I would be doing handsprings out to New Westminster. "Okay," I said, "but unless the meeting is simply to confirm my appointment, I'll walk out."

The next day I hied out to general manager Ron Bremner's office to see the assembled management. It was over in a flash. Ron said, "We're here to deal with the afternoon show, and I understand that Doug recommends Rafe be the host. Is that right, Doug?"

"Yes," said Doug, so Ron asked me if I would take the job. I said, "Yes," and it was a done deal. Why had I behaved that way? Because this a very tough business and I am an independent contractor, not an employee. Media management will run all over those whom they can run over, and the woods are full of performers who thought they could get ahead by kissing management's ass. It's no accident that most of the good performers are independent cusses.

The years between 1986 and 1991 were for me the days of George Garrett, CKNW's ace reporter, and me covering the crazy goings-on in Victoria while on my own I covered the Meech Lake Accord. The Vander Zalm years were bizarre and it is not my purpose to begin trying to cover them here. Suffice it to say that there was so much going on that George Garrett, whom I referred to as "the intrepid reporter" so often that the name stuck and who had hitherto specialized in police-related stuff, became a regular on my show, dealing, often editorially, with provincial government affairs. If it wasn't one thing, it was another. Vander Zalm waded into the abortion controversy. While abortion was and is a federal matter, Vander Zalm, a devout Catholic, wasn't about to let that get in the way of his giving his opinion, and since the enforcement of the Criminal Code is delegated to the attorney general, this opinion embarrassed Brian Smith greatly and no doubt contributed mightily to his decision to quit. He finally resigned after the premier demanded information the attorney general did not feel at liberty to discuss, namely whether the premier himself was under any sort of police investigation. Grace McCarthy also quit because of interference from the premier's office. Four MLAs left caucus to sit as Independents.

Then there was the pub licence granted to a very dear lady friend of one of the premier's staunch pals, political and otherwise; and the Philippine billionaire whom the premier entertained at Government House as he tried to flog his theme park, Fantasy Gardens, to him. It just went on and on and on with ministers resigning, senior bureaucrats leaving under a cloud, and a bag containing $20,000 being handed over to the premier late one night in a hotel room. (Not illegal but surely unusual!)

One of the more interesting moments came in October 1988 at the Socred annual convention in Penticton, which I covered in part for CKNW. Many rank-and-file members wanted the vote of confidence in the premier at the start of the convention to be more than the usual perfunctory blessing. They wanted a real debate with a secret ballot because many didn't dare expose themselves by voting by the usual show of hands against their leader. However, the premier's forces went to work, and when the motion to hold a vote of confidence was taken to the floor, it was for a vote by open ballot! By the time Flying Phil Gaglardi, Bennett Senior's controversial highways minister, and former cabinet minister Don Phillips (also known as leather lungs for his loud and endless filibustering in the legislature) had done, the meeting was cowed into rejecting the motion for a secret ballot. Over a drink the previous night I had talked about this subject with Bill Bennett who said presciently, "No party can survive if it denies democracy to its members." Clearly Bennett hadn't thought much about the federal Liberal Party, but he knew the BC Social Credit Party very well indeed.

It took until the Spring of 1991 for it all to catch up to Premier Vander Zalm, but after a report commissioned by the premier himself had found him in serious conflicts of interest, he resigned to be replaced by Rita Johnston. This was a curious event because the caucus was to select Mr. Vander Zalm's replacement on an interim basis, and the question arose as to whether the person selected should also be candidate for the permanent job, to be decided that summer by a leadership convention. (Some years later the same problems arose with the NDP when Glen Clark resigned and they, with hindsight sensibly followed, selected an interim leader, Dan Miller, who promised not to run for the job permanently.)

It was a critical decision, for if the Socreds' selection for premier was able to seek the job permanently he, or as it turned out she, would have a very substantial advantage over any rivals. The caucus had a choice. Russ Fraser, a senior minister, offered to take on the job with the understanding that he would not run for it at the convention. A former attorney, whose advice over the years had wisely been taken by the government, in a strange lapse of political judgment advised that it would compromise the lieutenant-governor if he knew that the person he was making premier was just a temporary appointment. This was nonsense, of course, as all the lieutenant-governor needed to know was that the person before him could form a government with a reasonable prospect of being supported by the legislature, and Mr. Fraser could have given that assurance. In any event, the caucus selected Rita Johnston who made it very clear that not only would she run but that she intended to win—which she did.

The leadership convention that summer of 1991 came down to

a contest between Grace McCarthy, representing the "liberal" wing of the party, and Rita Johnston, who had the support of the "conservative" wing including what had been affectionately dubbed the "Zalmoids." It was a close race but Rita Johnston prevailed. As the convention closed, Jack Webster and I, covering it for BCTV, looked down from the balcony of the Convention Centre and concluded that what we were seeing was the Red Sea parting—to the left were the "liberals," bound, in fact, for the provincial Liberal Party; to the right were the conservatives, bound to go down in flames as Socreds before the NDP.

My covering this convention for BCTV was a minor story in itself. Doug Rutherford had decided that Bill Good would be the CKNW anchor and that I would report to him from the floor. This pissed me off for not only was I host of the flagship show and had experience covering Socred and other conventions, but I had not been consulted (consultation never having been big with CKNW management). I refused and contacted BCTV (curiously, part of the same media family) and contracted my services to cover the convention for them at $800 per day. I know it seems like petty bickering, but I was convinced then as I am now that if you once let management dictate to you, they'll do it every chance they get.

Not long after that leadership convention, Premier Johnston called an election for October 17, 1991. She hadn't much choice as the Socred mandate had all but run out. Although she is a good egg and a pretty good cabinet minister, she didn't have a prayer. It wasn't that the NDP beat her because they didn't. Her own troops, fleeing to the provincial Liberals under the leadership of Gordon Wilson, are what did her in. But she deserved to lose and she knew it. She came on my show the following day and apologized to British Columbians for letting them down. A class act especially since it was not she who was to blame. The fault lay with the Social Credit Party for not selecting Grace. I don't believe she could have won the election—though she might have—but at worst she would have led a healthy Opposition. That would have eliminated the amazing revival of the Liberals under Gordon Wilson and would have, in my view, insured that after one term of the NDP Grace would have been premier. There would have been no Premier Glen Clark, no fast ferry scandal, and no Premier Gordon Campbell.

Grace didn't win the nomination for a couple of reasons. For one thing she stayed out of the race until the very last minute. On air and privately I had urged her to get into the race, but she knew this was a divided party, and she wasn't sure she wanted to—or even could—reunite it. When she did decide to run, she was too late. Second, while Grace had a hell of a lot of friends in the party, she had enemies, too, especially the right-wingers who saw her as the reason Vander Zalm fell. She represented the middle of the party and would have stopped the party's left wing making a mass exodus to the Liberals. Moreover, she had been in politics a long time and you can't be a successful, tough and resourceful minister for as long as she had without arousing both anger and jealousy, often both at the same time. Some, like me, could fight like hell with Grace but still see what a superb person she was and just write off the fighting as part of the political game. Others bore grudges. Unfortunately for Grace, too many fell in the latter category, and she became one of the great might-have-beens in our political history.

What a different picture politics in BC might have been had Bob Skelly not stumbled as he began his 1986 campaign against Vander Zalm and instead served a term as premier with a hale and hearty Socred Opposition on the benches dogging the NDP's every footstep! But, alas, it was not to be.

# 8

## Meech and Charlottetown

FOR THE SIX YEARS FROM August 1986 until October 26, 1992, my radio career, when not centred on the political goings-on in Victoria, was dominated by Meech Lake and the Charlottetown Accord. Although I have dealt extensively with these two constitutional initiatives elsewhere, especially in *Canada: Is Anyone Listening?*, I now have a better time perspective on both of them.

First, some background. While in government I had spent nearly four years acting as the minister responsible for constitutional affairs although my only title in that regard was Chairman of the Cabinet Committee on Confederation. I also served as chairman of the Western Premier's Task Force into Federal Legislative Intrusions. My colleagues on that task force were Lou Hyndman, then Alberta treasurer; Roy Romanow, then Saskatchewan attorney general and later premier; and Howard Pawley, Manitoba attorney general and later premier. During those years I was privileged to have a very close association with the late Melvin H. Smith, QC, one of the top constitutional experts in the country. As a result, I had developed one rigid conviction: vetoes in a constitution are a very bad thing. A constitution must be difficult to alter, but it mustn't be impossible. If it's too easy, political fashions of the day can be nation wreckers of the future. If it's too hard, the body politic becomes constipated. Moreover, I became very aware of the dangers of locking current political solutions into the constitution. It seemed to me then as it does now that these axioms should guide all constitutional considerations.

Let me give an example of the dangers inherent in vetoes. Because Quebec can now effectively veto the establishment of a new and fair Senate, there will never be one unless whatever power Quebec must give up—such as that province's present 24-6 domination over BC in the Senate—is compensated for (and then some!) in another form. Neither, for that matter, would Ontario allow it to happen. By the terms of the Charlottetown Accord (which I will henceforth refer to as Charlottetown), Quebec would agree to a pallid Senate (which because of her about-to-be formalized veto she could prevent from ever being changed again) the province demanded and nearly got 25 percent of the House of Commons seats for all time.

If you entrench such things as a certain percentage of seats in the House of Commons to a province or constitutionally embed the right of a tiny province like Prince Edward Island to always have at least four Commons seats, you lead to an inevitable distortion that makes a mockery of representation by population. And in Canada we have made this problem even worse by a 1978 law that prevents any province from losing seats by reason of population shifts.

An international example is also apropos here, I think. After World War II, when the French left Lebanon, the constitution provided that the presidency alternate between Christians and Muslims. This worked fine in the beginning when the populations were relatively equal, but when in the 1970s and '80s population figures moved closer to two-thirds Muslim and one-third Christian, all hell broke loose. We all know what happened to Lebanon, though, granted, the reasons were more complicated than just the method of determining the president. But this example underlines another axiom that must never be forgotten: power, once achieved, will never be voluntarily surrendered and can never be taken away or even diminished except by force or a bad bargain.

And so we come to the day that never happened in the Alice in Wonderland set-up that is the Canadian political system: October 26, 1992. By some sort of miracle Canada's establishment has obliterated from record and memory all evidence of this day's events. The Tories, who were in power that day, the Liberals, who mostly supported them, and the NDP, who did support them, act as if this day never happened. It's a blank in the memory of the political parties of all the provinces; the artsy-fartsy "higher purpose persons" (to use Denny Boyd's wonderful phrase) have no recall; neither do business and labour.

Allow me, therefore, for the sake of the record, to review what this date means or should mean to Canadians from coast to coast. It is a story that should be impressed on the brains of every Canadian alive and those not yet born for it is one of the two or three most important dates in our history. Let me tell you the story as one who was in it to such an extent that Prime Minister Mulroney called me a traitor, senior cabinet minister John Crosbie opined that I was Canada's most dangerous man and the government of Canada deliberated over whether or not a special tax audit should be done on me and my family.

The story really begins with Confederation, but it picks up in earnest when Pierre Trudeau "patriated" the Constitution from London to Ottawa, those discussions starting in 1976 and ending in 1982 with the new Constitution and the famous (or infamous) Charter of Rights and Freedoms. There were a lot of issues around Sections 91 and 92, which divide powers between Ottawa and the provinces, but the most vexing question at that time was: how do you amend this new Constitution? Up until then any amendment had to be done by the British House of Commons because the British North America Act (BNA Act) had been a British statute. Most amendments had been done by consent of all parties, but many people, particularly in Quebec, held strongly to the view that the BNA Act needed consent of the federal government and all the provinces and held this to be a condition of bringing the Constitution "home." There had been several efforts to come up with an amending formula but all had failed, and this became the sticking point, with Quebec in the ludicrous position of calling for the Constitution to stay in London where they thought their rights would be better protected because the British Parliament would honour their claim to a veto. When the deal was finally struck in 1982, it was taken without the approval of the Quebec government led by René Lévesque, though it was approved, under a heavy whip to be sure, by Quebec's members of parliament. At one point Lévesque had agreed with a solution to the amending formula conundrum proposed by BC, then by others, that would break the deadlock over how to amend the Constitution. In fact, I have seen his signature on that document possessed by BC's constitutional deputy minister, the late Mel Smith, QC. I believe it now can be found in the collections of the Mel Smith Foundation at Trinity Western University. However, after the deal was done, Lévesque said he disagreed with it and would not sign on, and he didn't. Notwithstanding the fact that the Supreme Court of Canada, with three Quebec members, unanimously made it clear that the patriation was constitutional and bound all provinces including Quebec, Lévesque and the Parti Québécois screamed that they had been cheated and swindled.

By 1983, the public, including that of Quebec, had tired of the debate. The feeling seemed to be that the deal was done so let's get on with life. Into this tranquility came Martin Brian Mulroney who, after stabbing Tory leader Joe Clark in the back, now led the party and was looking to defeat the Liberals in the next election. To do this, Mulroney, a Quebecer himself, knew that he had to make great inroads into Liberal influence in Quebec, and he did it by co-opting Quebec's separatists. These were not "sovereigntists" or whatever other weasel word comes to mind, but separatists like Lucien Bouchard who would later, as premier, lead his province in a referendum to desert Canada. The price for these separatists' support was that Mulroney must get them what they had always demanded: special status (in every sense of that word) in Canada. And so the phrase "distinct society" came into the Canadian political lexicon.

In August 1986 something happened that must have blown Mulroney's mind. It certainly did mine! That August in Edmonton the premiers, including the newly minted Bill Vander Zalm of British Columbia and Robert Bourassa of Quebec, met to talk of many things including constitutional arrangements. At a private lunch, with no advisers present, the premiers agreed to postpone all their constitutional claims to give precedence to those of Quebec. To use Mulroney's nonsensical phrase, they agreed to make Canada "whole" again by getting Quebec to sign on to the newly minted Constitution. They declared, one and all, that this meant settling Quebec's claims before their own. What is incredible is that all nine premiers outside of *la belle province* somehow overlooked the fact that in doing this, they would confer a veto into Quebec's hands whereby that province's government could nix any and all constitutional proposals thereafter submitted. Think on that! Such matters as Senate reform would now be subject to a Quebec veto, and everyone with an ounce of savvy knew that the very last thing Quebec would agree to was a new Senate unless (a) it was useless, and (b) Quebec got something very substantial for any concessions made or (c) both. However, armed with the provincial conviviality engendered by the Edmonton Conference, Mulroney trotted the premiers off to Meech Lake in May of the following year to see if some settlement could be reached to "make Canada whole" and coincidentally appease the captive separatists in the Tory caucus.

By this time, my radio show was becoming more and more involved in this constitutional scam as it unfolded under the chairmanship of Brian Mulroney with Joe Clark at his side as the sorcerer's apprentice. At their little party at Meech Lake, Quebec was promised many things, the most important of which was a "distinct society" designation within the Constitution. Churlish observers like me immediately asked a simple question: what does this phrase mean? If it confers powers, what powers? If it doesn't confer powers, why does Premier Robert Bourassa set his hair on fire every time this question is asked?

All the premiers signed on to the Meech Lake deal, but the Constitution required that the provinces officially consent by acts of their legislatures. The Canadian public was then expected to docilely support the legislatures as the approval process was conducted. But the heady promise of the Meech Lake Accord, as this deal was called, began to fade when Premier Clyde Wells of Newfoundland and Labrador took over from Brian Peckford and rescinded his province's approval and put it back on the order paper. He then spent time all over the country gauging opinion, and he came on my show numerous times, sometimes by phone, sometimes in person. In fact, he came close to becoming one of my show's regulars, and he and I began to feel the comradeship that comes from fighting the same battle against the same enemy. Consequently, in developing my own opinion, though I had relied upon my considerable experience in the field as well as the advice of the late Mel Smith and of Gordon Gibson, I gained a lot of insight by speaking and corresponding with Premier Wells. Later I was informed by Deborah Coyne, Well's constitutional adviser (and later mother of Pierre Trudeau's daughter), that during the fall of 1989 and the spring of 1990 he had received over 10,000 letters and faxes—and flowers—from BC alone, mostly from my listeners, in support of his stance! And this was before e-mail!

During this time I was so consumed with this constitutional horror as I perceived it that for the first time the management of CKNW asked if I didn't think I was being a bit excessive. "After all," program manager Doug Rutherford observed, "no one really cares."

"Doug," I replied, "they will care, trust me! And when they do, the story will be ours." And so it proved.

Premier Wells scheduled debate in his legislature on the motion to approve the Meech Lake Accord for the day before it was due to expire if it was not totally supported by the provinces. However, it turned out to be Manitoba, which for some reason nobody had been watching, that spiked the deal, not Newfoundland. It was in the Manitoba legislature that a government backbencher by the name of Elijah Harper embarked on a filibuster over a procedural matter to make sure that the question on Meech didn't come up for a vote until after the deadline for the deal to be ratified—June 23, 1990—had passed. And so Meech Lake died.

To their eternal disgrace, Mulroney, Senator Lowell Murray, John Crosbie and other Tory leaders placed the blame for the failure of Meech Lake on the shoulders of Clyde Wells, even though a vote in his legislature would not have mattered because Mr. Harper had made the point moot. Furthermore, Mr. Wells, who must be presumed to know his own politics, maintained that the vote would have failed in his assembly anyway. But I have always believed that Mulroney found it easier to blame Premier Wells because Mr. Harper is an aboriginal.

Now Brian Mulroney had a problem. He was nearing election time, and he had to have Quebec on side. He also knew that he couldn't front a new deal, so he selected his most famous victim, Joe Clark, to restart and retool the process and have a new deal in place before an election in the fall of 1993. The result was an agreement in Charlottetown in the spring of 1992 destined to go to the electorate by referendum on October 26, 1992. Why a referendum when none had been used for Meech Lake?

Mulroney was forced to it by Quebec and, curiously, by British

Columbia. Rita Johnston, though a "footnote premier" in BC, had left one lasting and important legacy. Seeing the way the federal government had crammed through the Meech Lake Accord and how unpopular the Vander Zalm decision to pass it had been, she brought in the Referendum Act which in short simple language made it obligatory that, before any constitutional amendment could be passed by the legislature, it first had to pass a province-wide referendum. I have no doubt that this came about in part because of the enormous opposition to Meech Lake by then Liberal leader Gordon Wilson, policy expert and writer Gordon Gibson, the late Mel Smith and myself. Ms. Johnston may have made other errors of judgment but she knew that a government that crammed a constitutional agreement down the throats of BC voters, after what had happened with Meech, would pay and pay big time.

The Accord itself is too long and in many parts too arcane to deal with here in detail. The nub of the matter originally was that Quebec would have a "distinct society" section of the Constitution and a veto over any future constitutional changes. There would be a new Senate that would be elected, scarcely equal and certainly not effective. In fact, then Liberal MP and constitutional expert Ted McWhinney called it a "damp squib." All this was bad enough but in mid-game Bourassa demanded that Quebec, in exchange for the loss of its power in the Senate, be given 25 percent of House of Commons seats for all time, and that this should be written into the Constitution and require unanimous consent to change. Mulroney agreed with him. Imagine the chances of that happening! But, never worried about the long-term in politics, Mulroney agreed with him.

When the campaign started, I was asked to be on CBC's "Journal," which in those days followed the national news. There were three panelists in the CBC's Toronto studio and me in Vancouver. The host was Bill Cameron and the other panelists consisted of a pollster and two newspaper columnists, one of them being Jeffrey Simpson, I believe. Of course, having no eye contact with the host or any of the other panel members, I found it difficult to break in at any point.

Cameron introduced the subject, namely the likelihood of the referendum passing and especially whether it would be supported by British Columbians. He addressed the pollster first, and I was astonished to hear her say that BC had been much in support of Meech Lake and would certainly support Charlottetown. I found myself gritting my teeth and silently shouting, "Bullshit!" He then moved to one of the journalists who also thought that the people of BC, being good Canadians, would vote yes, and again I restrained myself from shouting, "Bullshit!" The next journalist—I think it was Simpson—opined that once the great captains of industry and people like the prime minister came to BC and explained the value of the Accord, the people would understand its importance. Again I kept my response under control. But when Cameron at last said, "And what about you, Rafe Mair out there in Vancouver?" I exclaimed, "Rubbish!" I told them that if they thought this deal had the faintest chance of passing in BC, they were all smoking something they ought not to. I went on to explain the flaws in the agreement that would be fatal to my province. And so we ended with the panel in a stalemate. But in a subsequent article, Jeffrey Simpson stated that while he supported the Charlottetown Accord, Rafe Mair had raised questions that had to be answered. They weren't.

My show now became the far western battle headquarters for the tiny group that was firmly and vocally on the No side. With the exception of Mel Smith, writing in the now defunct *BC Report*, and Gordon Gibson when he could find someone to listen to him—which on my show was often—I started out as the only person regularly on air and in print in the country to oppose both Meech and Charlottetown from start to finish.

Two politicians who stood firmly on the No side from Meech through to the end were Preston Manning, who led the then fledgling Reform Party, and Gordon Wilson, then leader of the BC Liberal Party. Like Clyde Wells, both were well informed and articulate, and both soon became regulars on my show. Manning gave the No side presence and dignity. Gordon Wilson was a clever, articulate and brave man. Though dividing his caucus as he spoke, he knew his brief, and when he was on my show, which was often, the Yes side took a very carefully administered thrashing.

Premier Clyde Wells became the sad side of the debate. Passionately opposed to Meech, he converted to the Yes side for Charlottetown, this new agreement being, in Mulroney's words, "Meech Plus! Plus! Plus!"

I believe that enormous pressure was brought on Premier Wells who had to look out for his province, the poorest in the country. My interview with him during the debate was the toughest I've ever done because I so liked and respected the man. Unfortunately for him, I had mountains of material out of Wells' own mouth that directly contradicted what he was now saying. It was a cross-examiner's dream, and I had to decide whether I went for the throat or played pussycat. I chose the latter. I simply let him unenthusiastically answer the questions and when he left, I thought I detected a sense of gratitude. After all, he too was a lawyer, and he knew the unfired ammunition in my armoury.

The government, needless to say, was pouring its considerable resources into the Yes side. But it backfired. When Mulroney point-man Jean Charest and his committee rolled into Vancouver, supposedly to find out what we thought, they fixed the meetings so that only high rollers for the Yes side got to speak. Their strategy was just so obvious that by the time I had analyzed it on my show, many who might have voted Yes saw that they were being stampeded and defrauded by the Mulroney government and the eastern establishment. As a result, his meetings became known as "The Charest Charade." Indeed, one might accurately dub the Charlottetown Accord "the deal that demolished itself through its own bullshit." Charest avoided my show like the plague because my guests and I were firing every gun at him, his Mulroney pals and his "higher purpose persons."

The debate on the Charlottetown Accord itself was really no debate at all except in Quebec and British Columbia. In the rest of the country it was a case of "Do as you're told, children!" They were bamboozled into thinking it was utterly unthinkable and downright unpatriotic to oppose this establishment manifesto. The prime minister was shown on national television tearing up the Constitution to show that without Charlottetown the country was done for. Joe Clark damned near killed himself making speeches that had nothing to do with what the deal would do but were laden with predictions of the catastrophes awaiting us all if the referendum failed. When he was on my show, he was so red in the face and so obviously distraught I was truly concerned for his health. I had known and liked Joe since his leader-of-the-Opposition days, when he had quite a different view of constitutional matters. Derek Burney, a former ambassador to

South Korea whom I had met there in 1979, told my audience—while clearly operating on a considerable hangover—that Canada would lose its trade with the United States the very next day if the deal failed, presumably because the Americans would see us as a fractured, third-world country. That *wunderkind* of Canadian politics, Frank McKenna, made a speech in Victoria to the effect that all the late veterans would stir restlessly in their graves if we failed them by voting No. He was so shattered by the response he received from his audience there that, when he came on my show shortly afterwards, he shook and shivered as if he had just emerged from an ice-water bath—which I suppose he had.

The media also bolstered the Yes side campaign. In fact, MacLean-Hunter actually signed on as part of the Yes side! Here was a media giant, bound by tradition to ask questions, that was not only not asking them but uncritically assisting the government and the rest of the establishment. The *Vancouver Sun* was 100 percent behind the deal and dubbed me "Dr. No" for my position. The central Canadian media, especially the tame parliamentary press gallery—with only Claire Hoy, always considered a maverick for asking questions, the brave exception—was for the deal as was the artsy-fartsy crowd led by June Callwood, Pierre Berton and Margaret Atwood. The Companions of the Order of Canada weighed in on the Yes side, thus involving the Governor General in the political fray, and this got me into a sideshow battle with Order-of-Everything Peter C. Newman. Labour leaders such as Ken Georgetti, then president of the British Columbia Federation of Labour, were for Yes (although amusingly his sister Judy emphatically and very publicly disagreed with him), as was IWA prexy Jack Munro. The British Columbia NDP government under Mike Harcourt was for the deal, and on the day of the vote, in breach of House rules, his caucus all wore Yes buttons. The premier, in fact, asked my producer, Patti, how poor old Rafe was going to handle it when BC voted emphatically Yes. She told him that Rafe hadn't considered that question because he didn't believe that would happen.

The NDP's Yes-man in BC was Moe Sihota, and he was, I must say, the only Yes politician who came on the show who really understood the issues. By his own admission, he was knocked out by the deal that had been made shortly before the referendum between Mulroney and Quebec premier Robert Bourassa in which Quebec would get, in exchange for the new Senate, 25 percent of the House of Commons seats for all time. I must admit I don't know whether BC might not have voted for Charlottetown had not this outrage been perpetrated, though I doubt it.

The result of the referendum was crushing for the government. Six provinces voted No and Ontario only narrowly passed it. In British Columbia the vote against was just under 70 percent. And why did the referendum fail in BC? I think that most of the British Columbians who voted No did so because they felt that their province was under attack. We are a proud people who have been hammered by central Canada since Confederation. We don't see Canada as an ongoing struggle between Upper and Lower Canada with the other eight provinces lining up like loyal little children behind Ontario. At the time of the vote they saw, rightly in my view, the Charlottetown Accord as a perpetuation of central Canadian hegemony for all time.

Interesting things happened in the aftermath. On the Sunday after the vote *Vancouver Sun* editor-in-chief Ian Haysom wrote a column asking how the *Sun* under his leadership could have so misjudged its readers. Jack Munro, never known hitherto as a crybaby, complained about CKNW's (that is, Rafe Mair's) coverage to the CRTC. In fact, we were only three hours out from giving both sides equal time, and that was only because we reserved the last three hours before the vote for Brian Mulroney because his people had demanded the right to sum up. But Mulroney had been, as I had predicted, a no-show.

One of the consequences of the referendum's failure was the obliteration of the Conservative Party in the election of 1993, reducing them from a virtual landslide victory in 1988 to two MPs. Former prime minister Mulroney still bitterly blames Preston Manning for splitting the vote in the 1993 election and causing the Tory whiteout. It never seems to occur to him that the Reform Party happened because the Conservative Party under his leadership failed its traditional supporters in western Canada. And the referendum results will continue to divide the new Conservative Party of Canada because the Tories always see Canada as the Upper Canada/Lower Canada debate while the Reform/Alliance, now their partners, believe in 10 juridically equal provinces. It will be interesting to see if that unmentioned "elephant in their house" becomes unavoidably visual in the new Conservative Party in the event of a future constitutional crisis.

And how do I regard the referendum a decade and more beyond? I stand with Gordon Gibson who was my comrade-in-arms and who said it was a very liberating experience for Canadians who finally had the chance to tell their masters to get stuffed and did just that. And just what might have been had all Canada except Quebec said Yes? That would, in my view, have been catastrophic because the rest of Canada would immediately have said, "Okay, we agreed and you didn't, so obviously we didn't offer enough. Let's go back to the table and we'll bring a whole new batch of goodies for you." But suppose only BC had said No and every other province, including Quebec, had voted Yes. I believe the pressure on BC from the feds, specifically financial pressure, would have been enormous. Despite that, I don't think there would have been a government in Victoria prepared to resubmit the question, knowing that British Columbians would have responded even more vigorously in the negative and would have punished any government that tried to bully them. Under this set of circumstances I don't think the country could have been held together.

Given the risks, then, am I not sorry that I opposed Charlottetown? No. It wasn't I who took those risks. It was Brian Mulroney and the entire governing class of this country. My opposition wasn't based on some esoteric plane or unsupportable demagoguery but on the huge and very obvious flaws in the agreement that would have locked us into an unamendable constitution. I didn't get British Columbia to vote No. I merely put forth serious yet basic arguments that the Yes side couldn't answer. In fact, midway through the referendum debate, Orland French, writing in the *Globe and Mail*, said in essence that Rafe Mair was asking the tough questions, and in order for the deal to pass those questions must be answered. Of course, they never were.

Do I think that Mel Smith, Gordon Gibson and I had an effect on the overall vote in Canada? I can tell you that Mel thought so and so does Gordon. But none of our voices was heard in Nova Scotia, the first province to vote No, or in any of the western provinces outside of BC. The view of my colleagues, with which I agree, is that as the days passed the rest of the country knew that BC was going to vote No because the polls showed a huge opposition—58 percent a week before—and this finally overcame the government's patriotism arguments and gave them the courage to consider No as a legitimate response.

Can Charlottetown be somehow revived? The answer is clearly no as evidenced by the so-called Calgary Accord of a few years ago. The British Columbia government, which I was privately advising (though this fact was known to all), simply killed it by loving it to death with additional clauses that spelled self-immolation for the Accord. The NDP government of the day, with the very savvy Andrew Petter in charge of constitutional matters, not only knew that Calgary was Charlottetown through the back door but, more importantly, was aware that the people knew it too and that they would slaughter the government that circumvented their wishes. I must, of course, qualify my answer to the question of whether Charlottetown can be revived since in politics anything can happen. I suppose that, because the huge dislike of politicians in this country threatens to dismember it, there are scenarios that could arise to breathe life back into Meech and Charlottetown. However, I am convinced that they would be rejected even more forcefully than before. And why do I believe that?

Well, it happened that when the campaign started, I received a letter from Monica and Bud Smith (no relation to Social Credit's Bud Smith) telling me that they and a dozen or so neighbours had formed a group called "Friends of Canada Voting No." I encouraged them to carry on. A day or so later I heard from them again: they had been advised by the Secretary of State for Canada that a "higher purpose" group was using the name "Friends of Canada" and they were to cease and desist. They weren't troubled by this and simply renamed themselves. Now it must be understood that we're talking here about a couple of retired schoolteachers with no resources, but by voting day on October 26, 1992, their little group had grown to 800 people working on the campaign. They were everywhere—bus stops, ferry terminals, you name it—handing out copies of editorials that had been written by me, articles by Mel Smith and Gordon Gibson, and anything else that would bolster their argument. And so referendum day came and they had proof that what they had done had made a difference. At that time I was writing a weekly article for *The Financial Post*, and my first article post-referendum was about the campaign. I closed it by saying, "In British Columbia you don't mess about with Bud and Monica Smith!" And that is why I am confident that another Charlottetown would be defeated in BC just as overwhelmingly as the first one was.

What is now fascinating is that October 26, 1992, has become the day that didn't happen! By some sort of miracle the establishment of Canada has obliterated from record and memory all evidence of this day's events. Bill Fox, Mulroney's head flack, wrote a book about his years with Mulroney in which there is only one note about Meech Lake, Mulroney's second-biggest failure, and nothing at all about Charlottetown—his biggest! So there it is, the day that never happened. If you can get anyone in the establishment to talk about it, they say something like "The people didn't understand what they were doing" (Kim Campbell). Or "Everyone had something they didn't like and that killed the idea" (Warren Allmand). In fact, it was a hugely important day. Canadians, especially western Canadians, told central Canada that they didn't take orders from it and they were damned if they were going to give central Canada that right in perpetuity.

The following spring the British Columbia Association of Broadcasters named me "Broadcast Performer of the Year." This was interesting because the next year, after I helped bring down the Kemano Completion Project and won the Michener Award—the most prestigious of them all—I wasn't even on the long list for the BCAB award. It makes you wonder.

# 9

## *Why I am an Environmentalist*

I'M A SO-SO CONSPIRACY-THEORY KIND OF GUY. By this I mean that I'm attracted to arguments that someone in the oil industry keeps buying up the new carburetor that would cut gas consumption by half or that some electric company has bought out the inventor of the light bulb that will last a lifetime (you know how all these theories go), yet I don't fully buy them. But there is one conspiracy theory I believe implicitly: the corporate world and much of the senior bureaucracy in Ottawa and Victoria want to dam the Fraser River and create for the province (and the country) untold wealth in terms of cheap power at home and oodles of electricity for sale to the United States. It's not a new idea. General Andrew McNaughton, a cabinet minister in the Mackenzie King government in World War II, wanted to dam the Fraser. Bruce Hutchison in his marvellous book *Fraser*, published just after World War II, talked about the immense benefits of such a dam, and plans were hatched for a dam just north of Lytton to be called the Moran Dam. So what has stopped them from constructing it? What stopped the great dam builder W.A.C. Bennett himself?

Salmon. That's what stopped them. And salmon are what has stopped the damming of all major rivers that flow into the Pacific Ocean. The question now is: will salmon continue to thwart the plans of those who put money ahead of all else?

Over my years I have had four great crusades to save salmonids, that large family that includes the Pacific salmon (which biologists now claim includes the rainbow and cutthroat trout), trout and char. The first happened in the 1970s while I was in government, but it was really a crusade by others, men like the late John Massey, Dr. Tom Perry, former House Speaker John Fraser and so many others. The Skagit River, which flows into Washington state southeast of Hope, had been dammed—the Ross Dam—on the American side decades earlier, but pursuant to an agreement made with the BC government in 1941, Seattle Light and Power had the right to raise that dam and flood the river north of the border. The ROSS (Run Out Skagit Spoilers), a group that never gave up, and many others fought this project tooth and nail against not only the government but its powerful hand-maiden, BC Hydro. But it was not the NDP under Dave Barrett who listened. It was Bill Bennett who, at my urging, at last ordered me to go to Seattle and pay what was necessary to buy off Seattle. I did and the beautiful Skagit Valley is there for all to enjoy. I want to make it clear, though, that the real heroes were the men and women of all political stripes who banded together and fought the tireless battle to a success-ful conclusion. I have suggested to government that the little parking lots along the river, now named for fruits (Strawberry, etc.) should be named after those who fought the good fight. The NDP government put up a plaque instead, which implies somehow that they had some-thing to do with the saving of the valley but this is simply not true.

Not the next crusade in time, but an important one all the same, was the proposed gravel pit on the Pitt River. There, unlike the Skagit, not only resident trout but significant runs of Pacific salmon, as well as the sturgeon that lived in Pitt Lake and spawned near the river mouth, were all at serious risk. Again the real fight was by others, the PRAWN (Pitt River Area Watershed Network) environmental group being the most influential. I simply contributed my microphone. But this time it was the NDP government of Dan Miller that listened and acted.

My next campaign was against Alcan's Kemano Completion Project, which would see the company lowering the Nechako River to about 20 percent of its normal flow in order to build up power output for their Kitimat plants. The issue was a simple one that Alcan and both levels of government had made complicated. Two major runs of sockeye salmon pass through the Nechako on the way to their spawning beds in the Stuart River system. Was there a reasonable chance that there would be a combination of heat and low water just as these runs were passing through, thus putting them at serious risk? The answer to that was clearly yes, but Alcan and the governments maintained that everything is a risk but this was an acceptable one. However, the short answer was one of logic: if you create an ongoing, never-ending risk, it is no longer a risk but a certainty that a disaster will occur.

I got into the picture late and by accident. In June 1993 I was in Terrace and interviewed Alcan vice-president Bill Rich. The company had already received approval for this second stage of their dam project in 1987, but knowing nothing about its possible repercussions, I tossed slow-pitch after slow-pitch at Rich, and he easily batted all of them out of the park. When I got back to Vancouver, I received a call from Ben Meisner, a talk-show host at CKPG in Prince George. "What the fucking hell are you doing, Mair?" he demanded. Meisner is one of those rather candid people you run into from time to time. "Do you know a fucking thing about the Kemano Completion Project?"

After a short cooling off period I admitted I didn't and asked him to send me some bumph. I couldn't believe what I was reading, and so I asked him and Bill Rich to do a debate on my show, which they did. This launched a further six months of heated debate, much of which occurred on my show. The more questions I asked, the more were raised. We built up a huge volume of background material, and it became clear that the government of Canada had defied its own biologists and sent most of them packing one way or another. These men, stoutly courageous, sent me reams of material, including a report on the project that had been written when it was first proposed—several hundred pages of why the Kemano Completion Project should not be allowed to go ahead. That report had been hidden by the government until I made it public.

There were so many people involved in this fight that to talk about any would certainly lead me to miss some key players. Suffice it to say that Native bands, labour unions, fish biologists, professionals, environmentalists and people from every other walk of life joined in the fray, and by the beginning of 1994 the battle was at a fever pitch. Then suddenly it was all over. The Mike Harcourt government called a halt to the project. Both Mike Harcourt and Opposition Leader Gordon Campbell are to be praised for taking the time to look at the evidence, but the highest praise must go to Mike Harcourt because he had to make the decision. Though I had come late to the fight, considering that I received Canada's most prestigious media award, the Michener, for my efforts, I must have had some impact. Alcan tried to get this award taken away from me because they said I had libelled fisheries minister Tom Siddon. And it is true that Mr. Siddon sued me. I was part of the out-of-court settlement discussions that ensued, and when it became clear that it was going to cost as much to win the case as to settle, the insurers made the decision to settle, a decision both my lead counsel, Wally P. Lightbody, and I thought was wrong. But Alcan never succeeded in getting my Michener award rescinded.

My fourth campaign is the ongoing fight against fish farms whose horrific impact on salmon runs is finally getting through the craniums of those who run things. It stuns me to think that our governments (and incidentally so much of the population) actually believe that fish farms will take the pressure off wild stocks. The evidence against that notion is staggering. Salmon farms, especially Atlantic salmon farms off the BC coast where these fish are aliens or "exotic species," are a calamity. Here are a few of the problems they present. 1. They escape from their pens by the thousands every year, and—not withstanding all the cozy reassurances of the industry and the government—they have spawned in BC streams and are replacing wild Pacific salmon on the spawning grounds. 2. Farmed salmon catch all the diseases of the wild and, because they are concentrated in such numbers in such small spaces, spread those diseases back to the wild fish, big time. 3. They attract and breed immense swarms of sea lice that attack and de- molish the smolts of wild salmon as they travel past the farms on the way to the sea. 4. Feeding them requires the decimation of small fish stocks off the coasts of third-world countries that consequently lose their own fisheries into the bargain. 5. They make a hell of a mess on the ocean floor. 6. Eating them is unhealthy.

I'm no Luddite trying to turn back the clock. The trouble is that in pushing the idea that the world's burgeoning population can be fed by increasing aquaculture we haven't looked closely to see what is good and what might not be good. In the case of Atlantic salmon farming we have left the decision to industry and let the science follow later. It's a sad story, one that would make a cynic out of a saint. As a broadcaster the first event that caught my eye was the arrival of several Atlantic salmon (obviously from cages, since they are not natural to BC) in several BC rivers. The Department of Fisheries and Oceans (DFO) first said that the fish couldn't escape. Then they said that if they did escape, they couldn't survive in the wild. Then they declared that if they did escape and did get into our rivers they couldn't spawn—and anyway if they did, the progeny would not survive and come back to that river. Finally, the DFO declared that if any runs of Atlantic salmon did get established, they would destroy them. On this last point, considering how many runs of Pacific salmon they have ruined, I believed them!

The facts, according to fish biologist Dr. John Volpe, were quite different. He could only check a handful of rivers near where the huge escapes of Atlantic salmon had happened, but he reported that there were hundreds of Atlantics in the rivers and they had indeed spawned. I should add here that even if these Atlantics do not set up rival runs, their presence on the spawning grounds crowds out the wild species.

In this connection I had a famous interview with the Honourable John Van Dongen, who gives new meaning to the term "stubborn Dutchman." He simply denied everything and asserted at the end of our conversation that only three Atlantics had been found in our rivers. A subsequent interview with sustainable resources minister, the Honourable Stan Hagen, brought a correction. His colleague, Mr. Van Dongen, had been wrong: only two escapees had been found. After that I discovered that the fish farming territory was chock full of through-the-looking-glass raging red queens and mad hatter knock-offs. It's not as if we had no other country's experience to go on. In Norway, Scotland and Ireland, wherever fish farms were established near rivers, the spawning wild fish were wiped out or their runs seriously damaged. Sea lice have become a huge problem in BC over the last ten years. Returning wild salmonids have always carried a few sea lice, usually on the tail. When the fish reach fresh water, the lice disengage and, having no alternate host, die. It's a cycle they've been following for eons. When, however, there are fish farms nearby, the lice have an unimaginable bounty of hosts and instead of dying multiply into the millions. Then fast forward to spring when the young wild salmon smolts, just three to six inches long, head downriver and out to sea, passing en route by or through the lice-infested cages of salmon at the mouths of their rivers. The lice eat the smolts alive.

BC's fish farmers stoutly denied this was happening. It was sunspots that were causing the young fish to disappear. Or global warming. Or unusual populations of mackerel. Or some mysterious disease. But biologist Alexandra Morton did some testing in the spring of 2002 as the pink salmon smolts were starting to migrate in the Broughton Archipelago area. She netted sample smolts and found them covered in lice. She immediately called the DFO, whose first move was to threaten her with a $500,000 fine for the illegal harvesting of immature salmon. Six weeks later, after the majority of the migrating smolts had passed on their way to sea, the DFO sent the wrong boat with the wrong equipment to the wrong place to carry out their own testing and announced that there was no problem. Meanwhile, Alexandra Morton came on my show to pass on her prediction that the entire run of pinks in that area would be wiped out. And so it came to pass. When the run of mature pink salmon returned in the fall of 2002, only about 140,000 of the expected four million returned. Not only was Alexandra Morton vindicated by this sad event, her science was verified by Dr. Brian Riddell, the noted local fish biologist. The following spring I met a delightful Irishman, fish biologist Dr. Patrick Gargan, who was in Vancouver for a fishing conference. The world's top expert on sea lice and their impact on salmon, Gargan looked at the evidence provided by Alexandra Morton and agreed: sea lice were the most probable cause of the failure of that run. Other world-class authorities also weighed in on her side but, most importantly, the esteemed Honourable John Fraser in his extensive report on fish farming vindicated Alex both in his report and on my show. However, the DFO, Mr. Van Dongen, Mr. Hagen and the fish farmers association were all still in denial, so I invited ministers Van Dongen and Hagen to my studio. It was breathtakingly unbelievable! Both of them continued to insist that there was no connection between the teeming masses of sea lice around the fish farms and the loss of the salmon run and claimed that their experts had assured them there was no problem.

"Who are these experts?" I asked.

They wouldn't—or couldn't—name them but said they had science on their side. It was like discussing the history of the Jewish people with a Holocaust denier. The plain fact was that all the scientists and all the science backed Alexandra Morton's findings, which have now been peer-reviewed and published several times. But I am getting ahead of myself. In 2003 the spawn of the survivors of that same pink run went to sea, and Alexandra went to work with her dip net again. I asked her to report on my show.

"Rafe, it's awful. There will be a virtual wipe-out again!"

At this writing the government and the industry remain in denial, but consumers are making their concern felt. It is now hard to find farmed salmon on the menu in any decent Vancouver restaurant. And the fight has been carried to California, one of the biggest markets for BC farmed Atlantics in the past. The fish farming story in BC hasn't ended yet but it will likely end badly.

But why this obsession of mine with salmon? It's certainly not the value of the fish. If you add up all the money made from commercial fishing, commercial sport fishing and sport fishing, you can never win the economic argument with the aquaculture freaks and the spoilers who would dam a horse peeing if they thought they could get a watt of energy out of it. The financial returns from one dam on the Fraser would put paid to all the economic arguments in favour of wild salmon and then some.

No, the argument is cultural and indeed spiritual. It is not just to Native people—though most certainly to them—that the salmon means more than just money or even food. The salmon is what identifies British Columbia. Because of the huge watersheds that drain so much of our province into the Pacific, this fish is part of almost all communities in the province. Except, of course, in the Kootenays, where once huge salmon runs came up through the Columbia River system, and where they have been almost wiped out by power dams. So British Columbians must ask themselves what it is that they want. Is it more and more people, more and more harnessing of natural resources, and more and more development with no end in sight? Or is there a point where we say this far and no farther?

Nothing gained is without its cost. Alternatives to hydro power, even such seemingly benign alternatives as wind and tidal power, have environmental costs. Contrary to popular belief, however, coal-fired power may with modern technology become the most environmentally sound way to make large quantities of power abound. So the question remains: do we want the Pacific salmon, our heritage, to be the cost of our lust for expansion and thus power? For this is what we face if we build more dams to generate power. Of course, no one is going to dust off plans to dam a major salmon river as long as the salmon are there. But how convenient for the power freaks of this province if the salmon are all gone! And that is why the telling argument against the Kemano Completion Project was that, sooner or later, it was bound to wipe out the sockeye runs through the Nechako. That having happened, and the remaining salmon runs being of small consequence economically, there would be no reason left not to dam the Fraser north of Lytton.

Killing the environment is actually an easy, short-term way to make money. If that is what we as a society want, why not repeal the laws controlling the dumping of human and industrial waste into our waters? That will lower taxes and, because companies will make more money, it will presumably raise our prosperity. But is this the legacy we want to leave? Dams where the salmon once were? Farmed fish on our plates where fresh sockeye or coho once lay? More Jet Skis to replace the boaters who used to troll a line? Artificial lakes instead of river valleys? Rotting buildings where fishing camps once flourished? Kids growing up without ever feeling the tug of a fish on a line except in some artificial fishing pond? And more than that, do we want it on our consciences that the natural and very much alive symbol of our province, the wonderful fish that leaves our rivers to scour distant waters, only to return right on time to its native river to begin the process all over again, that this incredible gift bestowed by our Creator, came to an end under our watch? I can't tolerate the thought that I will die with this on my conscience, and that's why I'll fight the bastards to the end.

But I will be in good company. I have only three heroes who are alive, at least that I can think of, and all of them are in the environmental movement. Paul Watson, founder of the Sea Shepherd Society, is a New Brunswicker who transplanted to BC and helped found Greenpeace. They were too tame for him—or more likely he was too active for them—and he formed his own group, bought a boat and spent the next 25 years making a bloody nuisance of himself with those who would do violence to the environment especially, though not exclusively, where it involves whales. As I described in an earlier chapter, I once interviewed Captain Paul as he was being chased by the Soviet Navy and buzzed by their air force after he and his crew had landed in Kamchatka and destroyed a mink farm that was using whale meat for feed. He has been in jail several times, including Canadian jails and is *persona non grata* in more places than he can count. He is a man of immense courage—I have never met a more fearless person— and utterly dedicated to a lifetime of saving whales. Paul is a great man, all the more so because the government of Canada and many other governments and arms of the world's establishments hate his guts.

Anthony Marr is a different kind of cat. Chinese by origin, British Columbian by choice, Anthony had spent his working life until age 50 doing very routine, capitalistic sorts of things, including selling real estate. At 50, some sort of light fired up his belly, and he decided to spend the rest of his life saving animals, especially saving them from cruelty. He started by trying to reverse the insane BC government policy that permitted trophy hunting of grizzlies. Now his energies are concentrated on stopping the cruel raising of meat for the table and the production of paints. He is lecturing all over North America, showing his horrifying videos of what we do in order to put food on our tables. His word-pictures alone of chickens crammed into small boxes where they are force-fed, young cattle virtually strung up by the neck so that food can be periodically poured down their throats, and little piglets squealing helplessly as they are jammed into wooden cells barely bigger than they are, literally turn the stomach.

Then there is Alexandra Morton. An American biologist, she came to watch whales in the Broughton Archipelago, that beautiful bevy of islands that sit in Discovery Passage, which separates Vancouver Island from the Mainland. She married a Canadian and, with their four-year-old son beside her, saw him drown under their boat in six feet of water when new equipment failed. She dived overboard and loosened his weight belt only to watch his corpse come to the surface. In recent years, although her primary interest is still whales, Alexandra became aware, mostly from neighbouring Native people, that the inlets in the archipelago were full of sea lice. As described above, it was her fearless determination to find answers that led to the exposure of the part that fish farms are playing in decimating the wild salmon runs.

All three of my heroes force me to think. Anthony, a vegan, makes me wonder why I eat meat. Paul would make the most hardened of socialites wonder how a woman could wear on her back the pelt of a seal pup that was skinned alive in front of its mother. Alexandra makes me think about raw courage. All three of them, though mostly Anthony, have forced me to ask myself about my lifelong love of angling. Never mind catch-and-release. What is the morality of torturing a creature just for your own pleasure? Is it any different than bullfighting or the bear-baiting of 100 years ago? Is there any ethical excuse for fishing or hunting, and aren't they simply different sides of the same coin?

Of course, I rationalize: the fish is cold-blooded and doesn't feel pain, or so I convince myself. And it's different from running down a fox with horses and hounds or shooting some helpless animal, isn't it? That's the trouble with real heroes. They make you confront yourself and that isn't always a whole hell of a lot of fun.

# IO

## Depression

BACK IN 1988, I WAS DIAGNOSED with clinical depression that manifested itself in terrible bouts of anxiety. I was very lucky that my doctor, Mel Bruchet of North Vancouver, knew something about depression because in those days not many GPs did. Indeed there is still a large knowledge gap in the medical profession when it comes to mental illness of any kind. But Mel was able to diagnose my problem, comfort me with the reassurance that help was available and find the medicine that would provide relief for me. He knew that scientists were saying that in many cases clinical depression could be diagnosed by a physical examination because it is often caused by a lack of serotonin in the brain, and that these levels could be physically measured. And, thanks to modern medicine, seratonin deficiencies can be brilliantly dealt with. And that is what my problem turned out to be. Clinical depression is not just the feeling that comes when you lose your job or a family member or a friend. That feeling is, of course, depression but not what is called "clinical" depression. This is a complicated illness, but I define it in the many forms it takes as the "inability to cope." For those who don't suffer, this doesn't mean very much. Many people simply react to someone else's depression with, "Buck up! You're not the only one who gets depressed! I get depressed, too, but I don't go running off to my doctor!" It is this kind of reaction, of course, that has created the stigma that stands in the way of so many depressed people getting the help that's available. It may help to know that statistics (which I believe are conservative) tell us that one in four people will suffer from clinical depression in his or her lifetime! But the point of what I am saying here is not to convince anyone that depression is real. Surely, from what our society knows now, there can be no doubt about that. The problem is how to get sick people to seek and receive help. To do that requires two main ingredients: first, the knowledge and help must be available and second, people must be convinced they can smash society's stigma and get that help.

About six years ago, the principal guest on my show one morning was a remarkable woman by the name of Dr. Theresa Hogarth. At that time she was in private practice in New Westminster and, while not certified as a specialist, she had started to take a special interest in mental health. Because of what she saw every day with her patients, she had come to know that many of the problems she was looking at from the point of view of physical medicine actually had their roots in the brain. On this particular occasion, Theresa and I were taking calls from listeners, and call after call was a cry for help. Most, though not all, were men who were afraid to make the "unmanly" admission that they could be depressed. Then all of a sudden I heard myself saying, "Look here, there is nothing to be ashamed of. There is help available and often this help is nothing short of spectacular. And I should know because I've been treated for depression for years."

What was I doing? What had I just said right out loud over the airwaves?

Well, what I had done was start to make a difference for a hell of a lot of people. I'm not being immodest here. I'm simply saying that when someone in the public eye makes a public admission of that kind, it offers encouragement to others and gives them an excuse, if you will, to seek help. When I now tell people that since being diagnosed and treated with depression, I have maintained a five-day-a-week talk show, written seven editorials a week plus a newspaper article, done three editorials a week on TV, made countless speeches, done a lot of ad hoc radio and TV and written five books, it lets people see that one can, if treated properly, deal with depression. It helps them overcome that terrible but quite natural reluctance to seek help. (I also tell people that one of the reasons I'm not shy to admit that I take a serotonin enhancer is because I also take medicine in another area where nature has shortchanged me: I am a diabetic as well.)

As the result of that first interview and call-in program with Theresa, we started to do an annual "Depression Screening Day" when, while we were doing an on-air broadcast on mental illness, we invited calls to off-air mental health workers who were waiting by their phones. This effort was very much the work of the British Columbia Branch of the Canadian Mental Health Association and its many volunteers. The response has been enormous. We have had substantial support from the medical profession, the BC Branch of the Canadian Mental Health Association (CMHA), private groups and, to some degree, the government.

One of the great frustrations in doing a depression screening day is that you greatly fear—with good reason—that you are offering false hope. The idea, of course, is to get those suffering from mental illness to speak out about it and get help. But we depressed people start out ashamed and our shame is often aggravated by the attitudes of others, and that very much includes our loved ones. But what is the use of bringing people the good news that help is available when what you really mean is help is available if you can find it? And it is this that makes the process of "coming out" so upsetting. You have admitted you are ill, you understand you can be treated, you are assured that you can be "normal" again, but there's no one there when you knock.

The principal cause of this problem is the way in which government plays on the prejudices of society while pretending to do the very opposite. It must be understood that for governments mental illness is very bad business. It costs money, and this is not good in these times. (For the mentally afflicted it always seems to be "these times.") It is, therefore, distinctly not in the government's interest to find more sick people to pay for out of Medicare. But though governments can tell you with considerable accuracy what it costs to treat someone, what they cannot figure out is what it costs not to treat them. And it does cost a hell of a pile to leave mentally ill people untreated, and even though the math is difficult, we must try. What, for example, are the policing costs involved? What about the social costs of people unable to maintain normal relationships? How much alcoholism—a huge impost on the public purse—results from mentally ill people self-medicating? How many wives and children—and husbands—are abused by the mentally ill? How many marriages break up? How much is lost in training people who never use that training because they are unable to do so? What is the cost to industry?

One of the reasons we can't answer any of these and many similar questions is that we have never really tried to. And one of the main reasons for that is that governments operate on one-year financial cycles that don't encourage long-term thinking or computing. I make the accusation here that I have made elsewhere that the government in Victoria balances its budget on the backs of the mentally ill. And it does that by making almost no effort to find those who really need help, and it is aided by the mentally ill themselves who avoid exposing themselves by seeking treatment. The NDP government appointed a mental health advocate in the person of Nancy Hall, but she made the mistake of doing her job too well—she actually identified areas where help was required—and the government of Gordon Campbell did not renew her contract. Instead, the new government created a new position, the Minister of State for Mental Health, and though the person appointed was well-meaning enough, the whole thing was a sham that did little but raise false expectations. It is scarcely in the interests of a new junior minister to go to the finance minister and say, "Guess what? I've found another half billion in health care costs for you to fund!" But what about organizations such as the BC Branch of the CMHA, great people with whom I work regularly? Unfortunately, the CMHA and other organizations who are trying to help must rely upon funding from the government, and criticizing that government for its lack of help is a lousy way to get their financial help. And so they work in silence.

There are four things that desperately need doing to help the mentally ill. First, there must be a new mental health advocate appointed who, like the ombudsman and the auditor general, will be appointed by and answerable to the legislature, not a ministry. The principal term of reference for this individual would be to seek out and guide the mentally ill and to evaluate the private organizations active in the field. Second, the Medical Services Plan must be amended so that physicians are properly rewarded for dealing with the mentally ill. It takes a lot of time to evaluate mental illness, and doctors ought not to be discouraged from the field because they cannot afford to give that time. I know a wonderful physician who took such great interest in mental illness that her practice became almost confined to it. But in order to live she had to give up her practice and go to work for a pharmaceutical company. This shouldn't happen. Third, the College of Physicians and Surgeons must require, as a condition of practice, that physicians take and pass a course on the recognition and treatment of mental illness—especially depression, which is so widespread. Fourth, the British Columbia Medical Association must compile a list of family doctors who will take depression patients so that those of us who do depression screening can not only offer hope but help.

I might add a fifth: that mental health be put back into the health ministry where it belongs and thus put an end to the hiving off of the mentally ill as if they were some sort of strange aberration that must be quarantined. Anyone who is sick wants to be well. Those who have a physical illness demand and get treatment, all that medicine can provide, at public expense, while those who are depressed or suffer other forms of mental illness are generally treated as if they have committed some crime. If those with physical ailments were treated by the system as are those with mental problems, huge and very angry crowds would be storming the legislature with blood in their eyes.

It was our annual depression screening day that eventually led me to consider a further question: if untreated depression was such a terrible affliction, how was it affecting the workplace? How did it manifest itself there? People who suffer physical disease don't, for the most part, feel ashamed. There is no social barrier to admitting their problem and seeking appropriate help. Depression is the very opposite. Not only does the sufferer not wish to admit the problem to others—especially to an employer—he doesn't want to admit it to himself. Though the cost to society in general of untreated mental illness is incalculable, many businesses and unions are now trying to determine some numbers. What does it cost a business, for example, to train promising employees only to have them unable to perform properly? To have them become constantly tardy? Unable to concentrate? Unable to deal with co-workers? How much injury and death at the job site is caused by mental illness, not just of the variety we saw in early 2002 when a senior office worker in Kamloops killed two of his colleagues, but the day-to-day tragedies that we put down to inattention or faulty equipment or improper procedures? What is the cost to the families of these workers? What is the cost to the government and to society at large? And the key question now being asked—thank God—more and more often by employers, union leaders and, finally, the medical profession: how much alcohol abuse is the result of self-medication by depressed people?

My father died at 59 of cirrhosis of the liver caused, without question, by abuse of alcohol. But he wasn't your classic alcoholic. Looking back at the father I loved from the perspective of a depression patient in chronic care, I know that my dad drank because it was the only way he could cope. I have no doubt that, had today's medicine been available, his doctor would have determined that his serotonin levels were at the root of a severe depression, and he would have been successfully treated.

As I was exploring this whole area of how mental health issues affect the workplace, I had a conversation with Bev Gutray, the executive director of the BC Branch of the CMHA, in which I suggested that she should bring together management, labour and the professionals to discuss the problem. As a result, in the spring of 2002 her BC Branch organized a seminar on depression in the workplace. It was a huge success in spite of some childish behaviour by the president of the BC Federation of Labour, who boycotted the event because Premier Gordon Campbell was speaking at the opening luncheon. And I am very proud to note that the luncheon was billed as the first annual Rafe Mair Luncheon. The second seminar and annual Rafe Mair Luncheon was held on October 3, 2003, and saw the full and most critically necessary support of Jim Sinclair, president of the BC Federation of Labour, and the union movement. This was a good start. We still may not have all the stakeholders (it's a horrid term but it seems to be the only one available) onside but we're getting there. And very much part of "getting there," I say with confidence, is the understanding that much of the alcohol and other drug problems we see in the workplace will only be properly dealt with when we accept that they are the symptoms of depressed people self-medicating because they fear being stigmatized as "mentally ill." For the average sufferer, admitting alcoholism, however society may condemn it, is much safer socially and economically in the short term than admitting to mental health problems.

I have received awards in radio but none so important to me as those awarded me by people and organizations in this field: the Canadian Mental Health Association (I shared their national award with Pamela Wallin a few years back) from the psychiatrists and the nurses. And I would be very remiss if I didn't acknowledge the full and important support of radio station CKNW for my efforts to bring attention to mental health problems over the years.

# II

## Life at CKNW

I HAVE ALWAYS HAD MY DIFFICULTIES with the brass at CKNW, but then they would complain that they always had problems with me. And I think we're both right. From the start of our relationship it was a company that held the contract with them, not me as an individual. This company (now resting comfortably as we have new companies to do our business) had been incorporated when I was out of work and was starting a consulting practice. Now it is a fact that if you are truly an independent contractor you must have an arm's-length relationship with the other side of the contract. This is important for tax purposes if you have incorporated in order to do business. In the first place, you can't incorporate just to avoid taxes, that is to say, you can't if you want all the advantages of being independent. The taxman doesn't care how your relationship is stated in your contract or what name you give yourself, but you must in fact be independent.

Of course, I didn't need to act independently of CKNW in order to make a point. That came naturally to me, and we had some humdingers of tussles as I consistently declared and acted out my independence. I should also say that I always considered CKNW to be a big part of our community and thus as eligible as any other public person or organization for criticism.

The station and I had "got sideways" over the issue of my replacing Barrie Clark back in 1984. Another spat began developing in

1988, this time more openly, over Gary Bannerman, who had been their morning talk host for 15 years or more. He is a very bright guy and had led CKNW to some very good ratings over the years, but by that time he had some problems, occasionally on air, with John Barleycorn, and as his ratings were showing it, the station let him go. It had always been understood that, if Gary left, I would take his position. Notwithstanding this, the station brought the by then retired Jack Webster in for two months as they pondered their position. This time they did me the courtesy of just leaving me alone. For my part, I wanted to do the morning show but it wasn't all that big of a deal. I had settled into the afternoon program well and knew that there wouldn't be any more money in it for me until my contract came due again in 1992. Then in early July just as I was embarking on my vacation, Ron Bremner, CKNW's general manager, and Doug Rutherford, the program director, asked me to come down to the BC Place studio. Why I had to drive all the way from North Vancouver to spend five minutes hearing myself asked to take over the morning show and saying, "Yes," I'll never know. At all events, I went and learned I was to take over the morning show at the beginning of September.

Time went by and early the following year Doug asked Patti, Shirley Stocker (who was the senior producer looking after all the talk shows) and me to a meeting where he wanted a consensus on a decision management had already made. This was typical of 'NW and probably of many other organizations: management makes a decision then consults. At any rate, it was explained that Ron Vandenberg, at one time the general manager of CJOR, and some partners were buying out CFUN to make it into a talk station. One of the partners, we were told, was Gary Bannerman. CKNW's management, having decided that Bannerman would pose a threat to our ratings, planned to hire him back to spell off my show whenever I was away, thus taking him out of the picture. Doug was sure we'd all agree and that the decision he'd already made was part of a consensus. I was much opposed to the idea. I can't honestly say whether this was due to some fear that Gary would challenge me for his old job back. Perhaps I was taking Jack Webster's advice to me too seriously. He told me once, "Never worry about the guy above you on the ladder but stomp like hell on the fingers of the guy behind you for he wants your job." My stated concern was that I didn't want Gary's style of broadcasting to replace mine when I was away. In any event, Doug announced to us all that he had achieved the consensus he wanted so he was going ahead.

That night I was watching BCTV news and this story was an item. So much for reaching a consensus before a deal was made! I heard Rutherford tell Tony Parsons that hiring Gary had nothing whatsoever to do with the proposed takeover of CFUN with Gary as lead broadcaster there, but was only because Gary was such a fine broadcaster that CKNW just had to have him back. This was a very large fib.

The next morning, as I was waiting to go on the show, I thought about what I would say when a caller asked about it because I knew that was bound to happen. Just before air time I came to a decision: I would make a peremptory strike. I came on air, referred to the BCTV newscast, then told everyone that the CFUN takeover was the real reason for rehiring Bannerman and that Rutherford was spouting a load of crap. I'm not sure now, looking back, that I should have done so. It resulted in some heavy words between the manager and me, punctuated by the manager saying, "Mair, you are responsible for 42 weeks of the year. You do as you wish with them. The other 10 are ours and we'll do what we wish with them." In a way, this was a good thing to have out in the open because it came to me that I could always use that firm statement of company policy if my independence was ever threatened (which, until my last year there, it never was). Gary did return to the station as back-up host and did a good job. He had licked his personal problems and I was glad because they had become serious medical ones by that time. I always liked and respected Gary, and it was good to see that he could take charge of himself and get his life back in order. I scarcely covered myself with any glory and was, in fact, wrong, but it all came out okay in the end.

In the early nineties I came off air one day to have Shirley Stocker tell me that the company was moving the two CKNW studios—the one in New Westminster and that at the old Expo site where our talk shows still originated—to the TD tower in downtown Vancouver. I had heard rumours of this but couldn't believe my ears. Not for the first nor last time, I minded someone else's business and called Doug Holtby, the big push at the WIC Corporation, which owned CKNW.

"Mr. Holtby," I said, "my name is Rafe Mair and I do a talk show…"

"Yes, yes, I know who you are. What do you want?"

"Well, Mr. Holtby, I have just heard that CKNW is moving its entire operation to the Toronto Dominion Building, and if that's true, I think you've taken leave of your senses. I know it's none of my business but that's what I think for what it's worth."

"But Rod Gunn [CKNW's general manager at that time] told me he had consulted with everyone, including you, and you had all approved of the idea."

"That's bullshit, Mr. Holtby," said I, ending the conversation.

Five minutes later I got a call from Rod Gunn asking if I could make a meeting at the Expo site, where I was anyway, at two that afternoon. I agreed. At the appointed hour I went into the boardroom on the walls of which were several blueprints. Everyone except Bill Good, who was on air, was there. Rod opened by saying that this meeting had been called at the special request of Rafe Mair, then pointed to the wall and said, "Rafe, that's where your new studio will be."

"Rod," I asked, "is this a done deal?"

"Yes," was the reply.

"Then what the fuck am I doing here? This is a waste of my time. You've all taken leave of your senses and I'm out of here."

"But, Rafe, we called this meeting for you!" said Rod.

"I don't give a good goddam where my studio is. This idea is the height of stupidity! Not only is it fiscally dumb, the station will never be the same again. . . and I'm outta here!" Which I was.

That move did turn out to be the height of stupidity. The rent for the new premises is a cool million a year, due to rise when the deal ends. Here is all that hugely expensive floor space being used to store the immense equipment it takes to run four radio stations. But the problem is more than that. The station was not the same again. The "down-home" feeling was gone, shattered by the huge executive offices in the four corners of the twentieth floor, each complete with an expensive telescope for the big guns to scan the unbelievable view. When Corus took over and started wholesale firings, the "family feeling" was already dead and gone despite all the slogans the new owners plastered the place with. With the move downtown, CKNW had abandoned its roots and had started the slippery slope toward being just another radio station.

Listeners often think there must be lots of communication between on-air talent, but in truth there is almost none. The "stars" of talk radio who were there when I arrived were Gary Bannerman and Barrie Clark who loathed one another. I had known Barrie from my political days when he had been the province's "rentalsman," a job that came under my ministry. I had always liked him, and when I started at CJOR, he and his wife Ingrid went out of their way to welcome Patti and me to the business. I thought his shows were deadly dull, though. I remember his annual programs on tinnitus—the ringing in the ears many suffer from. Deadly dull. If you didn't have tinnitus before the show you sure as hell did afterwards!

I only knew Gary Bannerman from the times I had been on his show when I was in politics. I didn't know him socially. I also thought Gary was dull as hell, but there was no denying his massive intelligence. Booze was his problem, as it is with so many in show biz and it kept him from being an even bigger force than he was. The promise he had shown in the seventies when he settled prison riots and reported from the Yom Kippur War was not fulfilled in the eighties.

When I took over the morning show in September 1988, Bill Good came from CBC to take my place on the then "Afternoon Show." I had appeared on his CBC show occasionally and knew he was a very decent man, but he lobs the kind of slow-pitches that Larry King does, asking all the right questions but never applying pressure with pointed follow-ups. But different strokes…However, I was frequently unkind to Bill, and those occasions seemed to be the only times he got energized. It so happened that it was my job at the end of my show to "promo" Bill's show. One day Paul Martin was to appear, and as I signed off I said, "Coming up on the Bill Good Show is Finance Minister Paul Martin who hasn't the guts to come on this show but prefers nice easy questions."

Well, it turns out that Martin was in the men's room at the time and heard this on the monitor. He came flying out, adjusting his clothes as he went, to stoutly deny what I had said. Unfortunately for Mr. Martin, my producer, Shiral Tobin, was right there with her appointment book and gave him chapter and verse on all the occasions his underlings had refused our invitation. Martin was clearly rattled, and he promised to come on my show the next time he was in town—

which he did—though never again! Appearing on the Rafe Mair show was guaranteed to send a bad sound bite or two rocketing across the country, and for Mr. Martin it was easier to handle the gibes of cowardice from me than hear his own voice answering tough and pointed questions. (It was interesting to note that, when Bill co-hosted the Jack Webster Awards on October 23, 2003, and I got a standing ovation from the 1,000 people present as I rose to accept the Bruce Hutchison Award for Lifetime Achievement, Bill remained seated. When asked later by a listener why, Bill replied that he had worked next to me for 15 years and didn't like me. Not too classy.)

Philip Till is a world-class broadcaster. He had been with NBC worldwide and in all the hot spots of the globe. I was one of the 'NW types assigned to approach Phil about moving to Vancouver, so while in London in 1987 Patti and I invited him and Fred Kennedy, his NBC sidekick, to lunch at the very posh and very Tory Carleton Club, to which I had admission through my membership in the Vancouver Club. They arrived without ties or jackets. Phil was in a pair of corduroys that looked as if they had been with him when he witnessed the bombing of Tripoli by Reagan's forces years earlier and a flak jacket that simply would not do. The hall porter rustled up old jackets and soup-stained ties so we could all repair to the dining room, whereupon Phil and Fred proceeded to work over the club's supply of hard drink. After lunch we adjourned to the lounge where the uneven battle with John Barleycorn continued, and I began wondering whether an offence committed against the Carleton Club's rules could be used against me at the Vancouver Club. But nothing bad happened. We just worried a lot as the waiters (as happens so frequently with English waiters) looked down their long noses, unable to comprehend how the two with the North American accents seemed to be behaving themselves better than these somewhat noisy chaps with the English accents! When Phil came to Vancouver for more serious negotiations, the 'NW brass wanted to hear him on air. Imagine the cheek of wanting an audition from someone who had been broadcasting to a billion people every night!

Phil came on my show for his "audition" at 10:00 a.m. In those days it was critical that I break with the network at 10:30 precisely for local news, but at 10:20 Phil launched into a story of being in a garret in Lebanon interviewing a sniper who was blowing the brains out of people he didn't like in the town square below. Suddenly a grenade flew through the window and became imbedded in the wall behind Phil and the sniper. . .and began hissing away. I was so absorbed in this tale that when I looked at the clock, it was already 10:35! I had missed the break! But so enthralled had the operators of the network stations been that they hadn't cut Phil off but let him ramble right through their news time. This man was clearly a world-class broadcaster. And he proved once more that radio is theatre of the mind. Before Phil left NBC I interviewed him as he was exploring Loch Ness (from a nearby pub, I suspect) for the monster. It was a hilarious interview and showed me that, while he was the kind of journalist who could win the Peabody Award (which he has), he could also be damned funny.

Phil always maintained that he didn't know anything about BC politics. Maybe not, but try that one on Gordon Wilson who in the spring of 1993 was alleged to be in a more than usually friendly relationship with his drop-dead beautiful House leader, Judi Tyabji. But even after the story came out in full, Mr. Wilson stoutly denied any impropriety. Because the story broke in the late afternoon, Phil got the first crack at it, and he asked Mr. Wilson whether he was having an affair with Ms. Tyabji, to which the answer was a firm "NO!" Then Phil asked if Mr. Wilson had ever had an affair with the lady and the answer was "No," again.

Then Phil asked, "Do you plan to have any personal involvement with Ms Tyabji?" Listening , I muttered to myself, "That's a stupid question, Phil. Of course he'll deny it."

But to my surprise—and I'm sure to Phil's and the audience's too—Mr. Wilson began to babble. "Well. . .of course. . .who knows what the future holds?" he said. "I'm not a clairvoyant." And so on. Gordon Wilson's goose was well and truly goosed by a broadcaster who knew that apparently stupid questions often bring very interesting answers.

On 9/11 the bombings occurred just before my show was due to go on air, and Ian Koenigsfest, the Number Two program man, came to ask me if I would use Philip. I immediately said, "Hell, he should take over my show, and I'll just hang around and comment when he thinks it's appropriate." And that's what we did. Phil, in the host's chair, ran my program and did it brilliantly, but pro that he was, he constantly reminded listeners that they were listening to the Rafe Mair Show. That show was good enough to bring huge accolades.

When the US bombed Baghdad with that immense crash in 2003, it happened in the middle of my show, and I immediately called Phil in to take my seat. Just in case you don't appreciate the size of this gesture, letting someone take over your show does not come easily to any broadcaster, let alone one like me. But so vast was Phil's knowledge and ability to handle what he knew so well that I gave him my microphone without the slightest hesitation.

When I was fired by CKNW, Phil, as one might expect, came directly and strongly to my defence, defying the station management who certainly didn't want the matter dealt with on air. When Phil demanded to put me on his show to give my side of it and the station turned him down, he told his audience the station had refused this bit of fair play. After intoning that this was a very sad day for CKNW, he proceeded to dedicate his program to open line on the subject, and it was not a pretty thing for the station to hear. Phil and I were never personal off-air friends but we admired each other enormously, so what he did that day didn't really surprise me. He is world-class in his profession and is a first-class fellow to boot.

Jon McComb, who is a very underrated broadcaster, also took on management with vigour after my firing, and for him it was pretty difficult since he isn't operating under even a short-term contract. But Jon also has guts aplenty. An example was the day in July 2002 when I was in a very public dust-up with Pacific Press, owned by the Asper family through CanWest. The triggering mechanism was the firing of Gordon Gibson by the *National Post*, an Asper paper, for daring to criticize the Chrétien government. This had come hot on the heels of CanWest firing Russell Mills, long-time publisher of the *Ottawa Citizen*, for a similar offence. I publicly resigned my column with the *Province*, which is part of CanWest's Pacific Press, and called upon people to cancel their subscriptions. This brought strong and ill-advised retaliation against CKNW by Pacific Press who publicly withdrew advertising from the station and ended their charitable joint ventures. After I broadsided Pacific Press for this nonsense, they demanded air time for their flack, Don McLachlan, but he refused my offer of air time. Then, since Bill Good wasn't interested in getting involved (too many friends in the CanWest Empire was the official wimp-out), McLachlan was offered to Jon McComb. Jon, in a classic interview, helped McLachlan cut himself to pieces. (Good journalism is exposing the truth. Brilliant journalism is getting the subject to do it for you. Jon's interview was brilliant.) The next day I opined at editorial time that Jon's interview should be played to all students of journalism as an example of how things should be done. The next day Mr. McLachlan wanted another chance on air but, when offered Jon McComb, somehow found that there was a scheduling conflict!

Jon has been at CKNW many years but, for reasons I can't fathom, has never been given a proper chance. Over and over I told CKNW management that he should be groomed to take over my spot, but as I went into my new job as host at 600AM in 2003, I thanked my lucky stars that it was Bill Good, not Jon McComb, who was my opposite number at 'NW.

I had an iffy relationship at best with the newsroom after Warren Barker left CKNW. I very much like Gord Macdonald, the news director who followed him, but felt that standards slipped a great deal. I was not above complaining on air at the newsroom's shortcomings, such as when a story happened on my show and wasn't picked up by the newsroom. But I was on excellent terms with a number of the news people and very much enjoyed working with Yvonne Eamor, Stephen Quinn, Mike Clark and others. The difficulty was that Gord didn't like his people editorializing, and I felt that while that was the proper approach for newscasts, it was different on an editorialist's show. One person, however, who had no qualms about giving an opinion was George Garrett who, during my stay on the "Afternoon Show," had been almost a daily visitor with his reports on the Vander Zalm government. George also did "The Year in Review" on New Year's Eve with me—a lot of hard work that was much appreciated by the audience as it was fleshed out by personal opinions from George and me. I well remember one year when the scripts, being finalized as we went along, were so screwed up that I was getting different copy than George was. It made for very interesting radio as I tried to move from George's last answer to the next item on my list, which wasn't on his at all! It's moments like that you remember why you're paid the big bucks! George's reporting was the stuff legends are made of, and he did it all with untouchable integrity.

I became a reporter myself for a brief time in 1989. Patti and I were in London that fall when there was a terrible fire in the King's Cross tube station. I happened to be sitting in our rented flat in Pimlico, miles from the action, waiting for the 6:00 p.m. news when the story broke at about 10 minutes before the hour. I immediately phoned my show (where it was 10 to 10 in the morning) and told the operator I wanted to go on my show, being hosted by Terry Moore, right that minute. Terry, likely misunderstanding what it was all about, demurred, so I was put through to John McKitrick, a superb newsman, who put me on his 10 o'clock newscast live, and we scooped North America on the story. The following day Patti and I had tickets to attend the House of Commons for question period, and we watched and listened as the entire tragedy was hashed out. After it was over, I went back to the flat and phoned John again and gave his audience an up-to-the-minute report on what Parliament was doing about the tragedy. This dreadful event had an amusing sidelight. For months afterwards, people would write me or stop me on the street to congratulate me on my bravery in covering the story, not realizing that the closest I got to King's Cross was my flat in Pimlico with the "Beeb" on the telly and a beer in my hand.

I also had another scoop for North America. I was in a bed-and-breakfast near Leicester in central England in 1990 when the story broke, again around the six o'clock BBC news, that Margaret Thatcher had not secured a clear first-ballot victory in the Tory leadership challenge, and when the camera panned on Mrs. Thatcher, who was in Paris, I placed the telephone next to the TV audio and played her speech to CKNW's audience. I was able to repeat this performance a couple of weeks later when John Major was selected. It was kind of neat to scoop North America three times while a mere talk-show host on vacation and nowhere near the action.

I've made some enemies along the way in my broadcasting career, of course, probably a hell of a lot more than I know about! One of them was Bill Vander Zalm, but of such stuff is he made that we became quite cordial again once he was out of politics. Bill is a super guy with a lovely wife and family and a heart of gold. I just thought he was a lousy premier and said so. But at my roast in April 2000, Bill attended and by his remarks and the song he led the audience in—a special version of "On Top of Old Smoky"—he proved just what a class act he is.

I certainly have an enemy in federal minister David Anderson. He likes to say that this is because I called his colleague, Hedy Fry, a political whore. In the 1993 federal election campaign Dr. Fry, who had forged applications for Pharmacare for patients and got away with it, gave a stirring speech on my show on how she would always put her constituency and province before political matters and would never allow Liberal party discipline to interfere with her duty as she saw it. Within days of being elected, she was so obviously kissing Chrétien's ass for a cabinet post, which she got, that I called her a political whore, a term used non-sexually to describe politicians who put themselves above their duty to the voters. (Although I meant nothing sexual about the remark, one of her former colleagues from her active period in the British Columbia Medical Association did fax me to ask why I had bothered with the adjective!) So while Anderson may have been miffed at me because of what I called her, his real problem is that he is mighty thin-skinned for a politician. He didn't like it when I commented on him putting his kids at the head of the line to see the Queen at the airport when she was deplaning; when I pointed out that he had absented himself from the Prince Rupert fishermen's blockade of the Alaska Ferry; and when I told my audience that he had failed in his job as environment minister when he didn't take on his colleague Herb Dhaliwal over the fish farm issue. He knows the problems with farming Atlantic salmon on our coast but doesn't have the stomach for a fight anymore. When that happens, it's time to retire.

There were and are, however, people in public life to whom I have given a hard time who have always understood the name of the game. Grace McCarthy is an example. We have always remained good friends no matter what issues we may disagree on. Most notorious, I suppose, is Ken Georgetti, one-time president of the BC Federation of Labour and now president of the Canadian Labour Congress, with whom regular bloodbaths have occurred and who always comes back for more, but has been a friend when I needed one. Kim Campbell and I also had slugfests. She not only gave as good and often better than she got, she never ever turned down an offer to be my guest. Mike Harcourt was always willing to step into the studio. This is also true of Premier Campbell, although after his drunk-driving incident he seemed to be a bit mike-shy for a while, which one can understand. Moe Sihota was always a good interview and was always armed with facts—or at least things he passed off as facts. During the Charlottetown referendum he was the only politician, save Gordon Wilson, who knew his brief. Joy MacPhail, both as a cabinet minister with tough portfolios and later as NDP leader, has never turned down an invitation to appear on my show. Neither did Ujjal Dosanjh. And there are others: Attorney General Geoff Plant, Christy Clark and Gary Collins come to mind.

But interviewing politicians is difficult work. Many come well briefed not necessarily to answer your questions but to run out the clock without any bad sound bites emerging. Answers that quickly divert attention onto more comfortable ground are features of "hip" politicians. By far the best at this was Mike Harcourt. In fact, during the Charlottetown debate I asked my producers to put him on for two hours. I figured he would tap dance for an hour, but my audience's questions would get to him in the second hour. And so it proved. In the second half they hit him with everything but the ring post.

And that leads me to the subject of callers. When I came into the business, the main litmus test of a successful show was whether it in-spired plenty of calls. I was never too happy with that because in my early days on CJOR I could count on callers whenever my guests were psychics or numerologists, and I couldn't tell whether the people who were not calling found the show interesting. But as my show matured and I dispensed with this sort of guest, the callers also became a more mature crowd.

Regular callers sometimes pose a problem. Over the years some have been very good and have sparked good debate. The problem was that many of them decided that they were actually part of the show and that it couldn't survive without them. In some cases, they did provide a decided yang for my yin, and I would be happy when they called. Mostly, if my mail was any indication, they irritated the other listeners. They all had their moments: Alex, the Scot (not heard in recent years); Hanoi Hanna; the man with the speech impediment; the two Garys—one fighting for better recognition for servicemen, the other always tooting the horn for the Palestinians; Dave, the right winger from the East Side forever battling injustices to his community from the West Side-dominated city council; Ken, the republican; and Ken, the amusing Englishman who would be even funnier if he could hide his dislike of non-White people. The list goes on. For many years I didn't screen calls, but I finally concluded that regular callers were a very minor help to the program and could become a hindrance, and we began screening out those who tended to dominate.

I am often asked about memorable shows. The trouble is my mind seems to erase shows right after they're done, much as one's mind erases the dream one is trying to remember. I must say I recall with pleasure interviewing J.K. Rowling just as her Harry Potter was setting all the records. It had to be conducted seriously so we set up a studio in the Waterfront Hotel. But she is a lovely and extremely interesting interview. As is the wonderful Dame Vera Lynn who was, during World War II, "the sweetheart of the armed forces." When I played her signature song, "We'll Meet Again," she and I sang along in studio. It was a great moment.

But I do recall two gems of radio magic. Back in the months leading up to Vancouver's 1986 centennial, when I was on the midnight to 2:00 a.m. show, lights were being installed on Lions Gate Bridge, thanks to the efforts of Grace McCarthy, and we knew they would be well within our vision from our studios on the top floor of the of Holiday Inn Harbourside. To help me record this thrilling event was Shirley Stocker. Our lines went something like this:

"By George, Shirley, I think I see some lights coming on!"

"Golly, Rafe, it certainly looks like lights to me."

"Yes, Shirley, I think we can officially report, right here on CKNW, that the lights indeed have gone up on Lions Gate Bridge, and what a credit it is to Grace McCarthy for this historic moment."

"And, Rafe, don't forget the Guinness people who with their kind donation made this wonderful, magic moment possible!"

Gripping stuff!

The other thrilling moment also involved Shirley. It was a couple of years later and we were reporting the tsunami that never happened. All the indications were that a huge tidal wave was going to hit the West Coast, and everyone went into preparation mode. The station engineers had connected us up to several key points on the coast and we were keeping in constant contact with the government officials who happened to be high and dry in Kamloops. We went into count-down mode, skipping around to our many reporting posts. Zero hour! And nothing happened. Not a damn thing. Not even a ripple. The only excitement was that the good burghers of Port Alberni, which would have been wiped out, all lined the Alberni Canal to watch! The whole thing reminded me of when I was environment minister and the Soviet space lab was going to hit the earth. Vancouver was smack dab in the line of fire and would suffer enormous damage if hit. I had pow-er to order the evacuation of the city, but what do you do when you realize that the orbit is about 25,000 miles long and the target area in Vancouver just a tiny fraction of that? I decided not to panic the Lower Mainland with an evacuation order because it really was a question of evacuate—where? And all was well because the space lab duly hit the ground in the massive and unpopulated desert of Australia.

There was one bit of truly exciting radio I'll not forget. In February 1990, Shirley Stocker and I went to Moscow to do three shows for back home. (This was the trip I circumnavigated the globe, fly-ing Vancouver, London, Moscow, London, Abu Dhabi, Singapore, Sydney, Brisbane, Auckland, Vancouver.) Our trip happened to coin-cide with McDonald's opening their first Moscow restaurant. It was a great year to be there—or so we thought. In fact, while we were there I received a call from Philip Till asking me to trace down a rumour of a coup in the Kremlin.

"Phil," I asked, "just how do you suggest I find out? Go to the pay phone in the lobby, deposit three kopeks, and ask for Mr. Gorbachev? All I can tell you is that I am looking right across Red Square at the Kremlin as we speak, and I see nothing out of the ordinary."

To do these three shows we paid a Russian PR company to line up our guests and ensure that they all spoke English. We arrived on Sunday night, and the next day Shirley discovered to her horror that not one of the guests who had been lined up could speak a word of English! Thanks to her calmness under fire, contacts at the Canadian Embassy and at British Airways, and the fact that McDonald's made the Canadian Brass available to us (they introduced each show with both national anthems), we wound up with three great shows. Our guests included the deputy mayor of Moscow, Joe Adamov; a veteran newsman from Gestelradio, the state radio system; several Russian academics; and, of course, the man from McDonald's. It was great fun. We were accompanied by a young man named Viktor and a young lady whose name now escapes me. Viktor, a Jew, was looking forward to the immense changes about to take place but was very worried about anti-Semitism and the return of pogroms if there was a breakdown in the social order. The young lady was not so sure things were going to get better and clearly had been brainwashed by the old regime. But the fun part was young people coming up to us on the street to practise their new-found freedom of speech by saying, "Down with Brezhnev!"—though their bravery hadn't got to the point where they were criticizing Gorbachev! Older people weren't so brave; they had seen too much in their years under communism.

We took the Metro, Kruschev's great accomplishment when he was mayor of Moscow, and what an elaborate work of art it is! And thanks to McDonald's, we were taken to an evening at the Bolshoi, which, I think, was to make up for the fact that they had taken us to a meat factory earlier in the day—a real thrill I can tell you!

The Russian system for doing business was interesting. At the National Hotel, right across Red Square from the Kremlin, there were a dozen or more clerks behind the check-in counter, whereas two or three at most would be behind a North American hotel's front desk. And they not only used a manual system for recording data, they did their arithmetic on an abacus! There were two women behind the concierge desk on every floor, one to hand you your key if your room was to the left, the other to give it to you if your room was to the right, all part of the Soviet make-work system. These women were also the gateway to the black market and could get you anything you wanted.

The huge GUM department store clerks also used the abacus. I went in to get one of those Russian genuine imitation fur hats and, after lining up, picked one out. "I'll take it," I said. Instead of being handed the hat, I was given a piece of paper and sent to another lineup where eventually I paid and was given another slip of paper. I took this slip to another lineup and was at last given my hat!

At that time the official exchange rate was one ruble to one American dollar. The "unofficial" rate at our hotel was 17 rubles to the dollar. In the subway in front of the National Hotel, we got 34 rubles for the dollar and, if we bargained, we could do even better. But the real exchange tool was a packet of Marlboro cigarettes and we used this as our medium of exchange at the taxi rank outside our hotel. When we first approached a driver, he would look up just long enough to say, "Nyet." He was too busy. Since he was being paid by the State whether he worked or not, why work? Ah, but produce a package of Marlboros? "Right away, sir, and where can I take you?"

But for all its strangeness I loved Moscow. St. Basil's in Red Square at night with the Kremlin in the background is magic. And the people, especially the young ones, were great fun to talk to. It's a place I would really like to revisit.

We were not permitted to take rubles into or out of the country. This meant that coming in, we had no rubles to get a cart for our baggage. No matter. Though the stated price was five rubles, we discovered that an American dollar or a British pound would do nicely. But on the way out, having a few rubles still in my pocket, I went into the duty-free where I saw a camera for 300 rubles—about 10 dollars. "Great!" I said. "I'll take it," and handed over my 300 rubles. "Oh no, sir," said the young lady. "You must pay in American dollars." At par, of course. I left the camera and illegally left the country with 300 rubles in my pocket. But it was a great adventure even seeing for so short a time the capital of communism just as the wheels were coming off.

# 12

## The New Socialism

C AN IT BE THAT THIS OLD SOCRED minister, this lifelong free en-
terpriser is a (are you ready for this?) socialist? I'm beginning to
think I may be. A socialist of the 21st century. The trouble is, no one
else has declared themselves to be one and I never was an "old socialist" and never could be. Of course, I was occasionally thought of as an
old socialist by members of the Social Credit Party who saw me as far
too concerned with social issues such as consumerism and the environment. I was often called "Red Rafe" in those days.

In government the old socialists were, if nothing else, impractical
to the point of political suicide. Teachers, carpenters and bus conduc-
tors, all nice intelligent people, assumed that becoming left-wing
cabinet ministers conferred instant experience. Suddenly, a cabinet
minister whose only understanding of electricity was flipping a light
switch became minister responsible for Hydro and immediately spoke
to all who would listen, including the media, as if he knew what he was
talking about.

The old socialist had dogma that was tighter than that of a clois-
tered monastery. The capitalist was always to be sneered at as termi-
nally bad. Making a profit was a sign that someone was stealing. Any
business that was big and profitable could be run better by a carpenter
and a lefty bureaucrat, usually seconded from some university's ivory
tower. Marketplaces weren't just to be policed so as to ensure fair play,

they were to be entered into by government with great gusto with any resultant and hurtful distortions explained away as machinations of destructive capitalists who won't play along. (Wage, price and rent controls are good examples of what I mean.) Public money was to be squeezed from business and the rich, if possible, without any regard for common sense and spent like drunken sailors on anything that looked like the right thing to do. The basement of the legislative buildings in Victoria, for example, is loaded with the art purchased by the Barrett NDP in the 1970s in their effort to support the arts, forgetting there must be some sort of quality involved if it's public money being spent. They also forgot that old communist Pablo Picasso's definition of art as "that which sells." Most of all, the old socialist never tired of a fight even though it had been settled long ago or was utterly impractical. When I was in government, the NDP tried for years to save an old mine that had been closed down (are you ready for this?) because there was no ore left! No matter. Jobs had been lost! The mine must be reopened! Peace for the old socialist was something you obtained by slogans, songs, banners and marches.

So what is this "new socialism" of which I am so far the only known member? The new socialist does not believe in lots of regulations and the nanny state. He does not believe that the government knows how to run anything very well, but that government is a necessary curiosity arising out of the democratic principle that the people have the inherent right to screw up and to pick the people to do it for them. He does not fight free trade or international trade organizations but demands that citizens have the full right to participate in decision-making and that fair and prompt decision-making tools are put in place. Moreover, the State has not only the right but the obligation to assist those who are side-swiped by the new world economy. He doesn't believe that either the corporate or union boardroom is likely to provide the fount of any, let alone all, wisdom.

The new socialist doesn't believe that any health care system can survive on its own amid the daily advances of science but does hold strongly to the view that no one should be denied reasonable health care by reason of impecuniosity. (Unreasonable might be paying for a new heart for a 70-year-old smoker who won't quit.) While he hates the very idea, his belief is that the health care system must make its deal with private capital now on our terms or make it later on theirs. He believes that we are our brothers' keepers and that those who can't help themselves—and even those who won't—must be fed and sheltered and, more than anything else, their kids must be cared for.

He believes (and this is really where the socialism comes in) that all natural resources belong to the people and their exploitation is a matter for the people to control. It follows that the new socialist believes that the public should be always consulted as to what they want done with their resources and that public guidelines ought to be sought and enforced as well as changed as times and opinions change. For example, how big do we want to be? How much of our natural possessions do we wish to see exploited and upon what terms? If, as is usually the case, environmental damage is to occur, will we accept that as a trade-off for short-term jobs and profits? The new socialist does not believe in the leave-it-in-the-ground policy propounded by the old socialist, but rather in a consultation process through which the people declare if they want the money or the trees, ore, or fish, as the case may be.

The new socialist does not believe that growth forever is inevitable but instead that, with suitable financial sacrifices by society as a whole, we can have limits accompanied by reasonable prosperity, leaving us with both an environment and jobs. The new socialist believes that the living environment was given to us by the Creator to sustain and pass on to our children; that a man-made lake full of Jet Skis and summer homes is not equivalent to a river full of salmon in a valley full of God's creatures; or that a dam creating electricity for cheap power at home and bundles of it for profitable export takes the place of the environmental values it destroys; that natural resources like fish and wildlife cannot and should not be measured in terms of the money that can be raised by exploiting them, but instead that they are priceless resources that must be protected and nourished for those to whom they really belong: future generations.

The new socialist loves money and the things it can buy but stops short of earning it in ways that trade short-term gain for long-term destruction. The old socialist, often because of the times, saw jobs now as the goal and collaborated in a devil's bargain with capitalists who saw profits now. The new socialist sees sustainability—not the phony sort that has become sloganized by the old left, but real sustainability where a tree grows for a tree taken and a fish is born for a fish killed—as the guide to all current activity. Above all, while deploring a government that runs business, he is equally alarmed at the job of government being taken over by corporations that use their pools of capital to usurp nearly absolute power. The new socialist doesn't fight globalism any more than he fights the weather but instead seeks democratic—thus social—influence on the decisions of those who own the capital. Thus, while he tries to profit from it, he takes care of those who might be side-swiped by it.

But doesn't Rafe Mair, the new socialist, believe in the marketplace? Hasn't he always preached that when government tries to interfere in the marketplace, it gets badly burned pinkies? Of course, I believe in the marketplace, the *free*-market place. The law of supply and demand is the best way to determine what a thing or a service is worth. One interferes with the marketplace only with great caution. The trouble with the old left has always been that they don't respect the law of supply and demand. Left-wing governments love to play in the market by deciding what the price should be, as in rent controls, or what the cost might be, as in wage controls. And the trouble with the right is just the opposite: they believe in the market but think it should be utterly without discipline. And that is about as silly as deciding that free market forces should govern road traffic, allowing users to decide from time to time and as circumstances dictate what side of the road to drive on, what speed is safe and what to do at intersections.

Markets generally work best when the supply side and the buying side meet and make final decisions very quickly. Where markets tend to break down is when the demand is there now but can't be supplied for six months, or conversely when the supply is ready now but it won't be required for an extended period. Things like lending institutions, architects and builders tend to need arrangements to be made with certainty and right now, whereas the demand and the supply may for very practical reasons not be able to fit such a tight schedule. Another serious problem of supply and demand occurs when the goods to be supplied are perishables.

However, there are other areas where the market, acting alone, must be subject to issues of public policy. The ancient rule of caveat emptor, "Let the buyer beware," is an excellent principle but it has its drawbacks. Perhaps it worked just fine with chariots—which, one assumes, were relatively easy to inspect—but it clearly doesn't work with the more complicated things the marketplace is now full of, such as computers and the software that runs them. Certainly it was the automobile that first attracted the government policeman in a big way, although I suppose upon reflection it might have been the heavily mined field of drugs and medicines.

At any rate, governments have moved into the market not just as players in the supply/demand game (where they invariably screw up) but as passers and enforcers of laws to govern that which is unfair and which cannot be detected as such by reasonably wary participants in the market. One thing I learned after being BC's consumer minister for nearly three years is that the seller of that crummy used car you got stuck with had to buy that heap somewhere and that his inability to easily inspect it in the first place was just passed on to you at his used car lot. It is because of this that as a society we have come to accept the right, nay the obligation, of government to police the marketplace. Some people will, of course, avoid such protection. After an English town invested its entire pension plan in a Vancouver Stock Exchange-listed company that promised huge profits from a scheme in which a giant clam in a Honolulu shopping centre would produce huge pearls, I editorialized, tongue firmly in cheek, that we should repeal all consumer legislation on the grounds that, if apparently sophisticated people were prepared to do things like that, there was nothing anyone could rationally do to protect them!

One marketplace almost beyond the protection of the government acting as our policemen is the area of insider trading and corporate benefits to insiders and managers. For one thing, the notion that we should do something about insiders is preposterous. When a person becomes a director and is offered stock options as remuneration, does anyone really believe that he won't exercise and sell those options based upon insider information? Of course he will. Probably 50 percent of the fortunes supporting homes in West Vancouver's British Properties with Porsches in the garage came from insider trading. What the law really says is, don't get caught insider trading if the information you received is too good (such things as a bad quarterly report coming out tomorrow morning, which will show that the company is about to go down the tube). Anything less than that and "Anything goes until the whistle blows" should be our guide.

Of even more concern are the huge stock options, bonuses and obscene salaries paid to company directors and officers, especially CEOs. The theory is, of course, that shareholders have the ultimate control over such matters. Yeah, sure they do! Public company meetings are as controlled as a Fidel Castro election. The proxies are in the bag and the public aspect of the meeting is for show purposes only. The ordinary shareholder has about as much power over how the company is run as the ordinary buyer has intimate knowledge of the inner workings of the computer he is buying. The argument is, of course, that in order to attract the best people you must pay competitive wages. And that is true. The problem is that the competition is too often a friendly one between pals, and based more on a buddy system than real values for bucks spent. It is very hard to convince the average shareholder that the company he has invested in should be paying more than a million bucks a year to get the very best executive when the president of the United States makes less than half that. How on earth one can justify salaries of 10, 20, 50, even 100 million a year or more—all of which comes ultimately and directly out of shareholders' pockets—is beyond me. And when the influence extends past the grave—as when the retired CEO of General Electric has the use of a downtown Manhattan apartment and the corporate jet, tickets to everything that matters, and six figures a year to consult PLUS his obscene pension—the situation becomes comical. At least it would be were it not for the fact that thousands of restricted income pensioners are paying for all this out of reduced dividends in their pension plans.

The newest scam in the stock market game is the one that President George W. Bush used to make his own fortune. It's a refinement, and not a very sophisticated one at that, of the old Ponzi scheme in which you use the money coming in to pay those to whom you have made promises, always skimming for yourself. The Enron scheme is a variation of this: say, you own International Widgets (IW), a not too profitable widget factory. Being a nice fellow, you don't pay yourself much of a salary, but to give yourself the incentive to work diligently on the behalf of the shareholders (usually yourself and some pals), you issue yourself and your friends lots of stock options. Suddenly out of the blue comes an order for a million widgets at a very nice price indeed. What to do? Why, you let the stockbrokers know about this so the public can see what a hell of a deal IW has just made! IW's stock soars, and you and your pals call your options and make a piss pot full of cash. One of the beauties of this process is that stock options don't show up as salaries or expenses so that IW's bottom line continues to look very good indeed. If you are very clever, you can do this several times. Eventually it will become known that the company buying the widgets couldn't go through with the deal, and stock prices will plummet, but you will have made your money. If you are unlucky, the shareholders will learn that—Surprise! Surprise!—you and your pals actually owned the company that placed the order for the widgets and that you never had any intention of carrying through on it. Now, most people would say this is pretty serious stuff. And when the Enron bubble burst, President Bush said that tough new rules would come in and would be enforced. Then this same President Bush leaned on Congress to go easy on the transgressors. Of course, most of the Enron shysters had stayed out of reach of the long arm of the law, anyway, and the scams continue as if nothing had happened.

I started this exercise by saying that I may be a "new socialist" and that, paradoxically to some readers, I also believed in the marketplace. I am and I do. But when the marketplace becomes a gigantic crooked wheel in which the little guy is forced by the system to play, and where the guys running the wheel fix the odds so that they always win big time, the moment has arrived when a policeman is needed. The capitalist will counter by saying that, when government butts in, it just means a lot of red tape. Well, that's the penalty when your conduct is egregiously greedy and the marketplace cannot provide fair play without a cop to see that it happens.

At political fundraisers right-wing politicians are fond of referring to "good corporate citizens," often in tones of deep admiration. This is interesting for no other reason than that there is no such thing unless you define the term so narrowly that it means only that none of the executives has recently gone to jail. These same politicians of the right (of which I once was) are fond of painting labour unions as grasping bloodsuckers that leech money from their memberships in order to defeat right-wing governments. They do not understand that unions are like companies—out there after their own interests. Unions that strike are seen as unreasonable unto irresponsibility; companies that lock out or make offers so contemptuous that a strike is inevitable are seen as trying to keep the lid on inflation. But most corporations are rapacious despoilers of the environment and fudge on their income taxes or avoid them outright. They use shareholders' money to bribe governments, for that is what attending big political party fundraisers is all about. None of this should shock or dismay anyone but it will because people forget what the concept of a corporation is. It is a group of people thrown together for one purpose only: making money. (It's little wonder people *do* forget this, considering all the tax-deductible advertising such companies throw at them.)

Fortunately, people who work in corporations can be good, and often, thank God, corporate executives who have done well behave (after suitable tax deductions) as philanthropists, generous with their time and their money. It's good company PR when good deeds are done, and a generous act does not become a sordid one just because the doer made something out of it. What is wrong is that we swallow their guff, usually with nary a critical thought.

Where my cynicism, if cynicism it is, becomes clear is in the environment. Most companies don't give a fiddler's fart about the environment. They never have and never will. What they are good at is making it appear that the whole idea of curbing pollution was theirs—even though they have just lost a gut-wrenching fight against a government temporarily concerned about environmental matters. Does anyone seriously think that pulp mills would have curtailed their emissions into the air and water had they not been forced to? Do any really believe that Japanese and Norwegian whalers would have cut back on their hunts had they not been forced to by other governments whose consciences were finally pricked by people like the Sea Shepherd's Paul Watson? Indeed, would corporations institute anything more than minimal safety programs were there not unions and government-run workers compensation laws?

Some years ago the Fraser Institute, a right-wing think-tank and a very good one, published the notion that all rivers ought to be in private hands because the fish in them would be safe, they being the highest available financial return on the water. This little bit of laissez-fairism was part of the notion that, left to its own designs, the marketplace would take care of everything, even the fish in the rivers.

The history of the use of rivers demonstrates something quite different: historically the highest use for any decent-sized river has been as a sewer for companies, cities and farms. Fish farms are an excellent example of the attitude of companies toward the environment. Everywhere that open net pen fish farms have occurred they have been a disaster. Fish escape and colonize rivers; penned in close quarters they breed clouds of sea lice that attack migrating wild salmon smolts; they create huge areas of disease; their waste, which includes not just excrement but antibiotics and colourants, is indiscriminately dumped on the ocean floor. All the while, fish farmers pay huge amounts to right-wing political parties, put out glossy magazine and newspaper inserts extolling their wares, and utterly deny all their sins.

This screed isn't in support of a return to the consideration of Marxism. Far from it. Communism as an economic system failed abysmally. And if you ever wanted to see the environment well and truly buggered up, a trip behind the old Iron Curtain would have done the trick. My purpose here is to lay out a reality recipe for dealing with worldwide environmental desecration. The notion that either labour unions, for whom their members' employment is all-important, or corporations, for whom the quarterly dividend is the holy of holies, give a continental dam about the environment is what has led us to our present disastrous position. Although we love to hate 'em, environmental movements have been all that have prevented even worse disasters than we have already seen. The argument that they are often excessive is pretty tough to take when you think what would have been had they not done what they thought was appropriate.

All the great captains of industry and many leaders of the labour movement wind up with Orders of Canada. The better exploiter you have been the higher up that ladder you go. Captain Paul Watson of the Sea Shepherd Society has devoted his life to saving seals and whales and without him and his unbelievable bravery this planet would be very much worse off. But Paul has consistently pissed off the Canadian government. What chance of an Order of Canada for citizen Paul? None. Absolutely none. Those who ravish the environment under the guise of being good corporate citizens and responsible labour leaders reap the honours. Those who truly serve the world and its citizens are reviled.

Now international business does largely what it wishes as governments have become virtually helpless in controlling capital and those who use it. In Tom Friedman's brilliant book, *The Lexus and the Olive Tree*, he describes how the "electronic herd," the term he uses to describe pools of capital, wanders the world looking for comfortable places to settle. "If you interfere," these new capitalists say, "we will take our money elsewhere." This, in fact, is precisely what the salmon farmers told the governments of British Columbia and Canada when there were suggestions that they might behave a bit more responsibly. We would have been money ahead and certainly environmentally better off if we had taken their offer and indeed helped them pack.

Union influence is on the wane today, and governments raise minimum wage rates at great peril. In fact, the gurus of the right believe that there should be no minimum wage at all. "Let the market decide wages," they say. It's not in the interest of large capital to pay attention to niceties like decent wages and working conditions and environmentally good behaviour. So who can blame young people for being skeptical?

Many years ago Sarah Cleghorn penned the following biting lines:

> The golf links lie so near the mill,
> That almost every day
> The labouring children can look out
> And watch the men at play.

She spoke of different times, of course, but how different were the children in her poem from what we are seeing today? Children, admittedly not as young as the ones she speaks of, work long hours in fast-food parlours and convenience stores for minimum wages. Children of small business owners tend stores for hours after school for little more than the right to shelter and food. Companies that see a better place to put their money simply abandon their workers and go elsewhere.

Environmentalism is fighting for its life. In British Columbia and Canada protection of the environment is now officially subservient to industrial development. When Gordon Campbell and his ill-named Liberals came to power in May 2001, the environment ministry was eliminated and what was left put into the hands of Joyce Murray who immediately made it clear that, far from being an environmental policeman, her job was to help "development ministers" do whatever they wanted.

Is there no hope? Probably not as long as Canadians are content to have governments under one-man dictators controlled by corporate money. The public has no say in how they are governed in this country at either the national or provincial level. This is the impetus behind the movement of (mostly) young people who protest at APEC and WTO meetings. They sense that they and most around them are the modern-day equivalent of the helpless workers made jobless during the Industrial Revolution. Today it's not a case of being Luddites and destroying evil machines but of seeing that the benefits of globalism are fairly shared. And it is not (yet) the sort of neo-communism that kills the bosses and puts the workers in charge, but it is a demand that capitalism be more than fat cats playing with stock options while the industries they are charged with running go broke. In short, the new, young activists believe that corporations that see their shareholders as their only responsibility are wrong, and that those who use capital also have an obligation to their workers, their workers' families and to society as a whole.

I said earlier that communism is dead. I devoutly hope that I'm right. But I depart on this thought: most of the ills of society that prevailed when communism was first being bruited about also prevail today. Child labour, poverty, environmental degradation, homelessness, racism, government out of the hands of the people and utterly irresponsible capital are all alive and prevalent. We have learned that communism doesn't cure these evils but often makes them worse and even creates new ones. But the evil conditions that spawned the likes of Lenin are very much here today with the added problem that, thanks to modern communication, those under the heel of capitalism at its worst know very well what is happening. The only difference between Ms. Cleghorn's people and those of today are that the children are less visible and the men do their playing on the ski slopes or on tropic isles away from the eyes of their workers.

Karl Marx and Frederick Engels, if alive today, would see this as a perfect time to publish *Das Kapital* and *The Communist Manifesto*.

# 13
## *The Love of My Life*

WE HAVE ALL HAD GREAT LOVES IN OUR LIVES. They range all the way from the little girl across the schoolroom to the suddenly blossomed woman of our junior high school class, though often these were just "lust affairs" and not worthy of the word "love." Far from being an exception, I have been married three times, and I must admit that until 1993 I was always possessed of an eye and other body parts that roved more than they should have. When at last I found the love of my life, my difficulty in dealing with this person who truly is the one I wished I had known so many years before and of saying so publicly was my legitimate fear of hurting others. Moreover, to relive the past would mean the erasure of many beautiful memories as well as dispensing with my children, stepchildren and, of course, my grandchildren.

My divorce from my first wife Eve was dealt with in *Canada: Is Anyone Listening?* and I'm sure she doesn't need to see it repeated. Suffice it to say, that the fault was mine. I couldn't handle the sudden death of our daughter Shawn, and I fell into other arms. Eve was and always has been a wonderful woman who deserved a hell of a lot better than I gave her. The happy news is that our union brought forward Kenneth Rafe II and his kids, Kenneth Rafe III, Kevin and Ashleigh; Cindy and her kids, Robbie and Karyn Leigh; and Karen and her youngsters, Tyrel and Trent.

My second wife, Patti, was for many years my producer. In June 1993 we reached the point where our marriage was one in name only. I am 16 years older than Patti, and at 62 I had the legitimate worry that if this was already happening, what about ten years hence? We both knew that while we might keep the marriage going, it was scarcely on the firmest of footings. I say all this without the slightest rancour; I wouldn't want to answer under oath for all of my behaviour during our marriage.

In any event, that summer of 1993 was a bit of a tough patch for me, and since I was leading a tour of the UK and Ireland starting in London on August 22, the management at CKNW gave me a couple of weeks off and suggested I go fishing in Scotland before I joined the tour group when they arrived in London. It was a very kind gesture and, since my stepson Steve—though mercifully, as it turned out, not his mother Patti—was going on the tour with me, I took him to Scotland for the fishing as well. I have always been very fond of Patti's two children, Kim and Steve, a feeling happily reciprocated. During this hiatus in Scotland, I thought a lot about my marriage. And I spoke to my daughter Cindy long distance to get her perspective. I just didn't know what to do.

On our way back to London, Steve and I stopped in Oxford and over a beer I told him I had decided to move out of the house when we returned. I explained that this wasn't an anger situation. It was just that if I was this lonely at 62, I would worry from then on about being alone when I got older, more needy of companionship and less able to care for myself, being both a diabetic and subject to depression.

The next afternoon we went out to Heathrow to meet the folks who were going to travel with me and learned they would only be with me for one week, not the three weeks that had been planned, because of a change in the rating period. As our group started to appear, I noticed a beautiful, tall and much younger lady helping some of the older folks. As we all introduced ourselves, I learned that her name was Wendy.

On the bus ride to our hotel, the St. George's in Langham Court at the top of Regent Street, I offered to take as many who would like to come on a short tour to St. Paul's while Steve took whomever so wished to Piccadilly Circus. I told them that I knew they were jet-lagged but that staying up as long as they could would be their best plan. We scheduled the St. Paul's tour for 4:00 p.m. and sure enough, when the group assembled, there was Wendy. At the Oxford Circus tube station a few blocks away I noticed that she was having trouble with the automatic ticket machine, so I gallantly intervened, and on the short trip to St. Paul's each of us somehow managed to get our life story out. I found that she had left a very unhappy marriage six months earlier, and I told her of my plight.

After St. Paul's, we all walked back to our hotel, and I found myself with Steve, Wendy, and one or two others having a pizza on Argyll Street, just behind Oxford Circus. Then, for some reason, Steve, Wendy and I took a long walk through Mayfair before getting back to the hotel. The next day, a day off for the tour group, I took Wendy to see more of London including—and we still laugh at this—a tour of the food hall at Harrods! That night when we went to a musical, I thought I had arranged it so I would be sitting next to her but wound up at the furthest point I could have been. I was pissed off but really wasn't sure why. At the intermission I found myself looking down the row for her and saw that she seemed to be looking for me.

The following day we all bused it down to Leeds Castle, then on to Canterbury before ending with a visit to Chartwell, Churchill's home. Back in London again, I asked Wendy to join me for a pizza (what a romantic, eh?), and after dinner we walked down through Soho and thence to St. James Park. On the way down we stopped, and I kissed her and told her that I was quite taken with her (see, I am a romantic!). We ended up under a war memorial in St. James Park, necking like a couple of kids, and when we returned to the St. George's, we went into the bar, and with the carelessness of all new love (yes, you kids, even later on in life) resumed our earlobe-nibbling there. The next night we were in Exeter, and I managed to slip us away from the throng to a lovely Italian restaurant called Gino's where I proposed. And she accepted! What sort of madness was this? A 62-year-old man and a lady who had just turned 50 agreeing to marry after knowing each other four days!

But we were in love and we both just knew it was right. For the next couple of days we skilfully concealed our new love from the rest of our tour mates (yeah, right!). And then it was time for me to leave the tour group, and we were washed by great sadness as I promised I would phone her at a certain time a few days hence. In fact, I phoned every day at least three times a day.

When I got home, Patti met me at the airport. After some early moments of understandable hurt and anger, she wished me well over a nice dinner and wine at Earl's Tin Palace in North Vancouver.

The night before Wendy was to come home, I realized that, having agreed at Gino's that I would move in with her, we had not settled on where we would meet. She was by this time at the Gresham Hotel in Dublin. It was five in the morning there when I phoned. A lovely Irish tenor voice wished me "Good Morning. This is the Gresham Hotel in Dublin, how can I help you?" He put me through to Ms. Greer's room. The receiver was slammed in my ear. I rang back. The same lilting Irish voice answered and connected me; this time a lady picked up the phone but it wasn't Wendy! Whoops, try again. I got the same lady who wasn't amused. I dialled again and there was the same soothing Irish tenor, whereupon I asked if there was anyone in that effing hotel who was sufficiently skilled on the switch board to connect me to Ms. Greer's room. This time, in fact, it happened, and it turned out that the first connection when the phone was slammed down had indeed been Wendy who thought it was a wake-up call! In all events, we agreed that I would meet her at the ABC Family Restaurant in Aldergrove (Wendy's apartment was in Abbotsford) that same evening around 8:30 since her plane wasn't getting in until 6:30.

I arrived at the ABC Restaurant at 7:30! Well, hell, her plane could have been a couple of hours early, couldn't it? With me were two bottles of champagne, not the same brand because the vintner had run out of the best ones, and eleven long-stemmed red roses, one having broken in transit. Eight-thirty came and went as did nine o'clock, and no Wendy. I began to get those chilling doubts when common sense starts to take over. Of course, she's not here! I told myself. What sort of nonsense was all this! Four days and agree to get married! Rafe, you're an idiot. . . .Whereupon who should show up in her '88 Mustang but Wendy! My love was here! After great hellos, hugs and a few tears, I got into my Cadillac with its 13 garbage bags full of clothes and one computer and off we went to Wendy's place! We then sat on her sundeck in the warm September evening, wrapped in each other's arms, and drank the two bottles of champagne!

Wendy and I lived in her apartment for about four months, but then we moved back into the house Patti and I owned (to the extent the mortgage companies didn't own it—which is to say not much). Here Wendy met another lover who was to be every bit as faithful as I—Clancy, my wonderful chocolate Labrador, who immediately bonded to her and she to him.

Who is this woman who swept me and my dog off our six feet? Probably the warmest, most caring person I have ever met. I don't mean caring in that saccharine sort of way that replaces deeds with oleaginous mush, but really caring. A nurse for 30 years, Wendy had seen life in the raw and knew what suffering, mental and well as physical, really was.

So there it is. Wendy and I met on August 22, 1993, we moved in together on September 7 of that year, and on July 29, 1994, we were married—to live happily ever after.

# 14
## Finding God

WENDY AND I, HAVING KNOWN each other less than a week, never doubted that we would get married as soon as certain impediments—two other spouses—were removed. On July 29, 1994, only days after being entitled to do so, we were married in St. Christopher's Church in West Vancouver by the Reverend Ray Murrin. But it wasn't a slam dunk that we could marry in the Anglican Church, both of us being divorced. Thanks to the advice of a lawyer for the church who lived next door, we had been directed to the Venerable Lou Rivers, priest at St. Christopher's, who would decide whether we could be married there. After a short meeting with this marvellous man who, with his wife, was to become a great personal friend, we were told that the Anglican Church and St. Christopher's would make us most welcome, but that since Lou would be away, his honorary assistant Ray would do the deed. And so it was a wonderful wedding with just a few friends in attendance and a lovely reception afterwards put on by my cousin, Ann Robertson, and her late husband, Clark.

When we returned from our honeymoon in Britain—where else?—we came home much in love but also delighted that our love had been recognized by the church I had spent so little qualifying time in. This pivotal event in my life was now leading me physically back to the church of my birth if only for a look-see. I was enormously impressed by Lou Rivers as a preacher and so for a while I tended to overlook much of the dogma involved. I had already resolved that there is indeed a God for, in my strange way, I saw the orgasm as ultimate proof that there is a Greater Power. If there weren't some regard for the act of procreation, it wouldn't take place.

Though science thinks it can prove everything, at its very best it only gets to where believers got long ago. For when scientists solemnly announced that the universe came into being by a large explosion of something no bigger than a golf ball, then smiled smugly and said, "There you are!" my question was "And just where is it that I am then?" What right have you people to suggest that you've answered anything that the ancients didn't answer eons ago? What was there before the explosion? What caused the explosion? If there was no atmosphere, how come there was an explosion? And, most of all, where did that golf ball come from? I guess my final comment might be: so you say that creation was an explosion creating from matter an enormous universe full of stars and planets, do you? Well, if that's not a bloody miracle, what is? And isn't this just as consistent with there being a Greater Power or God as it is with there being this amazing explosion in what was hitherto nothingness?

Now scientists, having convinced themselves that they are right and that the universe was the result of some sort of magic spontaneous combustion, must then explain how oxygen and hydrogen came to be and how cells somehow happened. Then comes the tough part: how did the vast array of life on this planet come to be—everything from almost invisible micro-organisms to elephants? And science answers this with two most unscientific of terms: evolution or, when talking to small children and adults who don't understand them (which is to say most of us), "mother nature." What we are required to believe is that somehow natural forces made life in the form of protoplasm in the water and that this "evolved" into things that had fins and tails and eventually, through "evolution" crawled ashore, developing over time lungs and feet and hands and so on. What science can't explain, and doesn't even try to, is not that it happened but how it happened. What force within that bit of protoplasm got it to become a fish? To say that it had to evolve is to beg the question. Nothing has to evolve unless you believe that Mr. and Mrs. Protoplasm woke up one morning saying, "This mad splitting into new bits of protoplasm must stop! We must develop! Here we are a billion years old already and have nothing to show for it. Get thee a tail, some fins and lots of scales, my love, and what fun we'll have then!"

But there is another thing that I say puts paid to the scientist's argument. What is the force that compels animals to breed? Don't say it comes naturally. Again that begs the question. What is this "naturally" business all about? As the scheme of Mr. and Mrs. Protoplasm moved forward, how did the notion of attractiveness of sex to opposite sex happen and who thought up the idea of an orgasm to top things off, so to speak? Higher forms of animals breed because opposite sexes are not only drawn to one another but have a hell of a lot of pleasure in the act of copulation. If there was not this drawing together and there were not this pleasure, Adam and Eve would have died of old age with the apple rotting and the serpent still back with legs, shrivelling into extinction, and that would have been that.

So Mr. Scientist, explain this thing to me that the rest of us have defined as love? What is it that makes a girl and boy so attracted to one another that they make public spectacles of themselves? And how did the great pleasure of the sex act, the orgasm, come about? Of course, you can explain how the orgasm happens in a physiological sense, but not for the first time your answer begs the question. The scientist can do many wonderful things, but not only can he not tell us where the golf ball came from, he can't explain the orgasm.

But my inquiries went further than this. After Wendy and I had settled into the habit of regular Sunday worship at St. Christopher's, I started to think about the things I was mumbling every week over my prayer book and asking myself if I could conscientiously state that I believed what my creed had me saying.

My foundation in Christianity wasn't complicated. I was brought up a nominal Christian in the Anglican faith. I was baptized (we called it christened in the old days and a better word it was) at St. Paul's in the West End (where my mom had likewise been christened and my parents married), went to Sunday school, sang in the choir at St. Mary's, Kerrisdale, was confirmed on March 18, 1945, by Bishop DePencier at St. George's School Chapel (I still have *The Book of Common Prayer*, somewhat dog-chewed along the way, with my dad and mom's inscriptions in it), and thereafter was part of the church when I wanted to be.

During my childhood, we had gone as a family to church at St. Mary's twice a year—Christmas Day and Easter Sunday. On these occasions my father would be clearly annoyed if anyone was sitting in the "family pew" when we arrived! I attended more regularly than the rest of the family because until I was about twelve I sang in the choir. I remember with great fondness the Reverend Jimmy Craig and after him Dudley Kemp, one of those rare Englishmen who appreciated baseball, a very important attribute as far as I was concerned. While at St. George's I attended Chapel every day but, after leaving in May 1946, found myself only attending Sunday evening services at St. John's, Shaughnessy, when a young lady I had my eye on also happened to be there. After I left high school and until I began to attend St. Christopher's in 1993, I simply did nothing formal in the way of worship. As an adult, I used the church for my needs: three marriages, the christening of one of my four children and the funeral of another. I don't imagine that after my first marriage on September 8, 1955, I went inside a church more than once or twice other than to attend weddings, christenings and funerals.

All those years I thought a lot about God and Jesus, yet somehow I was able to remain in constant denial that after my death I might rue not having got better acquainted. I was like that English lord who wrote his vicar to say, "I have just been told by my doctor that I have six months to live. I had always assumed they were going to make an exception in my case. What now?" As with most people, my thoughts of religion were usually confined to somewhat boozy "learned" discussions with others who thought that boozy learned arguments substituted for serious thought. Being an avid golfer and later an equally avid fisherman, I consoled whatever conscience I had on the matter of religion with the comforting thought that my church was the "great outdoors." I was, like so many, put off by the great grief the Christian Church had caused and continued to cause over doctrinal disputes. I could never satisfy myself that I could belong to anything with such a brutal background. From Lou Rivers, I learned the concept of the "corporate church," that being the organizations set up in Christ's name by man but quite distinguishable from God's church, and I could now accept my own compromise that God's church was eternal and good, while man's corporate church could often be very evil and that, though many of the evils were done in God's name, God could scarcely be blamed. It wasn't God who sent crusade after crusade into what is now Israel and Palestine, slaughtering innocents by the thousands. It was not God who set brother against brother over the question of whether the bread and wine of communion became the actual flesh and blood of Christ upon ingestion. It wasn't God who hanged witches. It wasn't God who burned people at the stake for what others called heresy. (One heresy, that of the Arians who accepted neither the Trinity nor the divinity of Jesus, has caught my eye of late. Arians asked why God would go into the wilderness for 40 days to be tempted by the devil. Why would God ask himself to "take this cup from my lips," and why would God as God ask "Father, why have you forsaken me?") While it is not for mere mortals to conclude what God intends, there would be no point to believing in God if that were the sort of "force" we were throwing our lot in with. When I think of this doctrinal nit-picking that has caused so many millions to die, I go back to Jonathan Swift's *Gulliver's Travels* where two nations are perpetually at war over whether one should crack the egg at the big end or the little end. If one looks at his satire fairly, the fight over the eggs perhaps makes more sense than the things over which Christians have killed themselves and others in the past and up to the present.

Then my thinking took a turn. I couldn't deny the words and goings-on in the Bible just because they defied belief because an all-powerful God could do anything. My question was, therefore: is it necessary to believe all these things—the virgin birth, the physical resurrection of Christ and Jonah in the great fish? I was struck by something almost like Saul's blinding flash on the road to Damascus, and though this revelation only had meaning for me, it was fantastic! The teachings of Christ were not complicated! They were in the language of the masses so that they, not the learned, could understand. They boiled down to love God and love one's neighbour as oneself. All the law and the prophets hang on that. This was Christianity totally contained within these few words. But to always love God and to always love neighbour and self? That was impossible! And the fact that it was impossible was the whole point, because the sins left over from our vain attempts to follow Christ's rules were those we could rely on being forgiven for if we tried, failed and confessed our failure. This was Christianity, if one defines that word as following the teachings of Jesus.

But could I just toss aside the Bible as an interesting, much-quoted contrivance of some bishops who got together for a council at Nicea in 325 AD? Could I just cherry-pick the things from the Bible I had no trouble with and ignore the rest? And what about the men—strangely all men, it seemed—who wrote these things, especially that most troubling of apostles, Paul? Were their words not just of holy men but of God himself? And, if that were so, did the articles of faith of each version of the "corporate church," as interpreted by mortals, end all debates? And what about miracles? I decided that whether or not they happened was irrelevant since an all-powerful God could do anything.

I puzzled over these points for several years. If I was right that the essence of Christianity was the simple laws Christ laid down, did I have to interpret them in the context of all the utterances in the Bible being the infallible word of God? Could I pick and choose those that supported my prejudices or could I say I don't know? That is, I just don't know if it is essential to my salvation that I accept everything laid out in the Bible, Old or New Testament, as God's commands. In my decision I took the logical path that told me that "all the law and the prophets" meant that I did not. This made it easy for me to deal with the homosexual issues the Anglican Church is wrestling with today for, if my approach to the teachings of Christ is correct, it's a non-issue; it's not for me or anyone else, for that matter, to decide if being homosexual is a sin. As I see it, no matter what your sexual preference, if you love God and your neighbour as yourself, you can call yourself a Christian for that's what you are. I would, of course, point to the fact that Christ didn't deal with homosexuality, although we must assume that it was as prevalent then as today and, in many societies of that day, as open if not more open than now.

But, say others, it's not so simple, Rafe. You see, Jesus commanded us to accept the teachings of the scriptures including the Ten Commandments. But the Old Testament also accepts slavery, the inferior position of women and incalculable violence. And this leads to the nub of the matter. Is Christianity merely following Christ's summation of "the law and the prophets" or are those words subject to the utterances of others, which utterances shall be interpreted unto us by a priest, pastor or what have you?

I must approach this matter a bit legalistically, in accordance with my training, and ask if there is enough evidence from the utterances of Christ to justify the interpretations put on his words by those who would judge me according to their interpretation of the entire Bible. Here, of course, I open myself to fair assault by those who have gone over each verse of the Bible with a fine-toothed comb. But you cannot support the argument that everything in the Bible is wholly writ by quoting from the Bible as authority for your contention. That's like me defending a thesis by saying it must be correct and use that thesis as proof of what I say. The truth of the Bible, say the fundamentalists, depends on itself for substantiation. To me that's an illogical and unsustainable method of argument.

Now it would be utterly wrong to infer from what I say that, a fortiori, whatever is in the Bible is unproven. Much of it, no doubt, is provable, but the conundrum is that we don't know which parts. Thus it is argued that we must simply have faith. We have to accept some things, even the rankest of hearsay. I know I was born on New Year's Eve 1931 because of the hearsay evidence of my parents and my birth certificate (now only my birth certificate). We can prove the existence of Jesus with much, much stronger evidence than we have for my date of birth. On the other hand, Tom Harpur in his book *The Pagan Christ* says there was no such person as the biblical Jesus Christ and that there have been at least 13 people bearing the name Jesus or one like it who have all preached the same message, often in precisely the same language. But I came to the conclusion that he did exist and that even if the actual existence of Jesus Christ cannot be demonstrated, it doesn't matter. It's the message that matters. Even non-Christians accept that Jesus was real and was a profoundly powerful teacher of an extremely powerful message. Many may not accept that message or may accept it but not to the point they feel bound to Christ. But that Jesus lived and pronounced his essential creed is all but unchallengeable. Most who would deny Christ as Saviour and might cast doubt upon his existence and his preaching of his message would say, "Even if there was no Jesus, the message is the only logical one to accept if one believes in an all-powerful and forgiving God." So as a lawyer, I would argue it's proven that Jesus lived, pronounced his creed, and had such a powerful message that his enormous influence is strong worldwide 20 centuries later. I submit that any judge or properly instructed jury would conclude the same.

I digress again to say that the same can no doubt be said about Mohammed and other "men of God." Mohammed by words and, unlike Jesus, also by force was able to conquer the minds of an enormous number of people over a vast area in a very short time. If anyone were to tell me that those who follow the teachings of Mohammed will never die, I wouldn't argue with them. I know this contrasts with Jesus's injunction that "No one comes to the Father except through me," but surely Jesus wasn't saying that he personally had to be accepted but that his message had to be accepted, which message can easily be inferred from Mohammed's teachings. Besides, if Christianity is an exclusive faith that denies salvation to good people who are not Christians, I'm getting out of this argument while there's still time!

Having accepted that Jesus lived, uttered his commandments and set in motion this terrific force called Christianity, I faced this unresolved question: is it enough that one believe that in order to gain salvation, or must one also accept as true all the utterances in the Bible—the corporate church's operating manual, so to speak. Or, if not all of them, at least most of them, keeping one's doubts to oneself? I think that to answer that we must divide the subject in two: the Old Testament and the New Testament. As lawyer for the "simple Christianity position," I say that not only is it impossible to know the answer to that question in regard to the Old Testament, it is irrelevant.

What? Cast aside all the Biblical teachings of the eons before Christ as irrelevant? No fair judge would accept that!

But I didn't say that all the teachings of the Old Testament were irrelevant. Many are very relevant. "Thou shall not murder" is as relevant today as it ever was. What I say is that accepting the irrelevancy of the Old Testament simply means that all that one can say about one's duty to God is summed up by "Thou shalt love the Lord thy God with all thy heart, etc., and thou shalt love thy neighbour as thyself, upon those two commandments hang all the law and the prophets." All the rest is, therefore, extraneous to your needs. Indeed, from another context I would argue that "that is all / Ye know on earth, and all ye need to know." I fortify my argument by repeating that Jesus did not try to convert the scribes, Pharisees and other establishment figures of his time. Clearly, he hoped they would listen, but he, in fact, preached to the ordinary folk. Had there been a more complicated message for the elite to be entrusted with for the teaching of the dull masses, surely he would have spelled it out so that they, in leading the community, could hold the masses to a higher standard than what he preached on the Mount. But he didn't do so. And there are lots of other things he didn't do either, such as preach about his virgin birth or how the wine and bread commemorating him would turn into his flesh and blood. He doesn't tell us that as an article of faith we must accept the doctrine of the Trinity. In fact, I would argue that the notion of his bodily ascension into heaven is an earthly inference, not an essential tenet of faith in Christ, although especially at Easter virtually all corporate churches make it clear that this belief is the very essence of Christianity.

Well, then, what about the New Testament and, in particular, what about the utterances of that greatest of all the apostles, Paul? I don't deny the conversion on the road to Damascus nor do I deny his holiness. What I say again is that this is not relevant to the essential faith in Jesus's commandments. If I am right that "upon these two commandments hang all the law and the prophets," how can anything else matter, save as it helps us obey these laws? But others tell me that is what Paul was all about—interpreting Christ's words. To this I respond that Christ's words need no interpreting because they are almost childishly simple to understand. It is never the interpretation of his words that causes us difficulty; it is obeying them.

Ah but, it will be said, that's where Paul and the other apostles come in. They help us to understand what we must do to love God, our neighbours and ourselves. My answer to that is the essence of my argument: Christ phrased his words such that, had there been the necessity of intellectual interpretation beyond that of ordinary mortals, he would have laid down a complicated catechism so that the never-ending priestly profession, unto whom these secrets would be vouchsafed, could lecture the masses while holding them bound to a mystery that the masses were too thick to understand! And this,

I think, is where my argument really rests. If I am right, the rest of the Bible, though interesting, often helpful and historically invaluable (indeed, of sacred value to Jews, and nothing I say should be interpreted as critical of that great religion), but in the true, unhyperbolic sense of the word irrelevant to being a Christian. To say otherwise means two things: either one accepts each and every word in the Bible or one decides which words must be believed and which need not be. I cannot believe that God intended mankind should be saddled with an eternal legal debate with Godly hairs being split over and over.

While the Christian Church didn't start with the Council of Nicea in 325 AD, the bishops of that conclave did set the rules by which Orthodox Christianity would thereafter abide. As a result, we tend to look back and think that this occurred pretty much contemporaneously with the teachings of Paul and his ilk. It didn't. Not by a long shot. (Think on this: it is also nearly 325 years since Britain was ruled by Charles II!) In today's terms that council at Nicea was just a political convention to decide what the Christian package was to be and how it was to be sold, who could belong and who would be heretics. What was needed first of all was a complicated set of rules only the elite priesthood would understand and thus be exclusively capable of explaining. The Church needed a mystique, chants and prayers to be delivered by high priests in fancy dress, a complicated system of rules and the approved books to make up a Bible. This Church needed to be the legitimate heir to some existing doctrines such as the virgin birth, the doctrine of transubstantiation, the Trinity and the resurrection of the body, but also have the right to expand on those doctrines and come up with a few of its own from time to time. All that remained was the drawing of a straight line between believing these doctrines and great rewards for followers if they did what they were told and the horrible consequences if they did not.

But none of this is necessary. Jesus Christ's teachings are valid without all this mumbo-jumbo and, if followed to the letter (which, of course, no one could possibly do), they would lead to the perfect person to be ready, in death, to be embraced by God. Being a lawyer by trade, I like to have the last word. But I leave the final summation to Elizabeth I of England who said, "There is only one Lord Jesus Christ and the rest is a dispute about trifles."

So where are Wendy and I now, ten years after we visited St. Christopher's Anglican Church because of its wonderful priest? Well, most of what I've written above could also have been written by Wendy for it is the view of Christianity that derived from lines of thought developed more by her than me. I think we both see ourselves as much enriched, not just by the marriage Lou performed for us, but by the search for God we have lived with since then. It would be nice—comfortable is probably a better word—if we were devoutly convinced of the teachings of the Bible, secure in the notion that every word is that of God. But we are not, though both of us have a much better appreciation of what Christ (or the 13 of them if you wish) taught. We no longer see complexity but simplicity. Most of all we have become better people for it, better life companions whose love continues to grow, better able to accept other people and other belief systems. We both still have fundamental doubts about who we are and where, if anywhere, we'll go, but I suspect the most devoutly religious people, if truth were known and souls bared, would admit as much themselves.

# 15

## Clancy and Chauncey

IN JUNE 2000 THE STARS ALL came together for Wendy and me. We sold the house on Montroyal Avenue and at the same time bought a townhouse in Lions Bay in a complex we'd had our eyes on for years. Not only that, it was the end unit, giving us on one side the beautiful English country garden of our lovely neighbours and on the other side a wooded stream. It was in terrible shape when we first viewed it. The previous owners had two dogs, several cats and two birds, and the place looked like it. But Wendy saw what could be done with it. I saw only the view: 180 degrees of beautiful Howe Sound with the spectacular Coast Range Mountains behind it. It took some money (actually quite a bit of it!) but after we had a sunroom built, a wooden patio with a hot tub installed out front, the bathrooms completely overhauled, the kitchen remodelled and a complete paint job, we had the home of our dreams.

Then in August 2001 Wendy and I had to do a horrible thing: we had to put to death our beloved chocolate Labrador, Clancy. As is always the case with this particular sept of this marvellous breed, Clancy was a great character. While it is true that there are often mixed colours in a litter I maintain, and many experts agree, that for some reason chocolates have a special craziness all of their own. Labradors have webs between the pads of their paws, and there's a good reason they're called retrievers—they love to swim and fetch things—and

Clancy had loved to swim more than anything else. Since we had a swimming pool, he could swim whenever he liked. But he also had other interesting habits. For one thing, when Wendy and I had our nightcap, Clancy would wait at her feet, nose stuck into her face, paw working her knee over, awaiting the ice cubes to be given him once the Scotch had all gone. He loved ice cubes. We had a rubber "kong" which we would throw into the pool for him, and if you had the patience to throw it, he would retrieve it all day long. The kong just barely floated and sometimes Clancy would, while grabbing at it, force it underwater, whereupon all we would see of him above water was the end of his wagging tail as he went after it!

He was a dog of immense courage. In his last days, riddled with cancer, he would charge down the steep bank of the stream by the house, roll around in the water, then run back up the hill. Back home, he would flop on the carpet all but unable to move. On that terrible Friday afternoon when we took "the Clance" to the vet for the last time, he first went across the street, down the embankment, into the water, then back up full steam ahead. We couldn't help but wonder if he still had a bit of life left to live. Back home, we got our answer. Clancy flopped on the floor, entirely out of breath and energy. It damned near killed me to hold him in my arms, with Wendy cuddling his muzzle, as Dr. Moe Milstein, the gentlest and kindest of men, injected the fatal substance. I wept unashamedly. So did Wendy.

I have a poetry book always at hand that, when I'm in the mood, I glance at for no special reason. One evening at nightcap time, with no Clancy begging for ice cubes, I opened the book as if it were pre-ordained to a short poem by Dr. Wilfred J. Funk of *Funk and Wagnall's Dictionary* fame. I had never seen the poem before, had never even heard of the author. I read the poem to Wendy.

> *Father in thy starry tent,*
> *I kneel a humble suppliant. . .*
> *A dog has died today on earth,*
> *Of little worth*
> *Yet very dear.*
> *Gather him in Thine arms*
> *If only*

*For awhile.*
*I fear*
*He will be lonely*
*Shield him with Thy smile.*

We wept. Openly and copiously.

What to do? Our small townhouse in Lions Bay had seemed big enough when we had Clancy. But could we handle another Lab, a breed known for extending puppyhood into old age? Yes, we could. We didn't just like dogs, we loved them and really couldn't do without them. Wendy, when she separated from her first husband, had to leave her black Lab, Teela, behind and the hurt had never gone away. We pointed out to each other that there were plenty of lovely walks around us and beaches just minutes away. So we made the decision. But where would we get our puppy from? I had been very lucky with Clancy, having bought him from a breeder's first-ever litter. Not a good idea, really, but I had lucked out. This time we didn't want to rely entirely on Lady Luck, and we called our good friend Ann Jackson, a dog trainer. Could she make a recommendation? Ann did our due diligence for us, found Big Valley Labradors in Aldergrove and gave us the website. In no time the owner, Agneta, and I were circling one another like careful boxers, I trying to determine that she was a reputable breeder, she making sure I was the kind of person she would let one her pups go to. The e-mails between us have been preserved, and they make pretty funny reading in light of the wonderful friends we all became and the protracted love affair a chocolate Lab named Chauncey and Agneta have enjoyed. But I'm getting ahead of myself. After Agneta and I had approved each other's bona fides, she told us that she had a chocolate bitch in heat and hopefully she had been bred. We put our dibs in for a chocolate male.

It was November 20, 2001, and we were ensconced in a hotel room in London when I got a fax from Ann announcing, "Congratulations! You're a father!" In the litter of nine there were but two chocolates and only one male. And the male was one of the chocolates. We found out much later that Agneta literally had to take this pup to bed with her, so weak was he. That changed, but Chauncey's love for Agneta and vice versa hasn't. When we got home from London, we started visiting our new pup to get to know him. Agneta, who had a special spot in her heart for him, told us he already knew his name. The problem was that now the entire litter thought they were named Chauncey!

We took our puppy home when he was eight weeks old, and upon walking in the door of our condo, he dove under my computer and pulled out a bunch of wires. (Fortunately one of my stepdaughters lives with a computer wiz.) Chauncey should have been named Hoover because he swallowed everything that he encountered, including four aspirins from which experience he damned near died. When he pooped, the sound went plink, plink, plink, plop—the plinks being the stones he had swallowed! But, all things considered, he wasn't nearly as destructive as most Lab pups I've had and he was a great character. He loved games, especially the many games of his own invention. And he loved to swim. The first time we took him to the beach he was about two months old. It was in the middle of January, but I threw a stick in the water and he dashed right in! When he could no longer feel the ground, he did turn around momentarily but then kept right on going. He was definitely a Labrador. He now swims at least once a day, summer or winter, rain or shine.

But it was a couple of nights after his first swim that it happened. We were having our nightcaps—a beer for me and a single malt whisky for Wendy—when this little brown guy sauntered over to Wendy, sat down in front of her, stared at her glass with the ice cubes in it. Then he stuck out a front leg and pawed Wendy's leg. "I would like an ice cube thank you very much," was the clear message and again the tears welled up in our eyes. Clancy was back.

And what a pal Chauncey has turned out to be. With his daily swims and many long walks and runs, he's fit as a fiddle. Moreover, he's handsome and well-bred as proved by the fact that Agneta, whom he adores, has him betrothed to a beautiful little black bitch whose mother was chocolate. The nuptials and hopefully the consummation followed by issue are to take place in a couple of years.

Chauncey's relationship with Agneta and her partner, Willie Taylor (the former football player who was on the Lions team when they won the Grey Cup in 1964) is such that when we go away, Chauncey goes out to Big Valley where he immediately leaps out of the car into Agneta's arms and runs off to play with Skookum, his grand-mother. Wendy and I sit there, a tear in the corner of the eye, thinking, "Aren't you going to miss us even a little bit?"

It's a wonderful life: we have a view from our condo many would kill for, a dog that is not only part of the family but fully one-third if not more of it, and the love of my life to share my work and my play. I am truly blessed.

# 16

## Travel

I THINK THERE ARE THREE REASONS to travel. Sometimes it is just to veg out and it doesn't much matter where, as long as it is warm. But when I go to these places I find I get very annoyed when people want me to join in the "fun." This is especially true of cruises where there is always a loudspeaker urging me to do something. Bingo, "horse" races, bridge games. Shore visits are too often a whirlwind city tour, a pre-arranged lunch and the obligatory stop at a tourist complex that has a profit-sharing arrangement with the tour guide. I get back aboard ship six hours after I left, sink into a stiff drink and say to my mate, "So that was Lima!"

Sometimes travel means seeing something you haven't seen before. In our early days of travel this was probably the main consideration. Wendy and I meet this need now by taking four or five days out of our annual November trip to London to take in a European city, and over the past five years we've been to Paris, Prague, Copenhagen, Amsterdam and Rome. The trick to doing it cheaply is to book it from a London travel agent because travel agents closer to home don't have the information or the connections. For two to stay in a two-star hotel (lots of them are available near the town centre, clean places with continental breakfast supplied) for four days is about $1,000 to$1,500 including airfare.

For many, travel means a warm island, a cottage by the lake or a boat. Wendy and I go to New Zealand every year to fly fish and see friends, and we usually take Christmas in Mexico. But the place we really go to relax, when all's said and done, is Blighty and, in particular, London. We've been together for 11 years and we have been to London 32—yes 32!—times in that span. Why, oh why, we're constantly asked, would you do that? Surely, there is nothing left to see! But there always is!

I don't know why I have this unquenchable love for London. It started back in 1964 when, as a lawyer, I stopped over on a business trip that took me to the Midlands and later Ireland. Though I was so excited that I couldn't sleep on the trip over, nevertheless when I arrived at my hotel, The Cumberland on Marble Arch at the northeast corner of Hyde Park, I felt as refreshed as if I had slept for a week. In my business suit and leather shoes I walked all over "the city." When I got back to my room, the tiredness suddenly hit. But that evening I went around the corner to my first pub, the Old Quebec, and had my first pint, and for the first time in my life was the object of a gay's attention and received an invitation to join him in his flat! I declined. On that first visit, I was in one of the very last of London's famous fogs. These horrible phenomena ended in the early sixties when the government put an end to burning coal within the city. The plethora of chimneys are still there, but what followed was a massive cleanup of public buildings. It has meant such a transformation that anyone who had last seen London in, say, 1970 simply wouldn't recognize the buildings today

Since that first visit, I have returned to London at least 80 times. (In November '02 I had the great privilege and enormous fun of guiding my youngest daughter, Karen, around London for her first visit. She had just a week to see it all, but it quickly became clear to her that she would need the rest of her life to really see this great city.)

My former colleague Gary Bannerman, an inveterate world traveller, once remarked to me, "Rafe, there are other cities than London." But there aren't, you know. In August 2002 when Wendy and I, having decided to stay close to home for my two-week vacation, learned that a baseball strike threatened our sole reason for going to Seattle for a few days, we looked at each other in that way we have come to know and said almost simultaneously, "What the hell, let's call our travel agent and see if we can get a couple of cheapies to London." Which we did. It's not just doing the things we love so much—going to Sunday Matins at St. Paul's, followed by a cappuccino at Covent Garden and listening to the string quartets and the opera singers; or taking the long walk through the four great parks (Hyde, Kensington Gardens, Green and St. Paul's) from Notting Hill Gate to Horse Guards; or going to Shakespeare's plays at the Globe. Or the wonderful bookstores. Or the shops like Hardy's, Lock the Hatter, or Harrods famous food hall. It's that every time we're there we discover something we haven't experienced before. But mostly it's because when the plane lands, I feel 20 years younger. No other place does that for me, and at my age this is a very important consideration, indeed.

London is a city that never seems to change yet, in fact, changes every day. One change in the past half-dozen years is unique in that a re-creation of the past has become a genuine must-see of today: the New Globe Theatre. When the American actor and director Sam Wanamaker first came to London in 1951, he asked where Shakespeare's famous Globe Theatre was. He knew, of course, that the original was gone, but he was horrified that nothing had taken its place and vowed to do something about it. Wanamaker was a man of dedication and he eventually acquired land about 200 yards from the original site and assembled the money to build a new Globe. Scholars from all over England were pressed into action to describe what the original playhouse looked like. Old pictures were consulted as were the records of the craft guilds. Eventually plans were agreed upon and construction was started. As in its original incarnation, all the timbers are split oak and wooden plugs were used instead of nails. The roof was thatched and the only concession to the 20th century was the use of a sprinkler system to conform to modern fire code requirements. Sam Wanamaker, who was knighted for his efforts, died before the first play was staged, but he did live to see his dream largely constructed.

One of the most interesting features of the Globe is the half-moon-shaped, covered, tiered gallery that faces the stage in front of which is, as in days of yore, the uncovered pit where in Shakespeare's day those who couldn't afford seats would stand and, if they wished, heckle the players. In fact, this tradition continues, as Wendy and I discovered when we saw our first play there in the year it opened, 1997. We were fortunate to be able to get tickets for the second of the theatre's presentations, *The Two Gentlemen of Verona*. In it there is a scene where Julia soliloquizes on whether she should take back the lover who betrayed her, and as she was asking herself whether she should forgive him, a loud voice from the pit said, "Don't do it, Julia. You'll be sorry!" When we saw *The Merchant of Venice*, Shylock was booed and heckled throughout, but at the end of the play when it becomes clear that, whatever his faults, he was the only principal character who wasn't a hypocrite, he was cheered. Since that year we have also seen Thomas Middleton's wonderful comedy *A Chaste Maid of Cheapside*, plus ten more plays by the Great Bard himself.

Over the years I have seen London from many vantage points, and I must confess that the relationship is like a true love affair—every day something new—though not all the changes are great ones. And there are some changes that I haven't liked much at all because there is about London, as about most things, the good, the bad and the some-things-in-between. What follows is meant as a bit of a guide, though a whimsical, certainly unscientific one, of what I have discovered of those good, bad and in-betweens of London.

The really good part of London is its people, probably the most cosmopolitan in the world. The bad thing is that they really don't know it. Streets have good sides and not as good sides. The south side is the best side of Brompton Road and Knightsbridge where Harrods, Harvey Nichols and most of the good shops are located. The north side has lost the Scotch Shop, Past Times and a couple of other neat spots but has gained Burberry and has long had Jaeger. But it's still no contest. The east side of Regent Street is better than the west side—just check out the crowds from the impartiality of the upper deck of a double-decker bus—although the addition of Swarowski and FCUK (a brilliant marketing ploy, that four-letter logo) along with Burberry has made the west side a bit more attractive. And the north side of Oxford Street west of Oxford Circus is superior to the south. Harrods is better than Selfridges by far and Liberty is much underrated. The best CD store is the HMV *east* of Oxford Circus on Oxford Street, though the one to the west, near Selfridges, is pretty good. Tower Records at Piccadilly Circus is also good. There's a wonderful classics CD store at the back of the South Kensington tube station; it also carries some jazz, and what jazz it does carry, often under the Naxos label, can be a very pleasant surprise.

The best entertainment for the money (it only costs a tip if you feel like it) is at Covent Garden on Sunday where, for the price of a cappuccino or a sandwich, you can hear off-duty opera singers, string quartets and the like perform, often brilliantly. You can also hear some good buskers in various tube stations, especially Piccadilly Circus.

Loos are few and far between. Fortnum and Mason has one of the best. Those at Harrods are clean and comfortable, and they've finally given up the one-pound charge for the privilege. Selfridges has biffies like those in the pubs—good in an emergency but otherwise to be avoided. Good hotels are also a haven. But the public toilets are crummy and often require coins that you don't have.

The best bus tour can be had from the Big Bus Company. They have three different tours and pretty good guides, though I catch an average of three mistakes and one blooper each time I take a trip, but that's much better than the others! Even though we go to London so frequently, Wendy and I often take the tour just for the fun of it.

The most overrated tourist trap? Without doubt Madame Tusseauds Wax Museum where the figures look like real people all right—real, dead people who have been worked over by a mortician's apprentice. The one in Victoria, BC, is much better. Save your money. The same can be said for the London Dungeon and The Clink.

The most underrated tourist destination? The City of London Museum at the Barbican in "the city." Its collections go back before Roman times, and much of the museum is bordered by the London Wall itself. Incidentally, the lower part of the wall is Roman in origin, the top part Norman.

The best bookstore? Clearly Waterstones on Piccadilly has taken over from Foyles on Charing Cross as the largest, but Blackwell's on Charing Cross is pretty darned good, too. Hatchards on Piccadilly has a very good Churchill section. Waterstones branch store at Harrods is also worth a peek. But don't buy any new book until you have checked one of the four Bookthrift stores that usually have the blockbuster of the moment at four or five pounds off the list price. The best used books are nearby on Charing Cross Road near Cambridge Circus, and

I find Quinto and Pordes the best. A tip for used book buyers: look in places you wouldn't expect to find what you want. Often patrons put books back in the wrong place, and sometimes the bookseller has a different idea of what the subject is than you do. And don't overlook the open air book stalls in front of the National Theatre on the South Bank.

The best walk in London? From close to the Bayswater underground station starting at the northwest corner of Kensington Gardens, past the Round Pond, over to the Peter Pan statue by the Long Water, over to Hyde Park for tea and a bun at the Lido on the Serpentine (which is an extension of the Long Water), down to Hyde Park Corner through the Rose Garden, over to Green Park, down past the Canadian War Memorial dedicated in 1994 by the Queen (Wendy and I were there) to Buckingham Palace, then into the prettiest of them all, St. James's Park with its beautiful waters and birdlife, including pelicans descended from those who entertained the Stuarts. The second-best walk is probably a tie among a thousand possibilities, but a good bet would be a walk on Hampstead Heath with its wonderful views of the city on a fine day. And there you'll find, tucked away where the tourist maps seem to miss it, Kenwood, the stately home of the Iveagh/Guinness family, the Irish beer people, long a political force in Britain. The art, in particular the Dutch masters, will throw you for a loop because in any other country this house would be a top-notch art gallery. And speaking of galleries, the Courteauld at Somerset House on the Strand has a huge collection of French Impressionists and its Wallace Collection is a potpourri of truly great stuff—paintings, pottery, sculptures. The biggest surprise of walking London? The beautiful little squares that abound, my favourites being Grosvenor Square, Berkeley Square and St. James's Square, with an honourable mention to Soho Square.

The best cheap meal? It doesn't exist. Eating out in London is hugely expensive and you'll just have to get used to the idea. The biggest rip-off for food? This is a big topic, but I would put the Fountain Restaurant in Fortnum and Mason at the top. This is a place we always used to go to, but the price for a few cruddy pieces of unidentifiable and barely edible plant life make it obvious that Mr. Fortnum and Mr. Mason, when they meet every hour on the clock above the entrance, can barely control their laughter as they bow to one another. And for goodness' sake, don't order meat there! No one's wallet is big enough for that! There are lots of quick lunch places, but this city really needs a White Spot, Milestone's or Earl's very badly. The newest thing in food is the revival of the coffee house, once a mainstay of 18th-century life, now most often manifested in a Starbucks or other chain restaurant.

The best way to get around London? Clearly the underground. I have had taxis let me off by a tube station because the surface traffic was too heavy. The Piccadilly Line leaves Heathrow for downtown regularly, and the trip from the airport to Piccadilly Circus costs about $10 and takes 45 minutes. By cab it's more like $120. The double-decker bus, if you're in no hurry, is the best bang for the buck.

The cheapest place to stay in London? Try a bed and breakfast through the British Travel Centre at Number One Regent Street where British Columbia House used to be. Or rent a flat which, if you stay away from the centre of town, can be reasonable. There are no cheap places to stay in London.

The best bargains? With the present state of the Canadian dollar there are none. Best to just pretend every pound is like a dollar, have fun and save your anguish for when the credit card bills come in. There are some anomalies. Sometimes a very good English shoe is cheaper in London than in Vancouver, but that's an exception.

The truth is that London is an expensive old tart, but once she hooks you, you're hooked for life. I can't leave her without talking about what it is like to shop there with Wendy. At home we seldom shop together, our schedules being so different that it just doesn't work out. But when we're in London, we have one, often two, and sometimes three shopping days together. And I enjoy it. I've often thought I should write a book about the ladies' shops with the best "husbands' chairs." I would put Jaeger and Escada in a tie for first, with perhaps the nod going to Jaeger because, in addition to a comfy chair and something to read, they often serve the waiting husband a cup of fresh coffee.

Wendy is a much better shopper than I am. I'm an impulse buyer, the kind who sees something he likes and has an Amex card on the table before he knows if he really wants it. Wendy, on the other hand, likes to reconnoitre for a few days or even a week so that she gets the lay of the land. Thus, unlike me and my kind, she never finds she's blown her stash after the first day in London. I wouldn't want to leave the impression, however, that Wendy is only a better shopper because of her patience. Oh, no, there's much more to it than that. She knows what the hell she's doing and I don't. And she has the necessary nerve to pull it all off.

Most men are terrified shoppers. I, for example, will go into a fly fishing store without hesitation if I have something in mind I want to buy, however minor. And if I've bought a few bits of fly-tying stuff, I will feel quite okay about flexing a couple of rods or spinning the spools of a reel or two. But to walk in just to look around and flex a couple of rods or spin a couple of reels under the watchful eye of the proprietor? No can do. I can feel his penetrating eyes and can hear his brain asking, "Is this guy going to buy something or just kick tires?" Wendy, on the other hand, can press the bell on the door of one of those jewellery stores that are so expensive they lock themselves in, then boldly try on a necklace going for 15,000 quid or perhaps a ring for 50,000. Then implying, without actually saying so, that there is another ring at Mappin & Webb or Gerrards—much more expensive, of course—that she's also considering, she takes her leave. Of course, she'll probably be back. (Yeah, right!) And the clerk seems delighted that my wife, who couldn't afford a single item in the joint, has deigned to honour the store with her presence.

What always bothers me when we're in the early tire-kicking stage of our London trip is how to try all those things on and make an empty-handed but gracious retreat. I'm a sucker of the kind P.T. Barnum could only dream about. It's as if I have broken the law or at least some sacred custom of the trade when I don't buy *something*! I just don't have the verbal grease that could take me from chatting happily with the clerk about his wonderful jackets to walking out the door empty-handed. When I want to disengage, I'm struck dumb! I can't admit I can't afford it. After all, why would I be there if I couldn't?

For Wendy, who's escaped all those bolted-up jewellery stores with ease and aplomb, it's no problem. "It does look so nice but I was looking for more of a greeny turquoise than a bluey one to match my skirt at home." (The clerk nods knowingly). "You know, this is about the loveliest skirt I've seen but. . .I don't know what it is. . .but it feels just a teeny bit tight at the waist." (The clerk completely understands.) At the end of perhaps an hour of this, Wendy leaves empty-handed with the clerk acting as if she's made her day!

I don't want to leave the impression that neither Wendy nor I buy many clothes in London. As the customs person at YVR can readily attest, our return would be a call for a corporate dividend if customs duties were a private affair. It's just that while Wendy and I both have a good eye for quality, Wendy has the ability (I think it's inherent in women) to be patient until her personal demand and supply curves meet, with the right price going for just the right item. It's an art, often possessed by woman, seldom possessed by man. At least, that's the way it works at our house.

# 17

## Tribute to a Dying Friend

T HERE IS, SAYS ECCLESIASTES, A TIME FOR EVERYTHING, and though
that's so painfully obvious as we get older, it's no easier to bear
on that account. Right now I have a sick and dying friend for whom I
am grieving. This old friend isn't a relative or a spouse. In fact, it's not
a person at all. And no, thank you for asking, but it isn't our chocolate
Lab Chauncey who is in fine fettle indeed. No, my old friend is a river.

The Tauranga-Taupo—affectionately called the TT locally—is the
third of four great fishing streams as you proceed south from Taupo
to Turangi along the shores of Lake Taupo, New Zealand's largest lake.
These streams are very different from one another. The first is the
Waitenahui, a sandy river perhaps most famous for the shoulder-to-
shoulder lineup of fishermen at its mouth, a phenomenon known as
the "picket fence." I have fished this river and been part of that picket
fence and enjoyed it immensely. The next is the Hinemaiai or the
Hatepe, which is a smallish stream, but has given me much piscatorial pleasure over the years, both along its bank and at its mouth. The
third is the mighty Tongariro, made so justly famous by Zane Grey 80
years ago. I haven't fished this river for awhile because it is hard for my
squash-battered knees to wade, but I remember some very fine days
on it in years past.

But it is the TT that I semi-eulogize here for it has become, far and
away, the river of my choice. This gem is bigger than the Waitanahui

and the Hinemaiai but considerably smaller than the Tongariro. Unlike
the other three, it can usually be fished the whole way up without the
necessity of making hikes ashore. Its colour, a deep green turquoise,
also sets it apart. It lies, in its lower regions, in a meadow filled with
willows, pines and Australian eucalyptus, its banks bordered with the
New Zealand pampas grass called Toe-Toe. As you move upstream,
you get into the almost spooky containment provided by high cliffs
where the echoes of the songbirds bounce back and forth into your
ears from all angles.

I first came to the TT about 20-odd years ago, brought there by
my guide and friend, Keith Wood. He got me right down to business
by walking me about three miles upstream to the Ranger's Pool, so
named because you can't fish above this pool in winter when the fish
are spawning. The pool itself is shaped like a buttonhook, and right
by the "eye" another small stream intersects. At this point even the
rankest of angling amateurs would know fish congregate to pick up
the goodies this little stream carries into the bigger one. Under Keith's
watchful eye, I cast into this spot, and in three or four casts was into a
beauty. The fish wasn't the only thing hooked by the experience. We
went no further that day, but Keith told me of the wondrous water
above and encouraged me to investigate. I did that for more than 20
years.

Since none of the pools above the Ranger's had names, I called
the one above the Ranger's the Cathedral Pool, and I'm glad to say the
name stuck. It's an eerie place with the cliffs rising a couple of hundred
feet or more on either side, and it's a spooky place to fish, but it always
holds fish and it's always a huge challenge to catch 'em. Above this is
a long stretch of fairly fast-moving water where a dry fly would often
pick off a fish. But these are also spawning grounds, and one must be
careful not to tromp on the *redds*, as they are called, which appear as
bleached stretches on the gravel bottom. Then comes a deep, fairly
swift trench that I dubbed "Rafe's Run" because I always did well there,
but that name did not stick. Above that, and past some fast water that
has often proved profitable for a quick cast or two as it was being ne-
gotiated, is a second cathedral-type pool where the combination of
challenges posed by fast water meeting slow then becoming fast again
always made it an interesting and often productive run. I know there

were more good pools and runs upriver, but I never went more than a half-mile further.

The TT holds wonderful memories for me: the time I broke my brand new Hardy's split cane while trying to extricate my line from the blackberries while playing a fish; the time I saw six trout, three by three, in Rafe's Run and managed to hook and land five of them; the eight-pound rainbow from the same run; the immense brown I lost in the upper Cathedral Pool. But my fondest memories are of introducing Wendy to the upper TT and seeing her catch her share of fish the only way that's possible—by persistent hard work.

But four years ago, a huge flood threw the middle part of the river completely offcourse, leaving a mile or more of what had been excellent pools just boulders and snags. For the first year after that, my fishing was unaffected, save that it was now a much harder walk to the upper pools as the flood had taken the old trails with it. Then a lesser flood struck, making the walk to the pools I loved a very difficult task, especially as my knees, bombarded by age and playing kamikaze squash for all those years, began to deteriorate. One trip up was all I could now handle. Still, the memories of that one trip would carry me through to the next year. And besides, we had discovered some lower pools below the flood damage that could provide some wonderful dry fly fishing with patterns to match the huge cicada beetles that often fall into the river. (Cicadas are poor flyers and even worse swimmers.)

Then came February 2003. Wendy and I were leading a tour of New Zealand that would leave us three days at the end all to ourselves at Turangi, just time enough to visit our beloved TT. Like an idiot, I had not e-mailed to ask our friends Pete and Stella Gordon, who own the big Caltex station on the nearby highway with its fishing store and tea room, about the river. We arrived there unannounced to find that the upper TT was now all but inaccessible. Bulldozers had been working our favourite lower reaches in preparation for redirecting the flood-created parts of the river back to the main riverbed. The pools were a mess. We tried it for an afternoon, each catching a tiddler, but it was obvious that there were no good pools left to hold fish.

The local Maori landowners along with other interested parties have now undertaken, with their own cash entirely, to rehabilitate the river and restore the access to the upper reaches, but they are opposed at every turn by the Department of Conservation which, though unwilling to do a thing itself, doesn't want to be shown up by the citizenry. Sound familiar? So there she lies, battered and broken. My candidate for the most beautiful stream in the world, the repository of an inordinate number of fishing memories for Wendy and me, is no longer and may never be again. To make matters worse, there are plans for a huge hotel near the mouth, meaning that the rich, sporting their brand new, never-been-tried Orvis clothes and equipment, will be all over our river, stomping on what redds still exist and making this faraway gem just another place for people to bugger up.

Miracles can happen, of course. Kiwis are resourceful and stubborn people. Maybe Pete and Stella, the Maoris and the other interested parties can put Humpty Dumpty together again. Maybe by next year....In the meantime a very old friend is very sick indeed and this old pal weeps but doesn't really care to visit. He'd rather live with the memories than sit by the deathbed and weep.

# 18

## Some Latter-Day Thoughts on Fishing

I T WAS MAY 1995, AND I WAS OFF to the Arundell Arms to meet Anne Voss Bark and her husband, Conrad Voss Bark, for many years the fishing writer for *The London Times*. Coming from British Columbia, I'd caught plenty of Pacific salmon, but until the bloody fish farmers arrived with their ever-escaping Atlantics, I'd thought very little about their wild Atlantic cousin, *salmo salar*. This was to be my first chance to catch a wild one.

My charming hostess sent me down to the fishing centre to meet the famed David Pilkington who was to be my ghillie. "I have a problem, David," I said. "As you can guess from my cane, I can barely walk." Indeed, a reactivated squash injury had me barely hobbling. "Well, Rafe," said David, "the only salmon I know in the river [the Lyd] is in an easily accessible pool nearby and, though it's a hell of a long shot, let's pass a fly through a few times from shore and see what happens."

It was a beautiful pool indeed, and from the top I worked a wet through the pool for about half an hour. "Bad luck," said my host. "Let's take you for a spot of trout fishing from a boat." I turned to my ghillie. "David, let me have ten more throws."

Ten, nine, eight, seven, six, five, four, three, two, BAM! On the very last cast she was well hooked and, if I may say so, well played, then expertly netted and released by David. Spot-on ten pounds on my last cast, my first Atlantic!

The postscript to this story is that, when I went back to the hotel with my tale of derring-do, no one would believe me because I had not killed the fish! I'm told that catch-and-release has caught on a bit since then!

I have always loved to fish. My mother's scrapbook contained a picture of me taken, when I was about four or five years old, at Grantham's Landing on the Sunshine Coast, sitting on the wharf fishing for shiners. By the time I was about 10 I had learned to convert them into rock cod bait. I would keep the shiners in a pail of water, then impale one on a large hook, lower it until the sinker hit the bottom, bring it up a few feet so that the shiner was in a tantalizing place for the prowling cod, then wait for that wonderful tug. I fished with my mom and dad for salmon and grew up to be a fair fly fisherman and fly tier—certainly an enthusiastic one. Several flies I have designed have proven effective enough for friends to ask for some of their own. I have designed a fly for sea-run cutthroat trout and one for New Zealand trout, both dry flies, which are very effective indeed.

But now I am faced with the argument that fishing is cruel. When I was a child, I did wince a little when I hooked up my shiner bait for cod, but it was never enough for me to pause and think out all the ramifications. As I grew older, I began to dislike hitting fish on the head. I still did it, but I was a pretty easy convert to the catch-and-release ethic. As the late and truly great fishing guru Lee Wulff said, "A fish is too valuable to be caught just once."

Then as the years passed, I began to wonder at the ethics of it all. I fished not because I needed or even wanted food—I don't eat fish—but in order to fool them. This process, even with catch-and-release, required that I torment—if not actually torture—my quarry. I did a lot of rationalizing, some of it not all that bad. If I and others like me, very much including commercial fishermen, didn't care about the wild fish, especially salmonids, who would? Wasn't the user of the resource its best conserver?

But the thoughts lingered and made it to the surface more often. I began to remember fish caught not for the thrill of the strike but for the release. Who the hell was I, it occurred to me as I eased my defeated foe back into the water, to put one of God's creatures through so much misery just for my own pleasure? Yet, on the other hand, what about all the wonderful people who had been absorbed by my hobby and had written so brilliantly about it—not just the fishing, but the whole experience of communing with nature. So many of them were parsons, too. If men of God could fish, free of stricken consciences, who was I to care? I thought about Izaak Walton and his masterpiece, *The Compleat Angler*, that great work about 17th-century England spun in a web that catches all of the outdoors, not just fishing. Could men like him and our own great literary contributor on the subject, Roderick Haig-Brown, be so enamoured of fishing and where it was done to have missed the ethical arguments? Surely they must have had misgivings. I can't be alone! Can I?

Now I must tell you, in my own feeble defence, that size hasn't mattered all that much to me since I was a young man (we're talking fish here!). Well before middle age I had begun to question the idea that marlin and their ilk were proper objects of piscatorial pursuit. With that kind of fishing, there was no looking into the water and trying to discern what insect might be hatching or be about to, and matching it with the appropriate fly. Marlin fishing was strictly a matter of looking for these monstrous fish, trolling a teaser past their bills and hoping for the strike. If you were lucky, you were in for an hour of hard labour. If you were unlucky, you had to sit quietly sipping a beer while your mate—or even worse, the stranger who shared the cost of the boat with you—played the monster on tackle geared to a very high success ratio. After all, if the skipper could sail back with all the right victory flags on his mast, he would enhance his reputation. No, I don't even want to go after the big Tyee, though I've done it in the past, preferring instead to chase smaller fish with the fly. But what right do I have to question the ethics of a sport fisherman who likes large quarry? How can I possibly sniff that somehow I'm ethical because I spend a lot of time looking at insects and trying to replicate them on hooks and turn up my nose at someone who simply wants to imitate the bigger prey of the larger targeted fish? It is irrational and I admit it. Yes, I'm getting less and less comfortable with what I try to do to a dumb animal who offers me no threat and would be happy to simply mind his own business if I would do likewise.

Still I like it! I look forward to drifting my own cicada pattern past the nose of a feeding trout in my favourite New Zealand river. I get a special thrill out of the excited waiting that accompanies fishing that wonderful lake of very big trout called Otamangakau near Turangi on the North Island. After I've had my first vicious strike and experienced the seemingly endless screeching of the reel that comes with a hook-up on that water, it's as hard to give up fishing as it is to give up drinking good single malt Scotch whisky. I still get that feeling of inner excitement as my pal Don and I toss dry flies after sea-run cutthroats on the beaches near the same Grantham's Landing where the fishing bug first bit me. And there's the Skagit, that graceful little mountain fly water that I had a hand in saving from the ravages of a downstream dam when I was in politics. How could I give up the pleasure of watching Wendy badly out-fish me on our Skagit? And, dammit, I have a hell of a lot of money tied up in fishing equipment! I must have a dozen or more graphite fly rods and a good working cane rod. Surely I must have the same number of reels, all murderously expensive. And what about my fly-tying hobby?

I need help. Though I'm beginning to see the need to forswear fishing, I just don't know if....Maybe the answer is in St. Augustine who, you will remember, asked God to give him all the requisite virtues such as chastity and the like but concluded his prayer with, "But not yet, Lord, not just yet." So, there's my answer. I pledge to quit trying to deceive fish then tormenting them, but not quite yet.

# 19

## A Consuming Passion

I HAVE THREE PERSONAL PROBLEMS that have caused me hell all my life. No, it's not a penchant for a life of crime. If nothing else, I am deterred by the thought of jail. My problems are that I am a type 2 diabetic, I don't understand the word "moderation" and everything I like to eat is bad for me.

There is scarcely a diet book I haven't read. I have interviewed dieticians and nutritionists by the score and have not heard from any of them the recipe for a lunch or dinner I would even make myself eat. Moreover, they piss me off from the start by saying something like, "A little turnip with some squash and vegetable marrow alongside a couple of slices of nice roast pork makes a lovely meal!" Lovely? I nearly threw up my lunch writing those words. Those ingredients may indeed be lovely for someone, but they sure as hell aren't for me. Can't I have carrots? Way too high in sugar! How about some lovely corn? Just as bad. Try some parsnips, peppers or zucchini instead. Urp! Just about tossed my cookies again.

Well then, Rafe, how about a lovely piece of cod or halibut? I hate fish, all fish, with one exception: a freshly caught trout at breakfast, fried in flour and butter. But you may have observed, no doubt, that it's not the way the dieticians of the world would have you cook it! So, with that one exception, I don't even like to eat my lifelong quarries, salmon and trout. Most of all, I can't even get canned fish on the fork without wanting to urp. I'd rather swallow live goldfish. I am very fond of shellfish since my boyhood days at Woodlands when it was my job to man the crab trap by baiting it, sorting out the undersized and the males from females, then throwing the keepers screaming into boiling water. I love oysters, clams, shrimp, mussels and the like.

Well, Rafe, they are not great choices but perhaps a little in moderation....What the hell is this moderation bit, anyway? When my dad and I went cruising on his boat, I had to dig the clams. I remember coming back with a pail of clams whereupon he would ask, "Aren't you going to have any?" Right. Back for a second pail. The Vancouver Club used to put on a marvellous buffet on Thursday nights that always had the freshest of shrimp, crab and oysters on the half shell. Faced with that, how could I not fill my plate past brimming, douse the shrimp and crab with thousand island dressing and flail away, only pausing to take a bite out of a passing bun smothered in butter. I mean, what's wrong with that?

As a diabetic, desserts are *verboten*. I remember when, after being diagnosed, I was dispatched to the diabetic clinic in the local hospital where I was treated as if I were at my first day of kindergarten, and I half-expected to have to sing the diabetic's version of "This is the way we brush our teeth, brush our teeth...." The ending seemed pretty good, though, because I was shown all the diabetic desserts I could have, including ice cream bars, for heaven's sake! I love ice cream! Then I learned that all these goodies were sweetened with aspartame, which I consider to be poisonous. In fact, I discovered later that if I drank diet Cokes sweetened with aspartame, my blood sugar soared.

What about fruit, I asked? No problem. A small slice of melon or papaya, perhaps ten or twelve grapes, a small dish of blueberries smothered in skim milk all make lovely desserts. You have to be joking! Ten or twelve grapes? What ever happened to grapes by the bunch and a big kitchen dish full of delicious blueberries smothered in sour cream? And doesn't everyone eat a whole papaya? And skim milk! What about having a couple of servings of cereal at breakfast, say that lovely crunchy muesli I love so much? Full of sugar, Rafe. Even bran flakes with lots of lovely raisins? The raisins will get you, although if you just have half a bowl with perhaps six or eight raisins, maybe you'll be okay. This to a guy who used to take his raisin bran cereal over to the raisin bowl and dump in a couple of additional handfuls.

Then there's booze. I am not a heavy drinker, at least I haven't been for years. But bloody hell, I don't want just a glass of beer or a small glass of wine, preferably white. Whatever happened to that nice picnic with sandwiches and a bottle of good wine shared between two? (With perhaps a second having to be opened when the picnic ran overtime?) Moderation, Rafe, moderation.

So what the devil does a guy do if he's diabetic, fussy as hell and doesn't know the meaning of the word "moderation"? And no, dammit, don't tell me about that lovely tofu dish swimming in a sea of rice. If I'd been born Chinese I would have starved to death as soon as I was weaned because of all the loathsome things they eat. With the exception of kidneys and any form of tripe, for me rice tops the list of horrid foods. So when the server in my favourite restaurant says to me, "Rafe, that's the sixth time in a row you've had chicken in a small Cæsar salad," I say shut up and serve. It may look tiresome, but it's the only thing in the bloody world, it seems, that I like and am actually permitted to eat. In moderation, of course.

# 20

## The Computer Age

BACK IN 1982 I MADE THE BIG PLUNGE. I got a computer, a Xerox, and I haven't the faintest idea what model number or stuff like that. It was black and white and used enormous floppy discs that had to be "initialized" before they would work. In preparation for this undertaking, I took a course at a barge down at Granville Island where I learned to play some of the rudimentary games that were becoming the vogue in that far-off time. This was supposed to make me understand. It didn't. I had a lot of problems. A very nice lady named Judy, from the outfit where I had bought the computer, came to my house on several occasions and was always available on the phone for me. But I struggled. I was always permanently erasing an editorial (this was in the days before the automatic "Save" function) and somehow getting myself into that fatal computer "Lock" from which there was no safe escape. I was frustrated and rather ashamed of myself, but I soldiered on because, with all the writing I do, the editing capabilities of that computer put it far, far ahead of my old typewriter. Then came Windows with its icons, mouse and multiplicity of features. And I was hopeless again. It took me at least twice as long to understand this new process as it did the colleagues around me. And I couldn't understand why.

The arrival of the Internet was the last straw. I simply could not work my way through all the incomprehensible icons and instructions. I remain convinced that the "Help" mode is not only the last place one should ever go for help but that it started out written in English, was then translated into Japanese by a Japanese person with a very limited knowledge of the English language, then retranslated back into English by a person whose Japanese was limited to the words necessary for locating a loo in Tokyo. I remember once accidentally clicking on "100 copies" when I went to print out an editorial instead of one then trying to find out how to stop the thing printing them all. I looked up everything under "Help" that I could find, to no avail. After shutting off the machine and enlisting all the other defences I could think of, I finally accepted my fate and threw 99 editorials out. Happily, getting on the Internet has now been simplified so much that even I can do it, and I've even learned how to stop the printer!

The other new tools of communication I can never understand are cordless phones, cell phones and television "clickers." I had a cell phone for three years without ever using it because I got all buggered up with my recorded phone numbers. Moreover, as with all these machines—from photocopiers through TV sets to computers—I became convinced I was being "nuked." (As the evidence pours in, it turns out I may not have been so wrong!) With my TV clicker I can never seem to avoid hitting buttons that utterly destroy my ability to get programs. I am constantly on the phone to Shaw Cable so they can tell me the right buttons to click to get the picture back and, over the phone, they patiently walk me through the process one more time.

Why, oh why, am I so incompetent? I asked myself. And that is when I invited the now famous David Chalk to appear on my show because I needed someone who could explain computers to my audience in terms I could understand. My theory was that, since I was the one person on earth to whom these matters could not be explained, getting me to understand would guarantee everyone else understood as well. The light went on when I asked David Chalk to explain to me what *digital* meant. Instead of explaining, he gave me a book that he said was really "Digital for Dummies." This is a famous book written by a man with a long Italian name that could be Negromonte, which means black mountain, which is exactly where I belong. But I can be forgiven for forgetting since I could not understand the very first line of the book. The first line! I was at sea before the explanations even started!

And here was the answer. My mind simply does not work along the lines that understanding computers requires. For example, to me the word *default* means something bad; it does not mean the regular setting. When I learn how to use a program, I haven't the faintest idea why I am making the moves I am; I'm simply learning by rote. My wife, Wendy, on the other hand, understands why certain things are clicked and what happens if you hit the wrong things. This is especially irksome since for three whole years she refused to use her new computer, so frightened was she of it. Here was I, haughtily critical because she wouldn't use her computer while I was humming away on mine, but as soon as she overcame inertia she was instantly my superior by a mile.

My problem is compounded by the fact that all these computerized devices give me far, far more than I want or require. I don't want all the fancy menu stuff the TV clicker gives me. I only watch TV for the BBC World Service News or to see Tiger when he's playing in a major. I don't want a bank of recorded phone numbers in my cell phone because there aren't a bank of people I care enough about to phone. And I don't need probably 75 percent of what my computer programs offer and this is a very good thing because, if I did want all these things, there's no way in the world I could access them. I have resigned myself to my fate. My science is political science and my clicker is the *Sunday London Times, The Economist* and whatever paper carries the comic strip "Luann." By all means teach me what to do but don't ever ask why what I did just worked!

But now that I've discovered the Internet and e-mail and learned how even I can work them, I can't believe I ever managed to work in broadcasting when such tools to locate information and communicate with others weren't available. The learning curve from society as I knew it and what I now know is immense. But this is all my little brain can deal with. If I ever broke through the barrier and learned why things work, I would probably be like the centipede who one day started wondering just exactly how all his legs worked and fell on his ass.

There are, of course, downsides to the Internet and e-mail. You see, I grew up in a time when you spoke of getting a loan only in the private confines of your three-piece-suited banker's office and when you got your sexual jollies looking at ladies' undergarment ads in your mother's magazines. There was always *Sunshine Magazine* for nudists and pictures of nubile, nude black ladies in *National Geographic*. Somehow we got by, though it was pretty tame stuff. But considering what now comes onto my computer screen every day I wonder how.

I average about 50 e-mails a day on my home computer (it's often in the hundreds at the radio station) of which perhaps 10 are expected. I suppose I should admit that some I don't expect I should, since I can scarcely blame all the book companies in the world for thinking of me as a sucker for their wares. I am, however, taken to be a man who badly needs a loan. Not only that, they think so much of me that it can be at as low as five percent with no questions asked and no security, and it can be a done deal in five minutes. And it's incredible how much these people think of the small condo Wendy and I live in because there's no end of mortgage money available, sight unseen. My loss of hair troubles a lot of these good folks because every day a nice lady, usually with enormous jugs, is looking at my hairline and longing for the days when I wasn't losing 100 hairs a day. Not this lady, but another just as kind, is very concerned about the size of my willie and is cocksure (oops!) that it needs another two inches. No exercises required (that shattered my hopeful thoughts, I'll tell you!)—just some pills. Interesting that they should know my requirements with such precision. Trouble is I've reached the stage in life where I take so many pills that a full meal of its own has to be set aside for the daily ceremony. Several ladies, in fact, are evidently worried about my penile "shortcomings," which makes me believe that somehow they must be sharing this information that, fortunately, was hitherto unknown to all but a few other women of my old acquaintance.

But it's my sex life that seems to keep most of these online visitors most interested. Not content to bombard me with new and better varieties of Viagra, they put moving ads before my aging eyes that portray all manner of provocative sexual postures. And, it seems, they know I'm not gay for the only homosexual behaviour they vouchsafe unto me is of the lesbian variety. But that, I have assumed, is the only limitation on how they evaluate my interests. One of these billets-doux features moving oral sex which, as one is wading through mortgage ads, hair-loss treatments and new books, does catch the eye.

In fact, the come-ons (the perfect word I should think in this context) put what I had hitherto considered hard-core porn in the same category as the ads in the *Ladies Home Journal*. I am told—though, of course, I don't know this for a fact—that if you proceed past the come-on into the "free" area, the fact of your continued curiosity (though it may be purely in the interests of science) is known to the message's source through one of the sophisticated scanning techniques available these days. This means even more great stuff will be on its way.

In any event, one has to admit that e-mail beats newspaper inserts (Ye gods! I'm even frightened to use that word in this context) or free flyers in your post office box. But I have one question for all of these people bent on improving my sex life: WHERE THE HELL WERE ALL OF YOU 40 YEARS AGO WHEN I COULD HAVE USED YOU?

# 21

## *The Passing of Sport as We Knew It*

SPORTS HAVE ALWAYS PLAYED A PART in my life. I have no doubt that I would have been a superb hockey player but for an accident—that being that I grew up in Vancouver and never learned to skate. But for many years and until quite recently, in fact, I've always been a fan of professional teams and of the game I loved to play and became pretty proficient at: golf. This enthusiasm was by no means entirely youthful. Into middle age I lived and died with the Canadiens, and this from a man who couldn't even skate. But I've found over the years that I've become less and less interested in professional team sports. And given my enthusiasm in the past for the Brooklyn, now Los Angeles, Dodgers and the Montreal Canadiens, this is some transformation.

What's happened? I think a lot of things. When I was a real fan, there was meaning beyond just the sport in an attachment to a team. I loved the Canadiens as much because I despised the Toronto Maple Leafs as anything else, even though I was 35 before I ever saw either of them play, except on television. And why did I hate the Leafs (which, if Conn Smythe, their founder, knew anything about grammar, would be the "Leaves")? I hated them because they stood for a Canada I despised. When I started following hockey in the pre-television days, Toronto's management would not even permit a French Canadian player on the team's roster. Conn Smythe once addressed an audience with "Ladies and gentlemen and Frenchmen…" And Foster Hewitt, that WASP version of a broadcasting saint, was a raw bigot. The great rivalry between the Leafs and Canadiens (which the Canadiens won hands down) was as much between races as cities and teams.

When it came to baseball, I cheered for the Dodgers because of Jackie Robinson, the first Black to play in modern organized ball. Since one of the very last teams to employ a Black was the Yankees and since in those days the Dodgers and Yanks regularly met in the World Series, there was no doubt for whom this liberal would be cheering.

What also happened is that the great baseball player Curt Flood challenged baseball's "reserve clause," which bound a player to his team for life unless, that is, the team, with or without his blessing, traded him to another team. Flood, who started what Dodger pitcher Andy Messersmith successfully finished, received dick-all for being the pioneer. But while I was for the players and their fight to break their shackles, their success meant the end of team adulation for me. It was quite impossible for me to maintain loyalty to a team whose players showed no loyalty to their organization, and it was even harder to build up the necessary hatred for opposing teams. The players' new freedom meant, of course, obscene amounts of money, but that part of it never bothered me greatly. With huge TV revenues, someone had to get the money, and why not the players? At least they should get a big share. On that subject, I think there is room for much improvement, including gate and TV equalization, but that's for another day.

I don't know who plays for whom any more. Before league expansion, I suppose I could have kept abreast, but I can't keep track of 23 teams, who they are, where they play and who's on the team. In the last few years we have seen two expansion teams win the World Series, but who can relate to a bunch of guys called the Marlins or the Diamond Backs, if those are even their names? I can't remember! And while it's true that you can hate the Yankees on a regular basis, it's not because of their intolerance but only because of their bottomless pit of money that enables them to buy the players they need each year.

Nowadays when I catch a line score showing that the Canadiens have beaten the Leafs (we'd settle for a tie these days), I get a bit of a buzz but nothing like the old days. I remember back in 1967 watching the Leafs beat Montreal for the Cup and feeling humiliated. I knew that everyone in Maple Leaf Gardens and on the subway home was laughing at me! Now if I see the Dodgers have done something good (rare since 1988) or the Yankees have fallen on their faces, I smile a little. But it's not the same, not by a long shot.

It's different with individual sports. I used to play squash, and sometimes found myself on the court with federal minister Marc Lalonde, who was a much better player than I am. He played the classic, well-positioned game while I played what my squash pro son-in-law calls kamikaze squash. One afternoon I was getting beaten at every turn, and Lalonde was one of those who loved to gloat. After I hit a bad shot, he said, "You fool!" as he put it away. A few minutes later the same thing happened and he sneered, "So sorry, old boy!" In the next exchange I took the ball in the back court and there was Lalonde standing right in front of me on the T, as it is called. I could have called "Let," meaning that the point would be played over, or I could have "boasted" my shot off the side wall. Instead, I hit Lalonde in the ass. As I did so, I said, "So sorry, old boy!" A squash ball going full-tilt can sting like hell and it leaves a nasty little bruise. Somehow we never got together for squash after that.

I also used to played competitive golf, and though for reasons I will explain I don't play any more, I still love the game. (They called it golf, so it's said, because all the other good four-letter words were used up.) It is an addiction every bit as tough to beat as cocaine, tobacco or booze. It manages, once it's hooked you, to suppress all common sense and sense of responsibility. It cost me a year at university and would have cost me a marriage had my wife not been a saint and ultimately become hooked by the game herself!

I took up golf a little later than my pals. My first game was at the Langara Golf Club in Vancouver when I was 16 with my late cousin, Hugh Bardon. I shot 136, though I'm not sure I counted all the whiffs! I had caddied at Point Grey Golf Club and the old Quilchena Golf Club as a youngster but, perhaps because my dad was urging me to do so, I had shied away from playing, just to be bloody-minded. But after that day at Langara, I was hooked—really hooked. Inside of a few weeks I was scoring regularly in the nineties and soon got it into the eighties. Then I got a junior membership at Quilchena and took a couple of lessons from Ernie Brown, one of the great characters of Vancouver golf.

One day, having never broken 80, I surprised myself and my playing partner, Dorothy Silcock, by shooting 74! Mrs. Silcock was a very fine player who took a great interest in young golfers, so it was only a few weeks later that I shot a 68 and got my name in the paper for it!

Lamentably, this great promise didn't continue. I became a pretty fair 0-5 handicapper, but I had an unfortunate temperament for the game. In short I got mad as hell when things didn't turn out as desired, and that happens a hell of a lot in golf. I was, and I'm ashamed to admit it, a club thrower and even on occasion a club breaker. I wasn't world-class at that, though damned near. The record I think belonged to a young junior with me when I joined Marine Drive who bought a new set of Walter Hagen irons and, in the course of his first round with them, broke every one. He later became a pro! I was in good company, of course. The great Bobby Jones had been a club thrower as had "Terrible" Tommy Bolt. Jones got over his habit and went on to greatness. Bolt never did, though he won a US Open. I played with Tommy years later in a Pro-Am at Royal Victoria (Oak Bay) in Victoria, BC, and he admitted to me that his career had been badly impaired by his inability to keep his cool.

In my thirties I went on to become a better golfer with usually a two or three handicap, going down to scratch for a brief period. I had an undistinguished tournament record, winning one club championship and coming second (eagling the last hole to do it) in a major local tournament. However, the real point of this story is to talk about the game that made me decide to quit.

Now this wasn't my last game, but it was the one that told me I should find another hobby. At the time I represented Kamloops in the BC legislature and was, in fact, the minister of health. I was past 40 by this time and was beginning to see my long game getting not quite so long anymore. And I was having trouble getting short putts into the hole. On this day I was playing the old Kamloops course. I was like a kid again and hit 16 of the 18 greens in par figures and got into no trouble on the other two, but I three-putted so many greens that I was, to say the least, a very unhappy 79. Unhappy? I was livid. I stormed into the locker room and threw my shoes into my locker. Unfortunately, my aim with my shoes was no better than that with my putter, and one of them came back at me, spikes first, and hit me in the face. I stormed into the bar, face covered with bleeding spike wounds, to have a quiet beer and get my composure back. And there was this guy standing at the bar buying drinks for the house.

He had, you see, broken 80 for the first time. I stood there, bleeding from self-imposed facial wounds, mad as hell at shooting 79, and across the room from me was the happiest guy in the world because he had shot 79! There was something very wrong with this picture! I did play a few times thereafter. I still love the game and follow it closely, but basically my personal contact with golf ended that hot August afternoon when two people at the Kamloops Golf Club shot 79!

# 22
## Electoral Reform

IN THE SUMMER OF 1999, WHILE browsing in a Seattle used book-store, I came across a copy of *Miracle at Philadelphia*, by Catherine Drinker Bowen, which told the story of the famous constitutional conference that allowed the United States of America to become a nation, not merely a collection of jurisdictions. As I read it, what struck me was how these amazing men (and that collection of genius gathered there under the chairmanship of George Washington was truly amazing when you consider that Thomas Jefferson, who had authored the *Declaration of Independence*, was absent in France at the time) actually made the process work. And it worked because the representatives of the state of Virginia brought with them a sample constitution that their House of Burgesses had approved. This document acted as a working paper against which comparisons and contrasts could be made. When I finished reading this highly readable account of the legal formation of the United States, I once again pondered the situation on our side of the international border. There seemed to be no prospect for reform of the Canadian Constitution. Thanks to the Liberals in general and Prime Minister Chrétien in particular, our Constitution was in a state of extreme constipation. But why not, I asked myself, reform the way that things were done in BC?

My thoughts turned to my two allies of past constitutional battles, Gordon Gibson and Mel Smith, and they agreed that it was a sound idea. Next we recruited former MLA Nick Loenen, who had long urged electoral reform in BC, and to former MLA and cabinet minister Gary Lauk, who had shown a keen interest in constitutional issues when Trudeau was patriating the Constitution. This small group began fairly regular meetings in a boardroom kindly donated by CKNW.

In the beginning the group's members presented papers on what we thought should be done in various areas of governance in the hope that we could come up with a constitutional model, and this produced some very interesting work. It was not long, however, before we realized that we were really in danger of missing the whole point. We could never possibly agree on a model constitution among just ourselves; the decision on how the people of British Columbia should be governed would have to be made by the people of British Columbia themselves. Our task we set ourselves, then, was to recommend just how the necessary public process could be accomplished.

Upon one thing we were agreed: there must be an assembly and we felt that it should be elected. But how was it to be elected and how would it be driven? There were many alternatives. We could divide BC into regions with so many assembly members to be chosen from each region. But this would mean some pretty arbitrary decisions. Besides, when and how would these elections take place? Eventually we came to the view that, however imperfect, it made sense to have one delegate from each constituency, meaning 79 in all. But should they be elected at the time of a provincial election or in a separate election? Would such an election then become political? We felt confident that even if it did, electors would take matters seriously enough to select the best qualified persons. It was then our thought that since this group would need a lot of technical assistance, they might among themselves select another 21 "expert" persons, making 100 in all.

Our next recommendation was that a constitutional commissioner be appointed by the legislature to quarterback the process. It would be his or her job to bring this constituent assembly together, make suggestions and generally act as the driving force behind the process. He or she would be given a long term to do the job and report, of course, to the legislature, not the government.

The argument would be raised that this assembly would be too large and cumbersome. We discussed this at some length but decided that there was no recourse if anything meaningful were to happen, and if the constitutional recommendations of this body were to reflect the wishes of all people, regions and groups within the province and represent *all* the people of BC, not just its elites. Besides, in this electronic age there would be no need for all 100 to meet face to face in order to make decisions. Moreover, it would undoubtedly be necessary to break the assembly into a number of committees, and these smaller units could meet more frequently.

It would also be said that all of this would be expensive. The four of us who met face to face for these meetings—Mel was by this time too ill to attend but constantly made his presence and ideas known—all had legislative experience and knew that the cost of the actual meetings of the legislature are very small in comparison to the big picture, and we felt that many of the "expert members," apart from the normal stipend given to all members, would probably donate their expertise. We did feel, however, that all members of this assembly ought to be paid. But in the end, I think I can speak for my colleagues in saying that our key recommendation was the appointment of a commissioner.

On February 5, 2001, our Ad Hoc Committee for Constitutional Reform in BC released its report, and among the people who received a copy was the then-Opposition leader, Gordon Campbell. A month or so later Mr. Campbell, in contemplation of the forthcoming May election and after making a commitment at the Liberal Party convention, came on my show and recommitted his party to a public process to look at electoral reform. I was frankly astonished at this promise, and I must say candidly that I didn't believe he would follow through. He made it clear that he was inspired to do this because of our report and the talks he'd had with Nick Loenen before this, but also because of his strong personal conviction that change had to come. He told my audience that he had advised his caucus and party that he was going to put in place some reforms that might well make it difficult for him to govern in the traditional manner. His program, he said, would also include the idea of fixed election days.

As we all know, Mr. Campbell kept his promises, announcing as he took office that the next election would be four years after the one he had just won. Then in November 2002, he asked my friend and colleague Gordon Gibson to recommend how a Citizens Assembly should be convened and how they should function. The following April the government announced that it would set up such an assembly, and on May 8, 2003, former Simon Fraser University President Dr. Jack Blaney was appointed chairman. In my view this was an inspired choice, for Dr. Blaney is a man of impeccable reputation who could never do other than his best to carry out his mandate. He is also possessed of great people skills.

The assembly that was subsequently convened, though not in precisely the same terms we proposed, can be directly linked to our ad hoc committee, and I believe that my browsing through that Seattle bookstore and taking my find to Gordon Gibson is the reason that this baby was conceived. Continuing with that analogy, I think that the glint in the father's eye was the night when I spoke at the inauguration of the Mel Smith Foundation at Trinity Western University. In that speech I explained that even though the federal constitution was probably unchangeable due to the mess we had made in our amending formula, there was no reason we couldn't alter the way we did things in BC. I said that if we did grasp the nettle, we had the opportunity to lead the way in Canada. (That idea has turned out to be prescient, with at least four provinces now contemplating a process of electoral reform.) But I then pointed out that there was a caveat: we all have the bad habit of making "the perfect" the enemy of "the better." There is no perfect government or perfect election process.

My hope now is that the assembly understands that our present system cries out for reform and that they do make recommendations for exactly that. In the meantime, Gordon Campbell deserves credit for doing what most politicians shy away from: he has sown the seeds of reform that may well make it difficult for his party—or any other party, for that matter—to win a majority government in this province. What he has done is called statesmanship.

# 23

## Is That a Swan I Hear Singing?

IT'S THURSDAY, OCTOBER 23, 2003, and I have just been presented with the Bruce Hutchison Award for Lifetime Achievement at the Jack Webster Awards Dinner. This is indeed a great honour. I didn't know Bruce Hutchison, though I did meet him in the late 1970s when he was advising Premier Bill Bennett and his cabinet how to deal with the forthcoming referendum in Quebec. He was kind enough to sign and inscribe his book, *The Far Side of the Street* for me: "For Rafe Mair, with admiration for his fine service to the people of British Columbia, January 1979." This came at a time when British Columbia, largely through my mouth, was telling its side of the patriation of the Constitution story to constitutional conventions, premiers conferences and first ministers conferences, while the media, centrally controlled, brushed our efforts aside as being childish prattle from the "spoiled child" of Confederation. I couldn't even get the editorial boards of the *Vancouver Sun* and the *Province* to interview Premier Bill Bennett on the subject; they just weren't interested. British Columbia had put forth a well-researched and superbly documented presentation the year before that had been studiously ignored by all other premiers and especially ignored by the federal government and Prime Minister Pierre Trudeau. As we were to find out in September 1980, at the constitutional conference that in the minds of us preparing for it was going to be the modern equivalent of the Charlottetown of

1866, the entire strategy of the Trudeau government was to make the provinces look like squabbling children and Trudeau the kindly but ever-stern father who saved the day for the family. Mr. Hutchison, a lifelong Liberal, saw through this and knew what our government had been doing and of the sincerity of our efforts. His little note on the fly-leaf told me that those who knew, understood.

Another time I talked to Mr. Hutchison about writing a column. I had been doing a political bit for the Kamloops newspapers and had begun to be enamoured with my own scribblings. He looked at one of my columns and said, "Minister, every column ought to have a beginning, a middle and an end…and there should be at least a faint line connecting all three." Even I understood that this was not a compliment! I hope my professional efforts since have followed his advice!

Jack Webster, of course, I knew well. As a lawyer I had been a guest on his old radio show back in the 1960s, and then as a cabinet minister I had appeared many times on his TV show. It was he who got me started in radio (a story I have told elsewhere). Like everyone who listened to Jack Webster, I considered him an icon. He was simply the best. Fearless, fierce, obnoxious, well informed, yet gentle as a lamb under the surface, Jack was rightly loved and admired by all. I had greatly enjoyed the tussles we had on air and I particularly remember the one when, after the show I remarked to Tony Stark, my administrative assistant, "I thought I came out of that rather well, Tony. I even bested the old bastard on occasion." With the tact so useful for a senior bureaucrat (which he became), Tony said, "You won all the station breaks, Minister!" I thought about that. Tony was right. The "old bastard" had kicked the shit out of me on air and allowed me to get even when we were off air when it didn't count! Just before I was to start with CJOR, Jack took me to lunch in a Vancouver East café—where everybody, and I mean everybody, knew and loved him—and he gave me three bits of advice.

"First," he said, "even if you're interviewing your mother, have a scrap of paper with 'Mom' written on it because otherwise you'll forget her name." Splendid advice as I was to learn the hard way by having that cold sweat break out as I tried like hell to remember the name of the person I was talking to. I learned that my mind could even draw a blank when it was someone important, like a premier, sitting across from me! "And be yerself, ye dumb bugger! Don't try to imitate Pat Burns or me or anyone else." Again good advice, especially as I had yet to find my "air feet." The temptation to imitate is almost overwhelming in the beginning, but I like to think that I generally followed his advice.

The third thing he had to say was not so much advice as a statement of fact. "Now we're enemies," he growled. He meant it and I understood. Jack didn't get to where he was by bowing sweetly as his opposition swept by. He was a slugger and a competitor from his head to his toes. As I proceeded into my new career, I got some ad hoc TV work but, until almost the very end of Jack's career, I never got work with BCTV where he plied his trade. This might sound a bit ungenerous, even chippy on his part, but it wasn't. It was the way of the business. Jack knew that the old baseball manager, Lou Durocher, was right when he said that nice guys finish last. Jack was a nice guy, make no mistake about that, but not when he was competing. By the early nineties when Jack had all but retired, we did a number of gigs together, such as covering the 1991 Social Credit Party leadership convention and the 1991 election. These times were a great honour and a treat but, meaning no disrespect, he taught me on those occasions that you didn't have to know a hell of a lot about your subject if you were an entertainer—and Jack often didn't because he was.

But recalling the Jack Webster Dinner and the Bruce Hutchison Award for Lifetime Achievement has given me pause for considerable thought. Some nice things have been said about me. Denny Boyd, one of the finest columnists of our time, has been kind enough to say that I proved to be better than Pat Burns and the great Jack Webster. I can only say that such comparisons are unfair. All one can ever hope to be is the best of one's own time, and Jack was that in his. That I am the best of mine I immodestly agree. But where does this leave me?

First, I'm a bit concerned about the "Lifetime" bit in that award's title. I'm in the second year of a three-year contract as I write this, and I intend to be around to discuss terms of a renewal when the time comes. But I have to be reasonable. I am, as I say, even par: 72. I believe I have the health and the mental discipline to carry on indefinitely but they all say that. The day comes when you're just not hitting .350 anymore and it's time to hang 'em up. So with the caveat that I may, in time to come, delete this message and write another much different one, let me play it as if this is my swan song as a full-time talk-show host (though definitely not as a political commentator, columnist or editorialist!)

I have had extraordinary good luck. Throughout my career at CJOR and then at CKNW I was able to say exactly what I pleased without any management interference, subtle or otherwise, and no one else in this business in Canada can say that. I have no right to take all, or indeed most, of the credit for this. I am, to put it mildly, of the prickly persuasion and wouldn't have lasted very long if I had been censored or even made to feel the need for self-censorship. But the credit goes to the two companies I was contracted to: the Jim Pattison Group and the WIC Corporation under Frank Griffiths, Senior.

Within weeks of going on the air for Pattison's CJOR the first test came. When I had been a member of the Bill Bennett cabinet, I had vigorously opposed the advertising of alcohol on the electronic media. I had told Premier Bennett that I would feel compelled to resign if such a change were to be made. Why this was so is irrelevant, though I haven't changed my mind, but the important thing is that all broadcasters wanted the huge revenues that would accompany a change in the law, CJOR as much if not more than most of them. Nevertheless, I came flying out of the box, railing on air against the decision to allow it when the ruling was made just a few weeks after I had left government. Then I waited for a management summons. It never came. Al Anaka and Frank Callaghan must have been sorely tempted to at least debate with me on the issue, but they ran a radio station, not a legislature, and they knew that even attempting to clip my wings would hurt my ability to perform at my best, and that wasn't in their interests.

Shortly after I moved to CKNW, owned by WIC, I made the very stupid comment on air about McDonald's that I described earlier, but again management stood behind me. Over the years, managing CKNW with Rafe Mair on air must scarcely have been an undiluted pleasure. The Vander Zalm years brought an unending stream of highly critical (to say the least) phone calls to management, all of which had to be dealt with. The Charlottetown Accord brought the wrath of everyone from the prime minister on down onto the heads of management. I can only imagine what sort of pressure they were under! The Kemano Completion Project pitted me not only against big business at the very highest level in Canada but once again against the government and the top politicians and bureaucrats at both the federal and provincial levels. Much of labour was mad at me as well because every community on the west side of the mountains hoped to benefit from this huge construction project. Again the pressure on the management of CKNW was unrelenting and heavily into abusive. Never a peep did I hear. (As so often is the case, if you live long enough you see some strange things, and I lived long enough to have the mayor and council of Kitimat agree in public that I had been right all along when I said that Alcan was principally in the power, not the aluminum, business.)

This brings a couple of names to mind. Doug Rutherford and Tom Plasteras were both program directors when all this was hitting the fan. They could not help but feel the pressure, especially from the people in the sales department who were getting it from advertiser/clients. Doug and Tom were, in a word, magnificent. So was Rod Gunn, the general manager during the KCP dust-up. While I disagreed with what he did in a business sense, he was superb when it came to backing me up. (I had been about to say "backing all his talk-show hosts up" but to be candid the rest of them didn't say much that would get anyone in trouble.)

But the man who to me was simply the best was Ron Bremner, later president of BCTV and after that general manager of the Calgary Flames, who was at CKNW during the Vander Zalm years. It was Ron who, in the midst of the legions of Vander Zalm fans screaming for my head, sent around a memo about free speech, what it meant and how CKNW was dedicated to it. That may not seem like much. It could happen, say, in an Asper newspaper, except everyone there would know that the message had a whole lot of unmentioned "howevers" involved. No, the memo from Bremner has to be seen in its proper context. It came at a time the station was being seen as anti-government, anti-free enterprise, anti-Christian, you name it. The kind of free speech Ron was talking about was undiluted free speech. But what is so interesting about this is that Ron came from the sales end, and salesmen aren't supposed to like anything that makes any customer anywhere unhappy. But he has a deep and resolute love of freedom and all that entails and not only was prepared to take a lot of heat, he revelled in it. When Bill Vander Zalm resigned, I got a call from "Brem" who was on a ferry to Vancouver and couldn't wait to call. He congratulated me on my courage in fighting what I thought was a very bad government, and I found myself spluttering, "But it wasn't me who had the courage, Ron! It was you!" But that was Ron, simply the best of a very good lot.

My omission of the Corus Radio Group, the new owners of CKNW, in my words of praise is no accident. They know nothing about talk radio and it continually shows. As a result, one of the happiest moments in my broadcasting life came when I left what had once been the best private radio station in the country, CKNW.

There is now, as there has been for a long time, great wailing and gnashing of teeth over the bias of media outlets. And so there should be. A must-read on this subject is *Editor*, (MacMillan) by Max Hastings, who for almost a decade edited the *London Telegraph*, mostly for Conrad Black. The tale he tells is littered with owner interference on all matters, some very trivial, many of great importance. But even more invasive and instructive was Lord Black's assumption that since he had hired Hastings for his conservative (both small "c" and large "C") views that the *Telegraph* would almost uncritically support the government of Margaret Thatcher and later that of John Major. This bias had to appear not only in the main editorial, which the Brits call the "leader," but should also generally be found in the paper's columnists. The sense is strong that Lord Black only employed editors who supported his view of the world, who in turn hired writers, both of news and columns, who wouldn't stray too far from that line. I think it's safe to say that Rupert Murdoch is even more interfering than our Canadian nobleman, and there is scarcely a London paper, save the deadly dull *Independent* (though it is improving, I'm glad to say), that doesn't pursue a preordained political line.

That this is true in Canada is equally obvious. The Izzy Asper media outlets are Liberal down to their pink undies. The *Globe and Mail* is mainly conservative (though whether that includes the new Conservative Party is questionable) but even more simply supports the Canadian (for which read Ontario) establishment. The CBC is so establishment in its news that I, for one, simply cannot watch it.

So what do we do about it? Nothing. Not a damned thing except know it and let the media proprietors know we know it. Whatever we try to do will only bring about a worse result, for surely the only force capable of disciplining the media is the government and that's the last thing we need. A government that censors can never resist the opportunity to censor that which is unkind to it. And that state of affairs would mean the end of freedom of the press and, without that, the loss of freedom of speech would quickly follow.

On that score, I would argue that absolute censorship by a malevolent government guarantees more freedom of speech than exists in Canada. Outrageous statement, you say? Not at all. Under absolute censorship two things emerge: satire and underground papers. Britain didn't get free speech until very recently (lord chamberlains still censored plays in the West End in the 1970s) and may not have it now. Certainly, with the possible exception of Canada, they have the most rigorous libel and slander laws in the free world, such that critics of the establishment must tread very carefully indeed. The French establishment, even more than Britain's, has had a long history of forgetting all about freedom of the press when it suits them. During the negotiations leading to the Treaty of Versailles in 1919, for example, when a reporter wrote something that offended Prime Minister Georges Clemenceau, he simply closed the paper down for awhile. And he was a journalist and a newspaper editor by profession! I suppose that the United States in its Bill of Rights is thought of as the pioneer defender of free speech, yet shortly after that bill became part of the American Constitution, the United States Congress passed the Sedition Act, which prohibited citizens insulting the dignity of the president.

What is so interesting, I think, is that so much wonderful literature was passed under the nose of censors. At the time of Shakespeare, for example, insulting the king meant the scaffold. But any reading of Shakespeare, Marlowe or other wicked pens of the 16th and 17th centuries discloses *lèse-majesté* of the most extraordinary sort. The absence of free speech bred satire that was in itself a language of its own. When these folks went to the theatre, which was often banned by authority, they knew the playwrights' lingo and knew when he was taking the mickey out of his betters. Censorship bred the likes of Jonathan Swift, whose *Gulliver's Travels*, not a child's book at all but brilliant satire, took on both the state and religion—not always the safest thing to do in those days. Alexander Pope, whose *Rape of the Lock* is a brilliant satire of manners and morals of the establishment, couldn't be written today because no one would know what he was talking about, but people then knew exactly what the likes of Pope were saying because they spoke satirically themselves as a defence mechanism. And the novel, developed in the 18th century, was another way the government could be criticized without being able to do anything about it. Despite their gentle appearances and tone of their novels, Jane Austen, the Brontës, George Eliot and later Charles Dickens and William Makepeace Thackeray were taking society, government and the establishment itself to task, often shredding them in the process, by the use of fiction. Why accuse authority of evil things when you could avoid the consequences of such rashness by cloaking the accusation of evil in a fictional story? At the end of the 19th century the incomparable Gilbert and Sullivan also laid it to that ever-present establishment, perhaps the best example being in *HMS Pinafore* where we hear about the admiral who never went to sea yet became "ruler of the Queen's Navee." Oscar Wilde, of course, shredded the upper crust brilliantly, especially in *The Importance of Being Earnest* and *Lady Windermere's Fan*. Comedy, going back to Chaucer (just read the *Wyf of Bath*) and beyond, has also been the weapon of the protest movement. During World War II a part-Jewish stand-up comic survived the Nazis by plying his trade as a master of irony and satire in a Berlin cabaret. I make no case for censorship, of course. I am a free speech rebel whose philosophical hero is not Burke but Tom Paine. I only observe that thanks to the ingenuity of mankind, oppression often sharpens the tongue rather than dulling it.

But to return to the subject of bias, there is a silver lining to it all: it has resulted in there being more information available out there than ever before. All major newspapers in the world now have an internet edition or actually put their entire issue online. Sometimes there is a charge for accessing this, often not. The variety of tv news is much more than it was before. Pro-American? Try CNN. If you don't like the pro-American position, try the BBC World Service. And there are increasing numbers of internet "newspapers," often damned well written by columnists looking for an outlet and waiting patiently for the day, if ever, that these issues will bear economic fruit. And there are all the networks plus overseas newspapers. Unfortunately, all news is biased, some intentionally, some accidentally, some subliminally. Every outlet has a different slant; even the questions the reporter asks and the angle the camera shoots present bias of some sort. The most balanced of editors will have private thoughts that intrude, however subtly, into his daily work.

There is an answer to the bias that covers the entire planet: consumer research. One simply cannot permit a single point of view to govern one's thinking. While it is comfortable to stay with papers or electronic outlets that please your own sense of what events mean, that confirm your own prejudices, getting informed means reading and listening to things that you don't much like. There is, of course, always the feeling that, while we ourselves can see through the media bias, others less sophisticated than ourselves will be swayed by an evil newspaper or television or radio proprietor. In addition to being a tad arrogant, this suspicion doesn't seem to be borne out by the facts. There are many examples ongoing but I am mindful of the 1992 Charlottetown Accord vote where all the media in the country—for example, the Maclean-Hunter group that includes the *Financial Post*— were for the Yes side, yet it failed abysmally. (I would point out, somewhat immodestly, that there was one member of the mainstream media who used his bully pulpit to question the deal often and loudly.)

There is another solution that can accompany wider research: knowing the bias of the newspaper you are reading, you can write your own balance into the issue. *The Economist*, for example, is solidly pro-American and conservative, so as I read it, I can take that into account. In the same way, Londoners know the politics of the papers they read and take what's on the page with a grain of salt, although it would be naïve to assume that there aren't people who consume the media that best confirms their own prejudices.

The bias of the media, very often the bias of the owner, is ubiquitous, but it's up to the public to deal with it through individual efforts to sort out the information. Better to tackle the views of biased owners than those of self-serving governments any time. Having said all this and as much as I stand for freedom of speech and of the press, no media outlet can permit, much less encourage, recklessness. Throughout the many battles I've been in, I always had the back-up of two of the best defamation counsels in the business, initially Jon Festinger, but more recently and more often Dan Burnett. I made constant use of them and no one will ever know how much grief, not to say money, they saved both the station and myself. But—and here's the important part—they did not see their jobs as preventing me from saying what I had set out to say but, instead, as finding a way it could be said. Looking at the big and broad picture, we've had a very happy and successful relationship although we did have two unhappy consequences over the years.

The first involved Ted Hughes, former judge and deputy attorney general, and Stephen Owen, former many good things and now MP for Quadra, arising out of the same broadcast. I think I can say that the libels weren't particularly egregious—the amount of the settlements would indicate that—and, in the case of Mr. Owen, a miscommunication meant that my recommendation that I issue an unqualified apology went astray, and I have every reason to believe that me simply saying I'm sorry, which I was prepared to do, would have ended the matter.

The other involved Tom Siddon, who was the federal minister responsible for giving Alcan the right to desecrate the Nechako River under the Kemano Completion Project. The basis of Siddon's case against me was not any single editorial, thus Dan could hardly be responsible—though I believe they had all been passed through him— but comments made mostly on the open line. Moreover, Siddon, rather than protest along the way, waited until the matter was over before he hit us with a long list of one-liners to which he had taken offence. We'll never know whether Siddon was libelled and would have won his case because we settled out of court. The point is that, as with all challenging forms of work, there are risks, and I think my record is not too bad considering how long I have been on the air. Part of that record, incidentally, includes winning the coveted Michener Award for courageous journalism for the Alcan story and being runner-up for that award on two other occasions as well as winning the Bruce Hutchison Lifetime Achievement Award.

So what now? If I am the person who took the torch from Jack Webster and carried it high enough to be honoured as I have been, can

I pass it to anyone else with any sort of reasonable hope that it will be carried high in the days ahead? Before answering, I think I must make plain the pressures journalists are under. It isn't just being good that counts. It's getting printed or getting a radio or TV station to air your uncensored comments. The main problem here isn't direct owner censorship, though one should not underestimate that. As Abbott Joseph Liebling once said, "Freedom of the press is guaranteed only to those who own one." But when an owner, such as the late Izzy Asper, insists upon a certain cast to the reporting and to the newspaper's editorial, bad though that insistence may be, it doesn't of itself mean that freedom of expression has been banished from his pages. It's far more subtle than that. As an example, take Leonard Asper, the son and heir, who appoints the overall publisher for his chain and the publisher of each paper. It is highly unlikely that these publishers will express views that don't accord with those of the owner. Similarly, each publisher will look for a "safe pair of hands" to be his editor who will select the departmental editors and those who report and express opinions in the paper. Here the scene gets murky for editors know that they must compete (to the extent that there is competition in this country) and that they must therefore employ both good and entertaining journalists. They also know that some of these journalists won't have quite the same enthusiasm for the Liberal government that Mr. Asper has and that there might be criticism.

Now we have reached the difficult point. Do some journalists working for Mr. Asper, therefore, employ self-censorship, at least to some degree, in order to avoid that early golden handshake most journalists so wish to postpone? Do they pull some punches as much out of habit as introspection? For example, when writing a column about the Middle East, is there any care taken by the writer to avoid offending Mr. Asper even slightly? I would say that it would take a very brave and probably independently wealthy journalist to avoid this temptation.

I have always been very careful not to criticize journalists who seem to pull some punches. I have to remind myself that one of the information feeders going into their brains as they ply their trade goes something like this: "I have a wife, kids, big mortgage, insensitive banker and we've planned this little holiday for ages." To this might also be added the cost of elderly parents, sickness in the family, special needs schooling and on it goes. These things are very big realities and make a phrase here or a *bon mot* there seem eminently avoidable when you know in your gut that the paymaster may be touchy about it. I've never been in the position where I had to consider the spouse, kids and mortgage when I ply my trade. I don't know what I'd have done if I'd had that sword of Damocles over me, so I have no right to be critical. And I don't know if there is a media owner left who says to all persons of independent views who have talent in the field, "Just go ahead and print or broadcast whatever you wish, my only caveats being that you must show some concern for good taste, be tested as to defamation concerns and are reasonably literate." In other words, Mr. or Ms. Journalist, short of using the "c" words or clearly defaming people or being inarticulate or unreadable, you can say or write whatever you damned well please. There may be such an owner but I don't think so.

This doesn't mean that there is no dissent tolerated in the media because there is. The restraining factor on the owner is that he must sell newspapers, and mindless mumbling of sanitized platitudes isn't enough. They need the Allan Fotheringhams, the Stevie Camerons and the Christie Blatchfords to sell papers, but just ask any of these journalists over a drink (free, of course, in the best journalistic traditions) what life has been like with Canadian owners over the years. Ask Russell Mills, for eons the publisher of the *Ottawa Citizen* until he had the temerity to make a speech that displeased the Aspers, *père et fils*, and was unceremoniously dumped.

Stevie Cameron, a close personal friend, is another great example of what I mean. Two of her books, *On the Take* and *The Last Amigo*, were both directly and indirectly highly critical of Brian Mulroney. Out of the latter book, as well as parallel to it, were ongoing police investigations into the activities of Karlheinz Schreiber, the Mr. Fixit of the Aerobus scandal, who at this writing is fighting extradition to his native Germany to face fraud charges. During the glacial dawdling of the RCMP's investigations came a writ to search Swiss banks for some evidence of a pay-off to Brian Mulroney. The upshot of that fiasco was we taxpayers forked out a cool million to Mr. Mulroney and another million to his lawyer.

Then in the spring of 2004 the *Globe and Mail* ran a short, matter-of-fact story that reported that shortly after Mr. Mulroney left office,

Mr. Schreiber had paid him $300,000. The editor, Edward Greenspon, admitted to me privately that Mulroney had asked him to spike the story in exchange for which he would provide the newspaper with an even better story! Simultaneously, and one must conclude not accidentally, the *Globe and Mail* commenced an attack on Stevie Cameron, alleging that during the writing of *The Last Amigo* she had acted as a paid, registered police informer. Not only did the newspaper editorialize on the subject, its top columnists, including former editor William Thorsell and Margaret Wente, piled on. That Ms. Cameron gave tidbits of information to the police from time to time she doesn't deny. That's a regular part of being an investigative reporter. She stoutly denies being paid and of knowing that she was "registered," if indeed she was. It's not my purpose here to defend Ms. Cameron but instead to ask the obvious question: why the hell did not the *Globe and Mail* follow up the Mulroney story with a vengeance? Here was a story screaming to be investigated. I don't suppose it could have had anything to do with the corporate relationship between the *Globe and Mail* and CTV, which has Ben Mulroney, son of Brian, as a high-priced host, could it? Here we have a $300,000 unexplained payment to Brian Mulroney, of all people, from Karlheinz Schreiber, of all people, and the *Globe and Mail* gets its knickers into a knot over Ms. Cameron's relationship with the RCMP! The Canadian establishment looks after its own. Interestingly, although both of Ms. Cameron's books were in part about Brian Mulroney, they have not brought a single defamation writ from that gentleman, his cronies, or anyone else involved.

Why is it that owners give a fiddler's fart what's written in their papers? It's called ego. Lords Rothermere, Northfield and Beaverbrook had it. The Asper family have it in spades as did the Thompsons and Conrad Black. American press barons like Randolph Hurst and Colonel McCormack had it. Even the crook Robert Maxwell had it. These owners think that they can improve the world by refashioning it in their own image. But in Canada, there is a special wrinkle: press barons, in addition to wanting to elect their own governments, have a peculiar notion that it is their duty to keep the country together. There is this box within which the establishment operates and the slightest attempt to move outside that box brings calumny and indeed ostracism. If your dissent is within the box, like that of Don Newman of the CBC or Jeffrey Simpson of the *Globe and Mail*, you get Orders of Canada. Just as did that eternal paragon of virtue, Toronto's perennial interpreter of the country, the late Peter Gzowski. (My friend, columnist and eminent policy wonk Gordon Gibson holds that no journalist can take an Order of Canada and remain credible, and I agree.) The zenith (or was it the nadir?) of Gzowski's contribution to the great Canadian debate was a TV show he did on the Supreme Court of Canada. Hushed as if he were in the presence of God, Gzowski walked us through interviews with the chief justice and others of the court's robed ancients, all in tones of obsequiousness and without a peep about the controversy that has surrounded this institution ever since the Charter of Rights and Freedoms made them Canada's social engineers, a role they have eagerly played since. But what can you expect? After the 1992 Charlottetown Referendum—which he supported through bleating outbursts of patriotism far more strongly than if he had just spat out, "Vote Yes!"—Gzowski interviewed me and asked why I, a strong No-man, had not instead used my microphone to "do good for the country." I didn't even try to explain to this icon of comfy Canadianism that I and all who voted No (nearly 70 percent in my province) thought that was precisely what I had done. But such is the Orwellian state of the smug central-Canadian mind that they continue to believe that majorities, contrary to what their betters demand, are misguided. Democracy, they have decided, means supporting what the establishment wants.

Why is it necessary that there be absolutely free speech in the media? You might wonder why such a question should be asked, but you might be surprised, nay staggered, at how many people don't like to see the motives of their betters questioned. The establishment has a lot of supporters, most likely because there are a hell of a lot of people who earn their keep from it. Moreover, everyone has his own untouchable subject. It's a case of "Go ahead and kick hell out of those guys, but touch mine and I'll punch you in the mouth." A somewhat inconsistent message.

But the question must be asked for a better reason that that. Much of what one reads and hears and all that drops from politicians' lips is horseshit. Some of the horseshit is raw, some of it has been tarted up a bit, and much of it has been carefully deodorized. But it's still horseshit. And I mean that. It often takes longer to polish and spin government policy than it takes to develop it. There is, in fact, no such thing as instant government policy. It all goes through a huge and complex exercise of spin doctoring, and bad stories are slid out if possible under circumstances that will tend to bury them or at least blunt the impact of their revelation.

But horseshit is by no means confined to governments, large and small. Industry pays enormous sums per year for people who know absolutely nothing about the product and don't need to know anything about it in order to put the very best face upon it. Much of the time there isn't all that much harm done. So the Chevy doesn't, as the man on television said, outperform the Ford. That's petty stuff. But what about when chemical companies and pharmaceutical biggies are making claims for their products? Is DDT a story from too long ago? What about thalidomide? IUDs? Breast implants? And what about the tobacco industry, which still gets around government rules against advertising by virtue of its well-paid, influential lobbying arm?

One of the problems that has arisen in the wake of these tragedies being exposed is that companies have become much better at producing products that initially pass muster. It's not likely, though by no means impossible, that a company will actually get another thalidomide to market again. However, other products with unforeseen long-term adverse effects are getting to market with government approval that has been based not upon independent testing, as most believe, but only upon examination of the material put out by company scientists. True academic testing involves maintaining a strong unwavering skepticism till all the facts are in, and you are unlikely to find that skepticism among highly paid industry scientists.

As an example, let's take aspartame. No, come to think of it, leave me out of this. You take it. Here is the diabetic's dream drug: he can eat sweet things to his heart's content. And no more worries about sugar-induced cavities in the teeth. This really is progress. But is it? Is it possible that it actually raises a diabetic's blood sugar as it did with me? Does it cause unexplained but very real ear troubles that vanish when the drug is no longer used, as it clearly did with me? What are the real long-term consequences of aspartame? The more important question, of course, is—is it too late to do anything about it? Was the real test tube for aspartame the general public, meaning the tests were too late and the damage already done? How the hell did Monsanto get it approved in the first place? Ah well now, therein lies a story and, if you're interested, just google the word *aspartame* and you'll have hours of enlightening reading. (Pay special attention to what Dr. H. Roberts has to say.)

Genetically modified foods also ring bells, especially in Europe where environmental groups have at least enforced labelling. The scientists (descendants of the men in white coats who once assured us about the universal benefits of DDT) patronize, denigrate and lampoon the efforts of the environmentalists. Trust us, we're told. We know what we're doing! Then there's fish farming. Quite the natural thing to do, we're told. After all, most of our food is farmed, so why shouldn't fish be farmed, too? Don't worry about the supposed bad consequences placed before you. They're merely the expression of the unfounded fears of the usual suspects, the greenies and their lot! Use your head, we're advised. This is how we're going to feed the ever-expanding world population.

But what do aspartame, genetically modified foods and fish cage farming have in common? Simply this: the test animals are the whole of mankind. You and I are the guinea pigs and the lab rats. Worse still, in all three cases, if science is wrong it may already be too late to prevent a worldwide catastrophe.

What has this to do with free speech? Everything. If there are no credible cross-examiners with appropriate places in the media, it will simply be the marginalized environmental movement who will be sounding the tocsin of potential trouble. So it is in the media that the fight must be fought, because as long as the mainstream media is silent, who will believe the lonely and shrill environmentalist?

It is very important to remember who provides the shield for the establishment: enormous public relations companies whose full time job is to conceal the truth and minimize the obvious. These companies, Knowlton and Hill and Burson-Marsteller come to mind, are huge houses of skilled benders of the truth. Back in the mid-1980s it was Burson-Marsteller that managed to make Union Carbide's "accident" in Bhopal, India, look as if the company had conferred a benefit on local folks. It was a masterful job of spinning, bobbing, weaving, distracting, distorting. In short, they did just what a PR company is paid the huge bucks to do. All those whose activities might be catastrophic—the chemical companies, the pharmaceutical people, the fish farmers—have one thing in common. They all pay huge annual fees to the PR spin doctors. And note this: these PR companies don't just go to work after a disaster. They probably earn most of their money helping companies plan future pr strategy, including advising them in advance what to do when disasters strike, disasters that are all but mathematically certain. How do I know this is true? Because back when I was fighting bankruptcy and wasn't too fussy about how I accomplished it, I did quite a bit of work for one of these PR giants, so I know what they do and how they do it. I'm not proud of that memory.

Why is this system possible? It is because business leaders, labour leaders, politicians, artsy-fartsy types and the media themselves all drink each other's bathwater—and love it. The media don't comment upon the despicable political system that perpetuates the rule of the small establishment clique in Toronto and Montreal because, for the most part, they are part of that establishment. They will on slow news days solemnly intone that they think a politician here and a business or labour union there is not playing cricket but never will you find them examining the system itself. That's because they are an integral part of that system. This isn't just happening at the top, of course. Every province, city, town and village has its establishment. It's a very natural thing, but it goes wrong when that establishment gobbles up its critics. And that has happened in Canada. But also understand this: there are establishment critics in this country and some are very good. The problem is when was the last time you saw or heard any of them go outside the box? They don't because they don't dare, and who can blame them? Ours is a benevolent dictatorship but no less a tyranny because it covers its claws with velvet. It's a tyranny in which you are permitted to dissent, provided you don't go too far. I daresay that 99.9 percent of those who read these words have no opportunity whatsoever to have an impact on those who govern them nor will they have access to anyone who is prodding around in the deep, dark recesses of the machinery by which we are ruled, trying to find out what's wrong and what can be done to fix it.

The public is not fond of the media but they still dote on it because there is no alternative. The media is blamed for carrying the message, and the sinners are easily forgiven in the result. And the media has a hell of a lot to answer for. In the US the square shooters of the past like Edward R. Murrow have been replaced by money-soaked martinets like Dan Rather. But that goes back to ownership. An Edward R. Murrow went outside the box and embarrassed not only the government but the owners as well. In pleading the case for the muckraker (an honourable description, I assure you, of those who dig deeply into establishment's assertions and actions), I plead for the public. For surely it must be better to have a media that is subject to all the human frailties than have one that is as independent as Pravda. In Canada our problem is, simply stated, we have no tradition of free speech in this country. We don't have a Howard Stern or Rush Limbaugh here because we put good manners and respect for institutions, however tarnished, ahead of free speech. Our defamation laws, like those of Britain (they're worse in France) protect the establishment. Unlike the United States, which actually believes in free speech, we only care for it if it's within certain reasonable boundaries, don't you know? In the US for a public person to sustain a defamation suit, malice must be proved, so the bar to claim damages is very high. People in Britain and Canada scoff at that. Why, that would mean that politicians and other establishment figures could get insulted if we're not careful!

Free speech in Canada? Freedom of the press? When the media, instead of standing outside becomes an integral part of the establishment whose feet should be constantly held to the fire, there can be no freedom of uncomfortable speech. And without uncomfortable speech, you don't have freedom of speech or anything remotely like it, no matter how hard the politicians try to tell you otherwise.

So this is the sad part of retossing that torch Jack Webster tossed to me. Whatever faults I may possess (and they are indeed many) I don't think anyone can accuse me of backing away from the powerful. In fact, the very opposite is the case, and having received the Bruce Hutchison Lifetime Achievement Award at the 2003 Jack Webster Awards Night, I think I'm entitled to stand as the remaining survivor of the shit-disturber clan in Canada. But is there any point in even tossing that torch? Can I pass it to anyone else with any reasonable hope that it will be carried high in the days ahead? With the bean-counters, ever sensitive to advertiser demands, now mainly in charge of the media, I very much doubt it. The Peter Gzowskis and locally the Bill Goods have won. Solemn, respectful, low-key interviews will carry the day. Hopefully I will turn my microphone over in a couple of years to one of the best, Shiral Tobin, who has the guts, tenacity and necessary abrasiveness to rank with the very best. Her only problem will be finding a media owner who still values those virtues, and I'm not optimistic about that.

It might be simpler and easier on everyone if I just toss the torch into the chuck and, with respect for what it once stood for, simply say, "Goodbye, old friend. It's not that we don't need you anymore. It's just that this country doesn't want you."

# 24
## The End of an Era

I HAVE NOT SPOKEN ABOUT MY LEAVING CKNW. That is because I'm in the goofy position of not being permitted to do so under the release I signed. I think it fair to also add that it was not I who asked for a release that forbade giving the details that led up to my firing. But I say goofy because all of the details were in the media and widely circulated before this release was presented to me to sign. The entire story was, in fact, countrywide news. On the day I was formally canned, papers from coast to coast reported the details and the first 13 minutes of the Global/BCTV6:00 p.m. news covered the story. It was interesting to note that the camera shot of the brass at CKNW showed them pushing the camera lens away, while that of me—it being Monday and the day I regularly sail—showed me with Wendy, Russ Fraser and our Labrador, Chauncey, all with smiles aplenty, leaving the marina on my sailboat for a relaxing day-cruise.

All I can tell you about this episode is that I performed extremely well throughout my career at 'NW and certainly wasn't starting to sag. The evidence of this is contained in a notice sent by program director Tom Plasteras to all employees and contract people on May 22, 2003, just a shade over two weeks before I was fired.

**Rafe Mair dominates the 830-11am slot with a 17.8 share, up from 17.0 last fall. Rafe has an amazing average quarter-hour**

**audience of 99,900!! The next closest station is QM-FM with a 12.1 then QM with an 11.6 share. The other news/talk/sports competitors break out as follows: CBC: 7.1, CKWX: 2.9, CFUN: 1.0, TEAM 1040: 1.0, MOJO: 0.5.**

The emphases in that memo are Tom's, not mine. The rest of his memo deals with other performers and other stations.

I consider it a shame that I couldn't have finished my contract with 'NW; it still had two-and-a-half years to run. However, I left on a good note and I harbour no hard feelings whatsoever. During the time WIC owned CKNW it was imbued with the spirit of the late Frank Griffiths. I have great memories of the feisty atmosphere there, as is always the case in a good media workplace, and the wonderful bunch of people I worked with.

When CKNW fired me, I was actually delighted because I went from CKNW over to 600AM. Ironically, I had started with CJOR (the predecessor to 600AM) and back in those days I also did three weekly editorials for CKVU—which is now CityTv and for whom I now do three weekly editorials. I had not, however, as speculated in the media, already made a deal with Jimmy Pattison and 600am before I left CKNW.

It was somewhat more complicated than that. When it became clear that my days at 'NW were numbered I asked for, and got from the manager, permission to look elsewhere. I needed to get permission because I would otherwise have been in breach of contract. I then phoned Jimmy and he put me in touch with the manager at 600AM, Gerry Siemens, with whom I had lunch. Gerry told me bluntly but nicely that he wasn't interested. That was fair enough. A week or so later I was fired and even though Wendy and I have an unlisted number, the phone never stopped ringing. As a result, the day of the firing was bedlam and the next few didn't look much better, so I suggested to Wendy that we get a couple of charter fares and go to London to give ourselves some breathing space. I must digress here to say that I hadn't felt so good and at peace for a couple of years. While we were away, Wendy and I had time to think and talk, and the decision was that I would try to get into another talk show, but that in all events I wasn't going to retire. There were a couple of reasons for this: I wasn't ready to retire, and I wanted to show that whatever the reasons for my firing had been, they had nothing to do with my competence.

On our return there were plenty of messages, and one was from Gerry Siemens. His station had changed its collective mind—or perhaps Jimmy Pattison had changed it for them—and they would like to talk. At this point Wendy and I had already decided to ask one of the truly great names in radio, Red Robinson, to act for me. I'm delighted to say he accepted the task. He did a marvellous and sensitive job that put me exactly where I wanted to be. There were several job possibilities and three probabilities. After doing his due diligence, Red recommended I accept 600AM's offer of a talk show, which I would host, and a deal with CityTv doing three editorials a week. I agreed and the deals were struck. I must mention the "probable": CKWX made a handsome offer for me to do a couple of editorials a day. The reason I didn't go further down that path was that I was determined to do a talk show. However, I must say that Paul Fisher, the manager, and George Gordon, the news director, are class acts. When I went on air on 600AM there was a bottle of (very expensive) champagne from CKWX waiting for me.

I had one more problem to deal with: I wouldn't be starting either spot until September 2. What on earth was I to do with myself in the intervening two months? Unhappily that was resolved when I took two falls (both when sober, I assure you). The first happened when I was tripped up by my very strong chocolate Lab, Chauncey; the second and much worse one occurred just outside the new studio on West 8th Avenue, where I tripped over some broken pavement. That one left me with a huge hematoma on the femur that put me into emergency for eight hours and grounded me for more than four weeks. This meant I couldn't sail and was confined to barracks. I just about went nuts, and so did Wendy. It was a case of the old line, "I married you for better or for worse but not for lunch!"

Finally September 2 came and I went nervously back on the air with Premier Gordon Campbell my first guest. You would expect that, at 72 years of age, all nervousness was behind me. Not so, I'm afraid. Now I'm not scared of my shadow anymore, but it's all relative. Whereas when I was a young lawyer I was nervous going into police court, now I'm nervous doing what for me are important interviews. I haven't changed, you see. The challenges have.

But it was like old times. Shiral Tobin was back as my producer, and I discovered that the two news guys, Cam McCubbin and Jack Marion, were class acts and Greg "Dr. Sport" Douglas was a gem. I was, at long last, back in an atmosphere that sounded like a real radio station. I'm now in the last two years of my contract. At the end of that, I intend to turn the show over to Shiral, provided that she and 600AM want it that way. I'm sure they will. Shiral is the Number One new talent in the city and probably beyond, and the outlook for her and the station is nothing short of spectacular.

When my contract runs out, I won't be retiring unless my health dictates. I will stay in the media, perhaps spelling off hosts or doing editorials or both. I may even have another book in me.

Whatever happens, it's been a slice!

# 25
## The Sting of Death

I HAVE THOUGHT ABOUT DEATH SINCE I was a little boy of three and one of my great-grandmothers died. My mom explained how Gran's body was going into the ground and her spirit to heaven. In those days I thought "body" meant one's hindquarters, and this added a new element to my innocent conjecturing. What, I thought, was happening to the rest of Gran?

As with most kids growing up, when I thought about death, I was very scared. Fortunately, there were lots of other things to divert my mind, but I was a Sunday School attender and when I learned of Jesus's horrible death, I was haunted by it. During World War II each week's list of casualties further confused me. I became not only scared of death but petrified by the thought of the process of dying. I still am. In my teens and twenties I knew I was immortal, invincible—and infertile. And events seemed to bear out my arrogance. I had numerous lucky escapes from accidents and the only person I impregnated was my wife.

Deaths occurred, of course. My father when I was 34. A friend of the family here, the occasional premature death of a friend there. But the strong sense of denial I was building seemed impregnable. I wasn't intended for death for a very long time, so why worry?

Then came 1976 and the death of my beautiful 17-year-old daughter Shawn in a car accident. How could this happen? Why her? Why me? And I became conscious of my mortality in a very real and lasting way. "They" were not going to make an exception in my case. And I recognized that from the moment of my conception I had started the long (I hoped) road to death. As I got older, I began to realize that just as happens to a spawning Pacific salmon, my body was slowly rotting away. Things began to go wrong. Knees hurt; the back got sore. I had symptoms that I interpreted in panic as the foretelling of almost instant doom. I got much better acquainted with my doctor—who seemed all of a sudden to have gone grey and developed a bit of a paunch himself. It occurred to me that every living thing about me would sooner or later die. A pretty gloomy assessment. The words of Dylan Thomas seemed so apt: "Oh as I was young and easy in the mercy of his means/ Time held me green and dying/ Though I sang in my chains like the sea."

I think I would be lying if I didn't admit that death is what brought me back to the Anglican Church, though that wasn't all. Because my church permitted Wendy and me, both divorced people, to have a church wedding, we both started to attend services there. I think I can say that initially it was because we felt a spiritual void in our lives. I began to understand what Jesus told us, as did Wendy, and we felt this was the example we wanted to try to follow. Yet it still had everything to do with death because the reward for following Christ was eternal life.

But my puzzlement with life and death increased as the years passed. Did we know that there was an afterlife because of the thousands of cases of near-death experiences that told of the spirit leaving the body, of feeling sublimely at peace as it reached to a distant light? Or were those experiences—as a "reborn" Christian once told me—not death but just the process of dying, which is quite a different thing? And what was this life everlasting all about? As one wit put it, many earnestly seek the afterlife who can't find anything to do on a rainy Sunday afternoon! Did I want this life everlasting? Or was I just worried that the choice was that or eternal perdition where things were permanently very hot?

I had also made an interesting observation along the way: those whom you might think would have the fast track to paradise—popes, archbishops and the like—seemed to die harder and take longer doing it than ordinary folk who are going to need a very great deal of help indeed getting past St. Peter. If heaven was so great, so much better than life on earth, why wouldn't the priests of that faith be dying (pun intended) to get there?

I recently visited the Mayan part of Mexico and learned that they had a game, watched by thousands in big arenas, that rather resembled basketball. It was as hotly contested as sports contests here, but the winners were immediately and painfully sacrificed to the gods. Now that is what I call faith!

I have come to a more peaceful contemplation of my fate. I am by no means certain that I will have an afterlife, although this whole business of life and the mysteries of the universe seem pretty silly without it. However, I believe that if there is a Bar of Justice awaiting me I will have a better crack at it now than I would have during those years I ignored all matters spiritual.

I am none the wiser for all my musing and I leave you none the wiser in the telling. I only leave you with this: there is only one thing that consistently puzzles us, bothers us and frightens us. It is universal. I suspect that those religious zealots and those who claim no belief are lying through their teeth when they claim they don't fear death.

Death is the great leveller. It puts the high and the mighty, the rich and the powerful, on the same level as those poor HIV-positive buggers in Africa, trying desperately to get a few more days of life. It is the universal conundrum that consumes us our entire lives, yet we haven't any idea what it means or if we will ever know.

Does it mean anything other than an extinguishment of life? Is there no more? If not, what a cruel and idle exercise this has all been. We can't find the answers until we die and if death turns out to be game over, there is no answer! What a bummer! But we have no alternative but to make the best of it and see it through. When Irvin Cobb, the great American humorist, was diagnosed with his fatal illness and a friend asked why he was so cheerful, he observed that life was like a party and it would be wrong not to celebrate the fact of the party as you walked out the door.

Death, then, is and will likely always remain The Great Mystery of Life.